New Frontiers in Translation Studies

Series Editor

Defeng Li, Center for Studies of Translation, Interpreting and Cognition, University of Macau, Macao SAR, China

Translation Studies as a discipline has witnessed the fastest growth in the last 40 years. With translation becoming increasingly more important in today's glocalized world, some have even observed a general translational turn in humanities in recent years. The New Frontiers in Translation Studies aims to capture the newest developments in translation studies, with a focus on:

- Translation Studies research methodology, an area of growing interest amongst translation students and teachers;
- Data-based empirical translation studies, a strong point of growth for the discipline because of the scientific nature of the quantitative and/or qualitative methods adopted in the investigations; and
- Asian translation thoughts and theories, to complement the current Eurocentric translation studies.

Submission and Peer Review:

The editor welcomes book proposals from experienced scholars as well as young aspiring researchers. Please send a short description of 500 words to the editor Prof. Defeng Li at Springernfits@gmail.com and Springer Senior Publishing Editor Rebecca Zhu: Rebecca.zhu@springernature.com. All proposals will undergo peer review to permit an initial evaluation. If accepted, the final manuscript will be peer reviewed internally by the series editor as well as externally (single blind) by Springer ahead of acceptance and publication.

Kan Wu · Defeng Li

Researching Translator's Functional Style

A Corpus-Assisted Approach

Springer

Kan Wu
Zhejiang University of Finance
and Economics Dongfang College
Zhejiang, China

University of Macau
Macau, China

Defeng Li
University of Macau
Macau, China

ISSN 2197-8689 ISSN 2197-8697 (electronic)
New Frontiers in Translation Studies
ISBN 978-981-95-1220-1 ISBN 978-981-95-1221-8 (eBook)
https://doi.org/10.1007/978-981-95-1221-8

This Springer imprint is published by the registered company Springer Nature Singapore Pte Ltd.
The registered company address is: 152 Beach Road, #21-01/04 Gateway East, Singapore 189721, Singapore

Acknowledgements Many people assisted us in the writing of this book, which is based on Kan Wu's doctoral thesis, and we are very grateful for what they have done for us. First, we thank Kan Wu's academic supervisors: Prof. Dechao Li, who guided him during his doctoral studies at The Hong Kong Polytechnic University, and Prof. Defeng Li, who supervised his postdoctoral research at University of Macau. Their advice and guidance were essential in developing the research methods and understanding of translator's functional style.

We also thank the production team for their hard work and dedication: Ms. Rebecca Zhu, Mr. Vijay Kumar Selvaraj, and other team members who helped bring this book to completion.

Our colleagues at the Center for Studies of Translation, Interpreting and Cognition, Faculty of Arts & Humanities, University of Macau, provided valuable support throughout this research.

Any remaining errors are our own responsibility.

Competing Interests The authors have no competing interests to declare that are relevant to the content of this manuscript.

Acknowledgments. Many people [illegible]

Contents

Abbreviations

ASL	Average Sentence Length
BNC	British National Corpus
CA	Cluster Analysis
COCA	Corpus of Contemporary American English
CTS	Corpus-assisted Translation Studies
DS	Direct Speech
DT	Direct Thought
FA	Factor Analysis
FDS	Free Direct Speech
FDT	Free Direct Thought
FIS	Free Indirect Speech
FIT	Free Indirect Thought
IS	Indirect Speech
IT	Indirect Thought
KRA	Keyword Rendition Analysis
LCA	Lexical Chain Analysis
MAT	Multidimensional Analysis Tagger
MDA	Multidimensional Analysis
MFW	Most Frequent Words
MFWS	Most Frequent Word Sequences
NW	Narrator's Writing
PCA	Principal Component Analysis
RC1	Reference Corpus 1
RC2	Reference Corpus 2
SFA	Semantic Field Analysis
SL	Source Language
SP	Speech Presentation
ST	Source Text
STTR	Standardized Type-Token Ratio
SV-I	First Variant of ST-oriented Studies
SV-II	Second Variant of ST-oriented Studies

TL	Target Language
TP	Thought Presentation
TT	Target Text
TTR	Type-Token Ratio
TV-I	First Variant of TT-oriented Studies
TV-II	Second Variant of TT-oriented Studies
TV-III	Third Variant of TT-oriented Studies
WP	Writing Presentation

List of Figures

List of Tables

Part I
Theoretical Foundations

Chapter 1
Introduction

1.1 What is Translator Style

The concept of translator style encompasses a complex array of interpretations and cannot be confined to a singular definition (Li, 2016: 103). It is broadly described as a unique way of translating that exhibits a coherent pattern of choices, setting a translator's work apart from others and identifiable across multiple translations by the same individual. More specifically, it may refer to the consistent selection of strategies within a single translation (Lu, 2013: 42).

Baker (2000: 245) defines translator style as consistent patterns of linguistic behavior rather than isolated acts of translation. Therefore, Baker (2000: 241) posits that translator style is manifested through a combination of linguistic and non-linguistic features, such as the choice of texts, use of prefacing, footnoting, idiosyncratic expressions, and characteristic language habits. Contrastingly, Malmkjær (2003: 39) and Boase-Beier (2006: 5) regard translator style as the translator's engagement with both the source and target texts. They emphasize understanding the reasons behind the translator's stylistic decisions, particularly how the style in the source text is interpreted, modified, or preserved in the target text.

Saldanha (2011) introduces a distinction between translator style and translational style, arguing that much of the scholarship in translation studies concentrates on the latter. She defines translator style as the stylistic idiosyncrasies that remain consistent across multiple translations by the same translator, irrespective of the styles in source texts (Saldanha, 2011: 31). Saldanha's definition of translator style emphasizes it as a recognizable, distinctive, and coherent pattern of choice with a discernible function, not attributable solely to the source text's style or the target language's conventions. This definition suggests that translator style is shaped by the translator's habitual behavior, observable across their body of work, and is not merely a reflection of the source text's style or the constraints of the target language.

K. Wu and D. Li, *Researching Translator's Functional Style*, New Frontiers in Translation Studies, https://doi.org/10.1007/978-981-95-1221-8_1

1.2 Why Studying Translator Style

The study of translator style occupies a significant niche within translation studies, offering insights into the nuanced and complex nature of translation as an interlingual and intercultural communication process. This scholarly pursuit not only enriches our understanding of translation as a creative and interpretative act, but contributes to broader discussions in linguistics, literary studies, and cross-cultural communication. The importance of studying translator style can be elucidated through several key perspectives.

Firstly, the study of translator style highlights the translator's role as an active agent in the translation process. Contrary to the traditional view of translators as mere conduits for cross-lingual transfer, examining translator style reveals the depth of their creative and interpretive involvement. As Saldanha (2011: 30) posits, translator style is indicative of a coherent pattern of choices that distinguishes a translator's work, highlighting the subjectivity inherent in translation. This focus shifts the paradigm towards recognizing the translator's contribution to the literary and cultural value of a text, supporting Venuti's (1995) advocacy for the visibility of the translator.

Secondly, analyzing translator style facilitates a deeper understanding of the interplay between source texts and their translations. Malmkjær (2003) and Boase-Beier (2006) emphasize the importance of exploring how translators perceive and transform the style of source texts. This emphasis not only sheds light on the stylistic and interpretative decisions made by translators, but also on how these decisions affect the reception and interpretation of translated texts within target cultures.

Thirdly, the study of translator style contributes to the development of translation theory and practice. By identifying and analyzing patterns of stylistic choices across translations, researchers can offer more nuanced descriptions of translation phenomena, contributing to the refinement of translation theories. Baker's (2000: 245) work, which delineates translator style as a set of linguistic and non-linguistic features, provides empirical evidence that supports the development of descriptive translation studies.

1.3 Corpus Stylistic and Translator Style

The rise of corpus linguistics in the 1990s revolutionized translator style research by providing corpus tools for analyzing textual data. This corpus-assisted approach relies on compiling large digital collections of texts (corpora) to investigate linguistic features and patterns across translated and non-translated texts. Corpus-assisted studies have enabled researchers to empirically investigate stylistic phenomena, such as lexical choices, syntactic structures, and pragmatic markers, on a much larger scale. Baker (1993, 2000) was instrumental in proposing the use of corpora to examine translator style, which catalyzed the development of corpus-assisted translator style research by highlighting how corpora can uncover the "thumbprints" of translators and their stylistic idiosyncrasies. The corpus-assisted translator style research has become a fundamental aspect of corpus-assisted translation studies, alongside the investigation of translation universals, norms, and pedagogical practices. Moreover, this branch of research has initiated a paradigm shift, enabling quantifiable analyses of translator style and facilitating comparisons across studies.

While corpus-assisted studies have advanced our understanding of translator style, they sometimes neglect its functional dimension, focusing instead on formal aspects characterized by various lexical and syntactic features. This emphasis on formality can result in a disconnect between linguistic analysis and literary appreciation within the domain of literary translation studies (Mahlberg, 2013). To bridge this gap, the application of corpus stylistics presents a viable solution, offering a comprehensive analysis that encompasses both formal and functional aspects of translator style. Corpus stylistics is "a particular focus of corpus linguistics, one in which the research questions being investigated and/or the analytical frameworks used are primarily concerned with issues of style" (McIntyre & Walker, 2019: 315). If we use corpus stylistic methods to study translator style, we can not only scrutinize the frequency and distribution patterns of linguistic forms characteristic of a translator's style, but also investigate the potential literary functions these patterns may serve. Such a corpus stylistic approach effectively bridges the gap between linguistic description and literary appreciation, thereby providing some functional insights into translator style. This integrative perspective forms the foundation for subsequent discussions and analyses in this book.

1.4 Overview of the Book

The entire book is divided into two parts. Part I, comprising the first four chapters, focuses on the theoretical issues related to the study of functional style. Part II, consisting of Chapter 5 through 12, presents a demonstrative analysis of functional style through a case study of the Chinese-English translation of *Er Ma*, a novel by the renowned contemporary Chinese writer Lao She.

In Part I, Chapter 1 serves as an introduction, providing an overview of the background of the study. Chapter 2 offers a concise review of corpus-assisted translator style research over the past two decades. Chapter 3 delves into corpus stylistics and reviews existing corpus stylistic research. Chapter 4 introduces the functional style by discussing its definition, categorization, and ways of analysis.

In Part II, Chapter 5 introduce Lao She and his story of *Er Ma*, specifically highlighting the two recurring themes related to the Chinese and Britons in the story. Chapter 6 addresses the methodological aspects of the case study, providing detailed explanations of the research questions, corpus compilation, and data analysis. Chapter 7 generates and categorizes keywords related to *Er Ma*, establishing the foundation for the subsequent analyses. Chapters 8 and 9 investigate translators' functional styles through the ways translators recreate the two literary functions (i.e., thematic construction, characterization) enacted in *Er Ma* within target texts. Chapter 10 examines these translators' functional styles by comparing how they create the textual function of "textual panorama building" in target text. Chapter 11 delves into some possible factors that contribute to the translators' functional styles. Chapter 12 concludes the entire research.

References

Baker, M. (1993). Corpus linguistics and translation studies—implications and applications. *Text and technology: In honour of John Sinclair* (pp. 233–250). John Benjamins Publishing Company.
Baker, M. (2000). Towards a methodology for investigating the style of a literary translator. *Target, 12*(2), 241–266.
Boase-Beier, J. (2006). *Stylistic approaches to translation.* St Jerome Publishing.
Li, D. (2016). Translator style: A corpus-assisted approach. In: Ji, M., Oakes, M., Li, D., & Hareide, L. (Eds.) *Corpus methodologies explained: An empirical approach to translation studies,* 103–136. Routledge.
Lu, J. (2013). *A study of translator style from diachronic and synchronic perspectives.* (Doctoral dissertation). Shanghai International Studies University.
Mahlberg, M. (2013). *Corpus stylistics and Dickens' fiction.* Routledge.
Malmkjær, K. (2003). What happened to God and the Angels: An exercise in translational stylistics. *Target, 15*(1), 37–58.
McIntyre, D., & Walker, B. (2019). *Corpus stylistics: Theory and practice.* Edinburgh University Press.
Saldanha, G. (2011). Translator style: Methodological considerations. *The Translator, 17*(1), 25–50.
Venuti, L. (1995). *The translator's invisibility: A history of translation.* Routledge.

Chapter 2
Corpus-Assisted Translator Style Research

2.1 Introduction

This chapter provides a concise overview of previous corpus-assisted studies of translator style. The overview is meant to outline the development of translator style research by focusing on how translator style is conceptualized and studied over the past two decades. In this way, we can identify potential research gaps in this research field, and clearly understand possible contributions of the present study to corpus-assisted translator style research.

The whole chapter is organized as follows: Sect. 2.2 will offer a brief overview of the research background pertaining to corpus-assisted translator style research. Section 2.3 will discuss various definitions of translator style employed in previous studies. Section 2.4 through 2.6 will examine the existing translator style research, with a focus on corpus designs, types of analyses, and interpretation of analysis results. Section 2.7 will summarize the key issues discussed in this chapter, and identify a possible gap in these studies.

2.2 Background of Translator Style Research

According to Savory (1957), "a translation should reflect the style of the original, meanwhile a translation should possess the style of the translator" (see Venuti, 2000: 393). Over decades, Savory's theory has motivated translation scholars to find out the nature of translators' styles, with particular emphasis on the definition, identification, and representation of these styles. Such explorations of translators' styles are meaningful, because they highlight translators' visibility and demonstrate translators' subjectivity in translation. With the rise of corpus-assisted translation studies (CTS) in the 1990s, researchers have begun to answer these questions through corpus

K. Wu and D. Li, *Researching Translator's Functional Style*, New Frontiers in Translation Studies, https://doi.org/10.1007/978-981-95-1221-8_2

methods. Against this background, there emerges the corpus-assisted study of translators' styles, which, together with studies of translation universals and explorations of translation norms, is one branch within CTS. Corpus-assisted translator style research is connected to the rest CTS branches through a shared ground: they all emphasize the authenticity of collected data and the descriptivity of applied methodologies. Nevertheless, the corpus-assisted study of translator style is different from these branches, because it primarily focuses on translators.

Baker (2000) is a pioneer in the corpus-assisted translator style research. In her study, she used corpora to investigate translator style by comparing three formal features, including standardized type-token ratio (STTR), average sentence length (ASL), and frequencies of report verb SAY, in several translations by Peter Clark and Peter Bush. The purpose of her study is to find out whether the two translators leave "thumbprints" in target texts (TTs). The results support her hypothesis that translators do leave "thumbprints", which she describes as their styles. Baker's study contributed to the field in two ways. Firstly, it introduced corpora into the study of translator style. Secondly, it views styles of translators as their "thumbprints"—the consistent linguistic choices that translators make in a target text which is free from source text influence.

Following Baker's seminal work (ibid.), numerous studies have employed corpora to investigate translator style, albeit under different definitions and through varied ways of analysis. The following sections will provide a brief review of these definitions and ways of analysis.

2.3 Approaches to Translator Style

Baker (2000: 241) asserts that the analysis of translator style should focus on whether individual translators demonstrate their unique styles, rather than solely on whether a translation accurately reflects the style of the original author. She thus defines translator style as "a kind of thumb-print that is expressed in a range of linguistic—as well as non-linguistic—features" (p. 245). These features cover the translator's choice of materials for translation, consistent use of strategies like prefacing and footnoting, idiosyncratic expressions, characteristic language usage, and individual linguistic habits. In essence, Baker (ibid.) argues that studies of translator style should emphasize prevalent or habitual patterns of linguistic behaviors, rather than focusing solely on isolated instances of intervention (p. 245).

However, Malmkjær (2003: 39) argues that the analysis of translator style needs to focus on the underlying reasons behind the specific shaping of a translation based on a given source text. Similarly, Boase-Beier (2006: 5) suggests that attention should be given to the translator's perception of the style in source text, particularly how the style is modified or preserved in target text. Hence, Malmkjær (2003) and Boase-Beier (2006) take a different approach by exploring the style of translated texts in relation to both source and target texts.

As such, Saldanha (2011) distinguishes between *translator style* and *translational style*. She argues that Malmkjær and Boase-Beier's focus is on the style of texts (translational style), which is considered a response to the source text. In contrast, Baker (ibid.) emphasizes translator style, which refers to "stylistic idiosyncrasies that remain consistent across several translations despite differences among their source texts" (Saldanha, 2011: 27). Furthermore, Saldanha (ibid.: 27) contents that "most work in translation studies focuses on the style of translations, as opposed to the style of translators." According to Saldanha (ibid.: 26), the style of a translated text emerges from the "combination" of linguistic features selected by multiple individuals, including the author(s), translator(s), and possibly editor(s). These features are expressed in a way that makes it challenging to discern the responsibility for the choices made by each individual. Saldanha (ibid) maintains that while style can be seen as an attribute of the text or the individual, an integrated perspective that considers both aspects would allow us to "attribute responsibility for stylistic decisions and to go beyond the source text in search of motivation" (p. 28). Thus, she offers the following definition of translator style:

A translator style is *'a way of translating' which:*

is felt to be recognizable across a range of translations by the same translator,

distinguishes the translator's work from that of others,

constitutes a coherent pattern of choice,

is 'motivated', in the sense that it has a discernable function or functions, and

cannot be explained purely with reference to the author or source-text style, or as the result of linguistic constraints.

(Saldanha 2011: 31)

Saldanha's definition suggests that translator style is unaffected by the style of the source text or the conventions of the target language. Instead, it is shaped by the translator's habitual behavior consistently observed throughout their translated works. As a result, the analysis of translator style should concentrate exclusively on the linguistic patterns that emerge from the translator's unconscious decision-making process. The following section will discuss how we use diverse corpus designs to analyze translator style.

2.4 Corpus Designs in Translator Style Research

Corpus designs play a crucial role in corpus-assisted translator style research. Different types of translator style research (Cf. 2.4.2) often adopt different corpus designs to examine the stylistic phenomenon (Li, 2016: 105). For instance, TT-oriented studies, which focus exclusively on target texts, often employ the comparable corpora design. On the other hand, ST-oriented studies, which consider both source and target texts, often utilize parallel corpora design. Therefore, it is essential to gain a clear understanding of the corpus designs used in translator style research before delving into the different types of research. The subsequent sections will provide detailed explanations of two corpus designs commonly used in existing research: the comparable and parallel corpus models.

2.4.1 The Comparable Model

The comparable corpus design (Fig. 2.1) compares the stylistic features of translations produced by one translator with those of the translations by another, as well as with those of a reference corpus of non-translated texts in the same language. This model is often utilized in TT-oriented studies, where the source texts for the translations can be either identical (e.g., Bosseaux, 2007; Winters, 2009) or different (e.g., Baker, 2000; Saldanha, 2011). When the source text is the same, it is referred to as the one-to-many mode, while different source texts correspond to the many-to-many mode. In the one-to-many mode, translations created by different translators are compared between themselves and/or with a reference corpus of non-translated texts in the same language. In the many-to-many mode, translations generated by different translators using varied source texts in terms of languages and/or genres are compared between themselves and/or with a reference corpus of non-translated texts in the same language.

Overall, the comparable corpus model is suitable for the analysis translator style through target texts.

2.4.2 The Parallel Model

The parallel corpus model (Fig. 2.2) examines the differences of selected stylistic features (e.g., formal features, functional features) between a source text and its multiple target texts produced by different translators, as well as the differences between these target texts. The parallel corpus model is predominantly employed in ST-oriented studies, which also consist of two modes: the single and multiple modes. The single mode (e.g., Bosseaux, 2007; Huang, 2015) includes a parallel corpus that comprises a source text and its several target texts. In this mode, some selected stylistic features in the target texts resulting from translators' choices are analyzed and compared with those in the source text, as well as between different target texts. The multiple mode (e.g., Winters, 2004) often incorporates two or more sets of such parallel corpora, where the analysis and comparison are performed within each set of parallel corpora as well as across different sets of parallel corpora.

In contrast to the comparable corpus model, the parallel corpus model not only focuses on monolingual comparisons, but also emphasizes bilingual comparisons in the analysis of translator style.

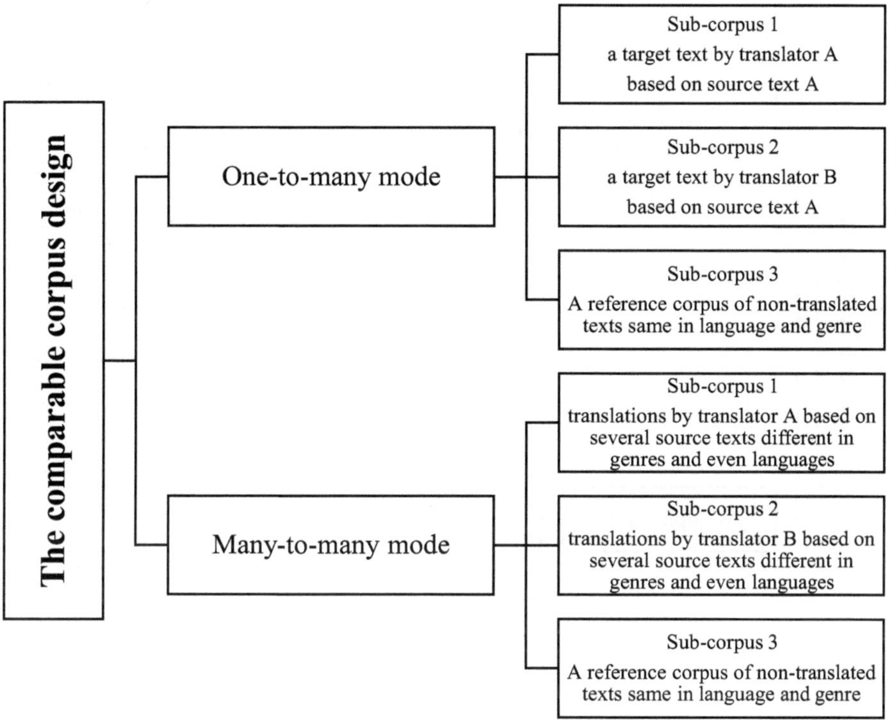

Fig. 2.1 The comparable corpus model

2.5 Types of Corpus-Assisted Translator Style Research

Saldanha (2011) classifies corpus-assisted studies of translational style/translator style into two distinct types: the TT-oriented and ST-oriented studies. TT-oriented studies revolve around target texts, while the ST-oriented studies place emphasis on both source and target texts (Saldanha, 2011; Li, 2016).

2.5.1 TT-Oriented Studies

The objective of TT-oriented studies is to identify and compare stylistic features in translated texts at various linguistic levels, such as morphemes, words, and sentences. TT-oriented studies (Baker, 2000; Olohan, 2004; Saldanha, 2011) often focus on the typical linguistic patterns observed in translations produced by different translators, in which a translated text or a reference corpus of non-translated text is selected as a benchmark for evaluating the styles of a single translator or those of multiple translators. Over years, numerous TT-oriented studies (e.g., Li et al., 2011; Li et al.,

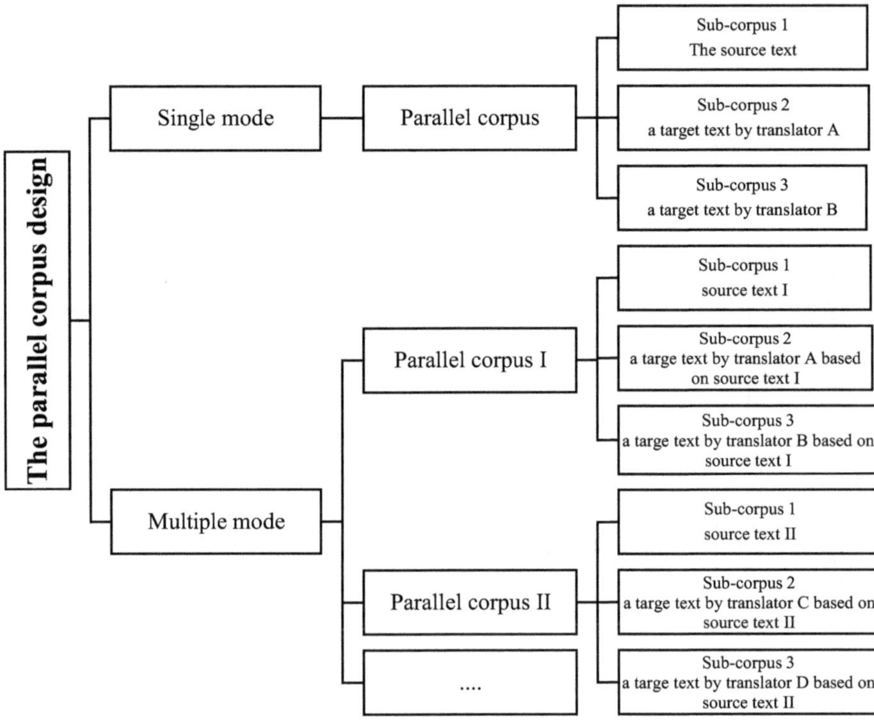

Fig. 2.2 The parallel corpus model

2018) have been conducted to compare the styles of various translators working on similar or different source texts. These studies differ in corpus design, and importantly the choice of stylistic indices used to capture a translator's style. This has resulted in three variants of TT-oriented studies, as depicted in Fig. 2.3

The first variant (hereafter as TV-I) of TT-oriented studies adopts the many-to-many mode and investigates translators' styles using the stylistic indices suggested

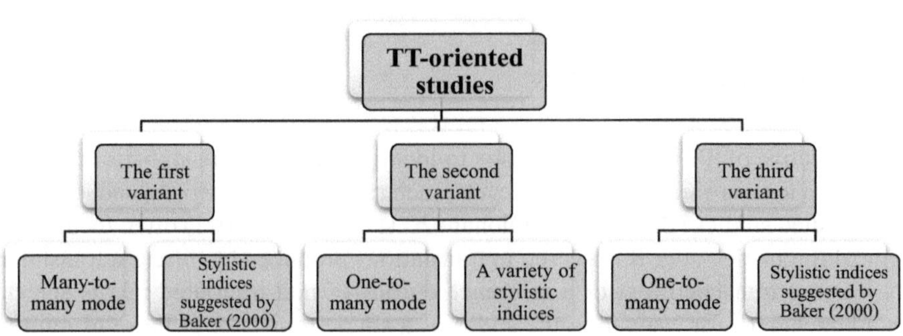

Fig. 2.3 Variants of TT-oriented studies of translator style

by Baker (2000): STTR (standardized type-token ratio), average sentence length, and reporting verbs. TV-I studies (e.g., Baker, 2000; Saldanha, 2011) compare translators' styles across their multiple translations of source texts in different languages and/or genres with those of other translators by analyzing these specific stylistic indices through comparable corpora. The primary goal of TV-I studies is to find out whether translators leave thumbprints in their target texts that are independent of the source texts.

The second variant (hereafter as TV-II) of TT-oriented studies examines translators' styles by using a wide range of formal stylistic indices, including the specific indices proposed by Baker (2000). This variant employs the one-to-many mode and analyzes various stylistic indices (e.g., STTR, reporting verbs, contractions, distal demonstratives, italics) that are capable of capturing translators' styles. Compared to TV-I, TV-II studies provide more flexibility in the selection of stylistic indices. The primary concern of most TV-II studies (e.g., Hou, 2014; Mastropierro, 2018; Wang & Li, 2020) is to identify stylistic diversities between translators working on the same source text, and explore possible factors contributing to these diversities.

The third variant (hereafter as TV-III) falls somewhere in between TV-I and TV-II studies. TV-III studies are similar to TV-I studies by using the specific indices proposed by Baker, but adopting the one-to-many mode, as in TV-II studies. As a result, despite employing the same stylistic indices as TV-I studies, TV-III studies (e.g., Olohan, 2004; Li, 2016) differ due to their distinct modes of analysis. Furthermore, TV-III studies also diverge from TV-II studies as they concentrate on a different set of stylistic indices, despite both types of studies using the one-to-many mode in analysis.

Overall, the discrepancies among the three variants of TT-oriented studies are minor, except for some differences in corpus design and the choices of stylistic indices that represent translator style.

2.5.2 ST-Oriented Studies

The ST-oriented studies investigate how translators transfer stylistic features from source texts to target texts and the possible stylistic variations across these target texts. These studies often employ the bilingual parallel corpora model in corpus design, with the option to use either the single or multiple mode (see Fig. 2.2). Over the past two decades, numerous ST-oriented studies (e.g., Winters, 2013; Huang, 2014) have been conducted to analyze and compare how translators handle stylistic features in source texts and examine resulting stylistic diversities in their target texts. Similar to TT-oriented studies, ST-oriented studies also show variability in the selection of stylistic indices that represent translator style. Nevertheless, this variability in ST-oriented studies is often related to the quality (e.g., formal, functional) of the indices rather than their quantity (i.e., the number of indices being selected).

As illustrated in Fig. 2.4, the ST-oriented studies have two variants. The first variant (hereafter as SV-I) examines translators' styles through the ways they deal

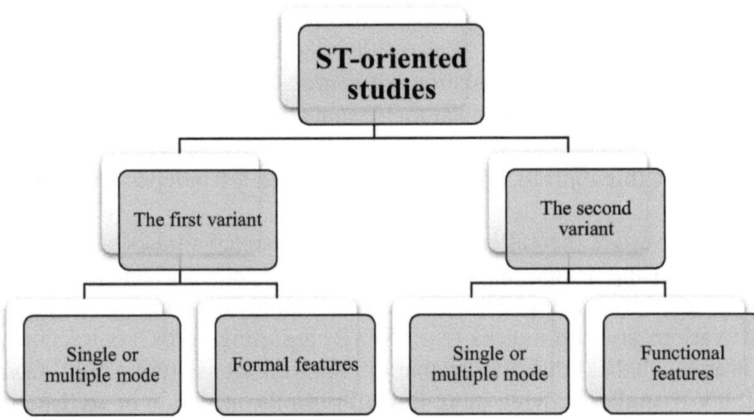

Fig. 2.4 Variants of ST-oriented studies of translator style

with formal linguistic features (e.g., lexical features, syntactic features) in target texts. SV-I studies (e.g., Liu & Afzaal, 2021; Chen & Li, 2023) utilize a predefined set of formal linguistic features identified in the source text as a benchmark to evaluate and compare translators' styles. These linguistic features are analyzed in different target texts of the same source text, where deviations from the source text are considered indicative of translators' styles. These SV-I studies also explore stylistic differences among different translators working on the same source text and analyze different factors that contribute to these differences.

The second variant (hereafter as SV-II) of ST-oriented studies investigates how translators handle literary functions (e.g., viewpoints, emotions, discourse presentations) in source texts. Unlike SV-I studies, SV-II studies do not exclusively focus on formal linguistic features. Instead, they examine how translators deal with the literary functions associated with these formal features and the resulting stylistic nuances between translators. This emphasis on functional aspects in translator style represents a departure from the use of formal linguistic features as stylistic indices initially suggested by Baker (2000). However, some SV-II studies (e.g., Bosseaux, 2004; Boase-Beier, 2006; Winters, 2013; Huang, 2014; Aldawsari, 2019) have limitations as they concentrate on "global"[1] literary functions, such as viewpoints and discourse presentations, while neglecting relatively "local" functions like thematic construction and characterization.

Overall, the present study argues that exploring these functional features could be a promising direction for advancing translator style research, which will be discussed further in Chapter 4.

[1] Definitions of the "global" and "local" literary functions will be provided and explained in Chapter 4.

2.6 Sense-Making in Translator Style Research

Pursing scientific rigor solely though excessive and unnecessary quantitative investigations is what we must caution against when conducting empirical linguistic and translation research (Baker, 1993; Tymoczko, 1998; Sinclair, 2004). Furthermore, Toury (1995, 2012) presents a research approach comprising three phases for systematic descriptive translation research. In this framework, the description of the translation product should be augmented by discussions concerning the wider sociocultural systems. Consequently, a reasonable and preferred corpus-assisted translation study should not merely reaffirm existing knowledge. Instead, it should explore the underlying causes for the patterns and trends that manifest in statistical data. This would require more than intuitive interpretations of the data, but rather thorough and well-substantiated efforts to make sense of the statistics, which incorporate at least the following characteristics:

> It does not merely present statistical results to prove the obvious and known.
>
> It goes further to explain the statistical results by looking at the causes for such tendencies as revealed in the statistical results.
>
> The explanation is firmly grounded in translation theories or other related disciplines, such as linguistic, cultural, literary, and sociological theories.
>
> (Li, 2016: 110)

The process of sense-making, as exemplified in Fig. 2.5, plays a crucial role in meaningful corpus-assisted translation studies, including translator styles research. Li (2016: 110) emphasizes that the sense-making process represents the final yet essential stage in translator style research, which involves establishing a connection between the retrieved statistical data and a proper comprehension of the translation process and products. This entails addressing inquiries concerning translation production, the evolution of translator styles, and their sociocultural influence on the target culture and language.

In translator style research, we can gain insight into the stylistic landscape derived from corpus analysis by examining two different categories of contributing factors: translatorial and extra-translatorial factors, as illustrated in Fig. 2.6. Given that translator style research primarily focuses on translators, an important human agent in translation, the classification of "translatorial" and "extra-translatorial" factors can effectively illustrate how various elements surrounding translators can influence their stylistic decisions. The "translatorial" factors are intimately linked to the translators themselves, including aspects such as their personal backgrounds, motivations for translation, attitudes towards the source text and culture, as well as personal stylistic and linguistic preferences. On the other hand, the "extra-translatorial" factors have less direct relevance to the translators and may involve external influences, such as patronizing intervention and post-translational influences.[2] As stated by Tymoczko

[2] Post-translational influence in this chapter refers to the possible stylistic influence of an earlier translation on a latter translation of the same source text by a different translator (see Ji, 2009).

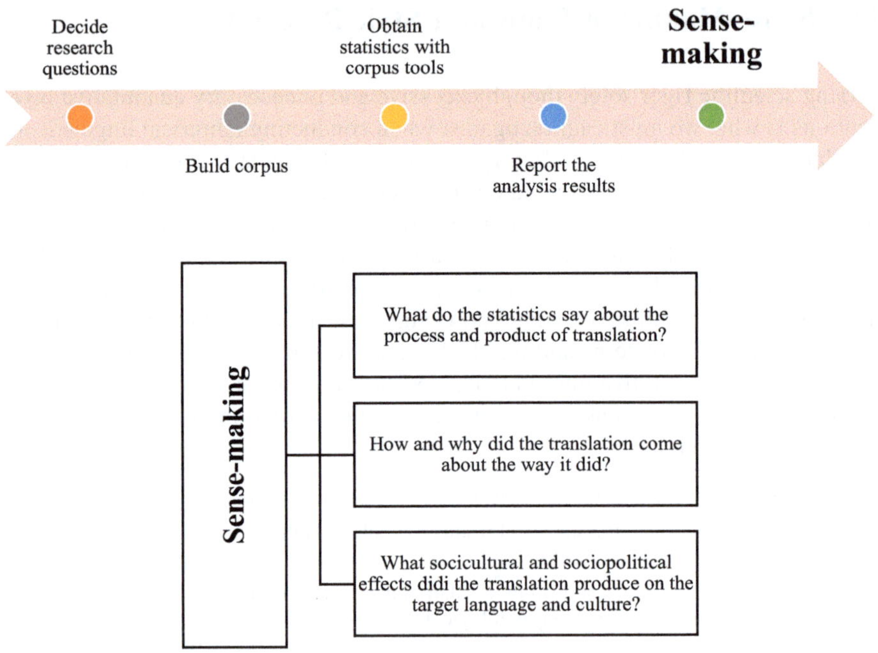

Fig. 2.5 Sense-making in corpus-assisted translator research

(1998), patronizing intervention represents a significant factor influencing translators' decisions, serving as one of the determinants of translation practice. Additionally, as discussed by Ji (2009), post-translational influence can also exert a partial impact on the choices made by translators.

To investigate these translatorial and extra-translatorial factors, important sources such as paratexts of translated works, patronage information, translator interviews,

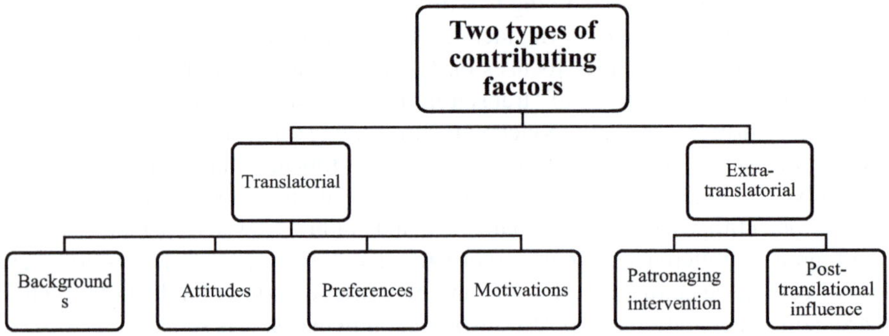

Fig. 2.6 Two types of contributing factors

and journalistic reports related to authors and translators are good places to start. Paratextual elements may include a publisher's promotional materials, correspondence between the author and translator, and scholarly reviews of translations (Genette, 1997; Li, 2016). Patronage information, obtainable from paratexts and publishers' online profiles (e.g., official websites), can unveil significant motivations underpinning translated works. Interviews with translators offer crucial insights into their backgrounds, attitudes, preferences, worldviews, and translation processes, which may shed light on their stylistic choices. Journalistic reports concerning authors and translators can provide additional perspectives on the translatorial and extra-translatorial factors that may exert influence on translator style.

2.7 Summary

Baker's (2000) introduction of the corpus-assisted approach has facilitated ongoing investigations into translator style over the past two decades. Various definitions have been proposed to understand what is translator style. While Baker (ibid.) defines it as a translator's "thumbprints" in target texts, Malmkjær (2003) and Boase-Beier (2006) argue that the source texts should not be disregarded in this definition. To unravel the nature of translator style, researchers have conducted different types of analysis (e.g., TT-oriented, ST-oriented) with such corpus designs as the comparable and parallel corpus designs.

While corpus-assisted studies of translator style have made significant progress in terms of corpus designs and ways of analysis, they are not without gaps. One of these gaps is that the functional aspect of translator style has been mostly overlooked in many previous studies, except for SV-II studies. These previous studies primarily focus on the formal aspect of the style, which are shaped by different lexical and syntactic features. In literary translation studies, this can lead to a lack of connections between linguistic description and literary appreciation (Mahlberg, 2013). To address this gap, a potential way is to employ the corpus stylistic method, which not only emphasizes the formal aspect, but highlights the functional aspect as well.

Hence, based on corpus stylistic theories and methods, the present study attempts to propose a novel type of translator style—translator's functional style. We believe that this new type of translator style has the potential to pave new paths for the development of corpus-assisted translator style research. However, before delving into the functional style, it is necessary to provide an overview of existing corpus stylistic research in the upcoming chapter.

References

Baker, M. (1993). Corpus linguistics and translation studies—implications and applications. *Text and technology: In honour of John Sinclair* (pp. 233–250). John Benjamins Publishing Company.

Baker, M. (2000). Towards a methodology for investigating the style of a literary translator. *Target, 12*(2), 241–266.
Boase-Beier, J. (2006). *Stylistic approaches to translation.* St Jerome Publishing.
Bosseaux, C. (2004). Point of view in translation: A corpus-based study of French translations of Virginia Woolf's *To the Lighthouse. Across Languages and Cultures, 5*(1), 107–122.
Bosseaux, C. (2007). *How does it feel? Point of view in translation.* Rodopi.
Chen, F., & Li, D. (2023). Patronage and ideology: A corpus-assisted investigation of Eileen Chang's style of translating herself and the other. *Digital Scholarship in the Humanities, 38*(1), 34–49.
Genette, G. (1997). *Paratexts: Thresholds of interpretation.* Cambridge University Press.
Hou, Y., et al. (2014). A corpus-based analysis of Howard Goldblatt's translator style: A case study of English translations of Mo Yan's novels. *Foreign Languages and Foreign Language Teaching,* (2), 72–78.
Huang, L. (2015). *Style in translation: A corpus-based perspective.* Springer.
Ji, M. (2009). Corpus stylistics in translation studies: Two modern Chinese translations of *Don Quijote. Language and Literature, 18*(1), 61–73.
Li, D. (2016). *Corpus-assisted translator style research: A corpus linguistic approach to literary translation.* Shanghai Foreign Language Education Press.
Li, D., Zhang, C., & Liu, K. (2011). Translation style and ideology: A corpus-assisted analysis of two English translations of *Hongloumeng. Literary and Linguistic Computing, 26*(2), 153–66.
Li, D., He, W., & Hou, L. (2018). A corpus-based study of Julia Lovell's translating style. *Foreign Language Teaching, 39*(1):70–76.
Liu, K., & Afzaal, M. (2021). Translator's style through lexical bundles: A corpus-driven analysis of two English translations of *Hongloumeng. Frontiers in Psychology, 12*, 633422.
Mahlberg, M. (2013). *Corpus stylistics and Dickens's fiction.* Routledge.
Malmkjær, K. (2003). What happened to God and the Angels: An exercise in translational stylistics. *Target, 15*(1), 37–58.
Mastropierro, L. (2018). *Corpus stylistics in heart of darkness and its Italian translations.* Bloomsbury Publishing.
Olohan, M. (2004). *Introducing corpora in translation studies.* Routledge.
Saldanha, G. (2011). Translator style: Methodological considerations. *The Translator, 17*, 25–50.
Savory, H. (1957). *The art of translation.* Jonathan Cape.
Sinclair, J. (2004). *Trust the text: Language, corpus and discourse.* Routledge.
Toury, G. (1995). *Descriptive translation studies and beyond.* John Benjamins Publishing Company.
Toury, G. (2012). *Descriptive translation studies and beyond (revised edition).* John Benjamins Publishing.
Tymoczko, M. (1998). Computerized corpora and the future of translation studies. *Meta: Translators' Journal, 43*(4), 652–660.
Venuti, L. (2000). *The translation studies reader.* Routledge.
Winters, M. (2004). German translations of F. Scott Fitzgerald's *The Beautiful and Damned*: A corpus-based study of modal particles as features of translators' style. *Using Corpora and Databases in Translation*, 71–78.
Winters, M. (2009). Modal particles explained: How modal particles creep into translations and reveal translators' styles. *Target, 21*(1), 74–97.
Winters, M. (2013). *Modality and translation.* University of Nottingham.
Wang Q., & Li, D. (2020). Looking for translators' fingerprints: A corpus-based study on Chinese translations of *Ulysses*. In: Hu K., & Kim K. (Eds.) *Corpus-based translation and interpreting studies in Chinese contexts.* Palgrave Macmillan.

Chapter 3
Corpus Stylistics

3.1 Introduction

This chapter offers a brief overview of corpus stylistics, which is closely intertwined with the present research on functional style. The primary goal of the chapter is to provide a clear understanding of corpus stylistics, particularly regarding its definitions and approaches. This will enable us to grasp the potential contributions of corpus stylistic theories and methods towards advancing translator style research.

The chapter is structured as follows: Sect. 3.2 delves into some key features in the "corpus turn" in stylistic research, and demonstrates how this "corpus turn" has facilitated the development of corpus stylistics. Section 3.3 reviews existing definitions for corpus stylistics and discusses some problems with these definitions. Section 3.4 outlines the varying approaches employed in existing corpus stylistic studies, highlighting the ways in which corpus stylistics can provide different theoretical and methodological support to translator style research. Section 3.5 suggests a way to move forward by interconnecting corpus stylistic studies with translator style research. Section 3.6 concludes the present chapter by summarizing the key issues that have been discussed, while also emphasizing the significance of the chapter in relation to other chapters in the book.

3.2 From Corpus Linguistics to Corpus Stylistics

The corpus linguistic approach to language research emerged in the 1960s, but gained prominence in the 1980s due to advancements in computer technology (Biber & Reppen, 2015: 1). This approach relies on computer software to identify linguistic patterns in natural language use, emphasizing the collection and organization of "real-world" language data (Biber et al., 1998: 4). The study of style within language

K. Wu and D. Li, *Researching Translator's Functional Style*, New Frontiers in Translation Studies, https://doi.org/10.1007/978-981-95-1221-8_3

research has been approached from various perspectives and with diverse methodologies. However, traditional stylistic research often heavily relied on the stylistic experiences and intuitions of researchers (Fischer-Starcke, 2010; Ho, 2011). The emergence of corpus linguistics has facilitated a noteworthy shift in stylistic research, known as the "corpus turn" (Leech & Short, 2007: 286). This shift can be partly attributed to the availability of a vast collection of electronic texts in English. We argue that the "corpus turn" represents a recent trend in which theories, models, and methodologies from corpus linguistics have been employed in stylistic research. This "corpus turn" in stylistic research has several key features that are worth discussing. In the following section, we will explore some of these features to understand how the "corpus turn" has advanced stylistic research and contributed to corpus stylistics.

The corpus linguistic approach could provide both theoretical and methodological support for the "corpus turn" in stylistic research. The corpus linguistic approach has demonstrated its effectiveness as a theoretical framework for stylistic studies. There has been an ongoing debate regarding whether the corpus linguistic approach should be considered a theory in itself or simply a method employed in language research. Stubbs (1993: 23) and Teubert (2005: 2) argue that the corpus is more than just a tool for linguistic analysis. They contend that the corpus is an integral concept within contemporary linguistic theory. In contrast, Biber and Reppen (2015: 1) primarily perceive it as a methodological guideline. They assert that the corpus linguistic approach differs from other approaches to language research by not aligning itself with specific "hyphenated" areas of linguistic inquiry, such as psycholinguistics or sociolinguistics. However, Tognini-Bonelli (2001: 1–2) maintains that the corpus linguistic approach serves as both a theoretical framework and a methodological guideline. She emphasizes that although the corpus linguistic approach is practical-oriented in language research, it is a pre-application methodology that establishes its own rules. The dual role of the corpus linguistic approach as a theoretical framework and a methodological guideline strongly supports the "corpus turn" in stylistic research, offering new possibilities for stylistic analysis.

The "corpus turn" in stylistic research places values the authenticity of collected language data and the descriptiveness in analysis process. Similar to empirical research, the authenticity of the collected language data is a crucial concern in both the corpus approach to linguistic and stylistic research (Tognini-Bonelli, 2001: 2). In essence, when we consider a corpus as a compilation of language samples, it should faithfully reflect language usage and, consequently, stylistic phenomena in real-world contexts. Biber and Reppen (2015: 2) note that the corpus linguistic approach strongly advocates the idea that language usage (and the resulting stylistic phenomena) can be better understood and illustrated when systematically described through empirical methods. Tognini-Bonelli (2010: 14) and Conrad (2002: 23) examine the descriptive and empirical nature of the corpus approach, highlighting its inductive logic. In this logic, theoretical assumptions about language and style are generalized based on observations of real language data. These assertions suggest that stylistic patterns within language usage can be more effectively described and understood when derived from real-world contexts.

The "corpus turn" in stylistic research capitalizes on advancements in corpus technology to expand methodological possibilities. The progress in corpus technology can be largely attributed to developments in computer science and technology (McCarthy et al., 2010: 5). In the era before electronic corpora, researchers engaged in linguistic studies had to rely on "human hands", manually collecting thousands of texts for case analysis. Consequently, the size of their collected language samples was often limited, and a corpus of a million words was considered significant (Rayson, 2015: 32). However, rapid advancements in computer technology have transformed this situation. Nowadays, researchers have convenient access to the internet, which enables them to collect hundreds of millions of language samples more easily. Meanwhile, the development of corpus software has provided researchers with efficient tools to examine language usage and variation. This technological progress in corpus linguistic studies has played a significant role in promoting the "corpus turn" in stylistic research. Methodological designs in stylistic research that were once unimaginable for stylisticians who adopted non-corpus approaches have now become commonplace (Davies, 2015: 11). An example of this is the use of reference corpora by researchers aiming to explore stylistic variations among different texts. In the past, such resources were unavailable for stylistic analyses before the advent of corpora. These reference corpora act as benchmarks or norms for language and style, enabling researchers to compare styles in texts and identify stylistic variations.

Therefore, it is evident that the corpus linguistic approach and stylistic studies share numerous similarities. Ho (2011: 7) aptly summarizes these similarities as both approaches emphasizing the importance of authentic linguistic evidence, such as language data retrieved from real-world communication and literary publications. Furthermore, both approaches require a scientific and rigorous analysis that leverages technological advancements to identify recurring patterns and situate findings within broader social, cultural, and ideological contexts. Therefore, it is expected that these two approaches will increasingly intersect, giving rise to an interdisciplinary field known as corpus stylistics.

3.3 Definitions of Corpus Stylistics

Stylisticians with an interest in employing corpora for stylistic research hold various interpretations of what constitutes corpus stylistics. Consequently, there exist diverse definitions of corpus stylistics. On one hand, some scholars view corpus stylistics as a form of quantitative analysis that centers on language and style. For instance, Louw and Milojkovic (2014: 290) propose that corpus stylistics can be characterized as the computational analysis of stylistic features. Similarly, Wynne (2006) defines corpus stylistics as a discipline encompassing multiple methods, including the direct utilization of digitized literary texts and the application of statistical analyses to literary works. On the other hand, some scholars see corpus stylistics as a framework that interconnect language and literature. Mahlberg (2007: 219) sees corpus stylistics as a means of bridging the gap between the study of language and literature. Corpus stylistic research often employs descriptive tools that align not only with linguistic frameworks, but also accommodate the literary qualities of texts. Carter (2014: 86) defines corpus stylistics as the application of corpus linguistic techniques in the literary analysis of different stylistic patterns, which may not be readily discernible through human intuition.

However, there appear to be several issues with the current definitions of corpus stylistics, especially the tendency to narrowly define it as the analysis of literary texts using corpus linguistic or computational methods. This restricted definition is endorsed by Fischer-Starcke (2010), Ho (2011), and Louw and Milojkovic (2016). However, if this is the sole focus of corpus stylistics, it would seem unnecessary to introduce a new label to describe it. Unlike corpus linguistic approaches, which concentrate on specific linguistic aspects, corpus stylistics should include more than just the application of corpus linguistic tools to literary text analysis. Corpus linguistics, regarded as a methodology by Biber and Reppen (2015), serves as a general framework for various linguistic analyses, such as identifying genre variations and detecting lexical differences. It employs the same methods and analytical tools regardless of the area (e.g., linguistic, stylistic, sociocultural) under examination. Therefore, for corpus stylistics to be truly what it claims to be, it must incorporate additional elements (e.g., an independent theoretical framework, specialized analytical tools) beyond the mere use of corpus linguistic methodologies in analysis.

Another issue with current definitions of corpus stylistics is the implicit assumption that traditional stylistics lacks rigor. Fischer-Starcke (2010) suggests that corpus methods offer new insights by studying data systematically and analyzing a larger number of units of meaning compared to the non-corpus methods. However, this argument overlooks the fact that traditional stylistic methods have always aimed for falsifiable, systematic, and rigorous text analyses. For instance, Stockwell's (2010) checklists for stylistic analysis stress systematicity, while Leech and Short's (1981/2007) *Style in Fiction* emphasizes rigor in stylistic analysis. Here, it is worth noting that a systematic stylistic study with methodological rigor does not necessarily have to rely on the corpus linguistic approach. Rather, these essential qualities should be inherent in any well-designed stylistic research. Therefore, corpus stylistics does not inherently possess greater systematicity than traditional stylistics, and the use of corpus techniques only offers additional ways to examine texts. In other words, while systematicity and rigor are necessary for corpus stylistics, it is not sufficient to differentiate it from non-corpus (traditional) stylistics.

A further concern regarding current definitions of corpus stylistics is the confinement of the discipline to the examination of literary language. Stylistics aims to identify linguistic features specific to literary language. However, it is evident that the term 'literary language' is misleading, as there are no linguistic elements exclusive to literary texts that cannot be found in other text types. Consequently, there is no inherent reason for stylistics to be confined to the analysis of literary texts alone. In fact, stylistic analysis extends to non-literary texts, as demonstrated by Feyaerts and Brône's (2005) stylistic comparison between literary and non-literary language, Fogal's (2015) stylistic analysis of pedagogical language use, Jeffries' (2017) critical stylistic studies. Stylistics is best understood as the linguistic examination of style and its interaction with non-linguistic factors, such as genre, authorship, and history. While literature remains the main focus for most stylisticians, there is no inherent justification for such exclusivity. Thus, defining corpus stylistics solely as the corpus linguistic study of literary language is excessively narrow. An appropriate definition of corpus stylistics should consider this broader scope while acknowledging that literature remains the primary subject of investigation for most stylisticians.

Fortunately, recent definitions of corpus stylistics have significantly broadened its scope, extending beyond the realms of both corpus linguistics and literary analysis. For instance, McIntyre and Walker (2019: 315) define corpus stylistics as "a specific focus within corpus linguistics, where the research questions under investigation and/or the analytical frameworks employed primarily concern matters of style". Similarly, Mastropierro (2019: 380) conceptualizes corpus stylistics as a "scalar", capable of "incorporating varying degrees of corpus methods to best accommodate the needs and objectives of the researcher". These recent definitions indicate that corpus stylistics can incorporate a wide range of stylistic analyses conducted using corpus methodologies. Consequently, corpus stylistic analysis offers the potential to triangulate results from diverse analytical perspectives and methods, enabling a multifaceted understanding of stylistic phenomena. In the subsequent section, the chapter will discuss the different approaches that have been employed to conduct corpus stylistic analyses.

3.4 Approaches to Corpus Stylistics

Due to its multiple definitions, corpus stylistics is currently quite varied in its "points of departure" and "ways of analysis". While some studies (e.g., Toolan, 2009; Fischer-Starcke, 2010; Mahlberg, 2013; Hoover et al., 2014) see corpus stylistics as a kind of corpus linguistic study for stylistic purposes, other studies (e.g., Leech et al., 2007; Jeffries & McIntyre, 2010; McIntyre, 2019) regard corpus stylistics as stylistic research assisted by corpus. Similarly, under the umbrella of corpus stylistic research, some researchers such as Ji (2009), Egbert (2012), and Rybicki et al. (2014) explore forensic features, while others like Semino and Short (2004), McIntyre (2015), and Louw and Milojkovic (2016) are interested in examining textual patterns. This diversity in perspectives and areas of interest underscores the multifaceted nature of corpus stylistics, a topic we will explore further in the following.

3.4.1 Points of Departure in Corpus Stylistics

The burgeoning interest in corpus stylistics has fostered increased interaction between corpus linguists and stylisticians. However, there is diversity in the "points of departure" when they approach corpus stylistics.

Some stylisticians (e.g., Semino & Short, 2004; Leech & Short, 2007; McIntyre, 2015; Louw & Milojkovic 2016) conceptualize corpus stylistics as a form of stylistic research that harnesses corpus technologies. They argue that corpus stylistics involves the application of stylistic theories and frameworks to corpus analysis, effectively amalgamating corpus techniques with stylistic theories and frameworks. According to McIntyre (2015: 66), corpus stylistics distinguishes itself from corpus linguistic studies of styles by integrating corpus methods into stylistic research. Semino and Short (2004: i) further propose that corpus stylistics illustrates how stylistics and text/discourse analysis can derive benefits from the use of corpus methodology. Therefore, these scholars perceive corpus stylistics as a branch of stylistics that employs corpus linguistic methodology.

On the contrary, a substantial number of scholars (e.g., Toolan, 2009; Culpeper, 2009; Ho, 2011; Hoover et al., 2014; Mahlberg, 2015; Mastropierro & Mahlberg, 2017; Čermáková, 2018) view corpus stylistics as a burgeoning field of stylistics that applies the corpus linguistic approach. They perceive corpus stylistics as a research domain that utilizes corpus linguistic methods to scrutinize stylistic patterns and features embedded within literary texts. For instance, Čermáková (2018: 122) asserts that corpus stylistics, rooted in corpus linguistics, relies on the comparison of recurring textual patterns and features in literary works. Similarly, Mastropierro and Mahlberg (2017: 79) observe that the term "corpus stylistics" is increasingly employed to describe research that uses corpus linguistic methods for analyzing literary texts. These scholars typically regard corpus stylistics as a specialized form of corpus linguistic research, emphasizing its focus on the examination of literary texts. Furthermore, they underscore the significance of establishing connections between corpus linguistic methods and stylistic analysis. Mahlberg (2013: 5) encapsulates this perspective by suggesting that corpus stylistic research applies corpus methods to analyze literary texts, with a particular emphasis on the relationship between linguistic description and literary appreciation. This viewpoint underscores the value of corpus stylistics in linking the corpus linguistic description of textual patterns to the functions these patterns may serve in literary appreciation.

These diverse "points of departure" have led to varying "ways of analysis" in corpus stylistic research. Some corpus stylistic studies (e.g., Ji, 2009; Egbert, 2012; Rybicki et al., 2014), advocate for a quantitative approach, with a primary focus on the exploration of forensic linguistic features through statistical means. Conversely, other corpus stylistic investigations (e.g., Semino & Short, 2004; McIntyre, 2015; Louw & Milojkovic, 2016) place a greater emphasis on qualitative examinations of textual patterns and their functions. The following subsections will briefly discuss these different "ways of analysis" in corpus stylistics.

3.4.2 Corpus Stylistics as Frequencies of Linguistic Forms

Burrows (1997: 186) defined style as "whatever marks the distinct identity of an author or a school, a set of loosely consistent features". Such identity and features include linguistic forms that can be quantified and categorized using corpus tools. Early studies in this domain include Binongo et al.'s (1999) stylometric investigation into the authorships of *Pericles* by Shakespeare, Tabata's (2002) examination of stylistic variation of Dickens' writings, Stubb's (2009) stylistic analysis of Conrad's *Heart of Darkness*, Hoover's (2007) corpus-based research on Henry James's styles, and Ji's (2009) stylistic exploration of two Chinese translations of *Don Quijote* through language archaism. These studies often involved the calculation of frequencies of linguistic forms such as words, n-grams, and sentences.

However, some recent research has shifted its focus to the linguistic behaviors exhibited by these forms, including aspects like repetition and co-occurrence. For example, Egbert (2012) employed Biber et al., (1998) multidimensional analysis to measure the styles of ten authors by investigating the co-occurrence of various linguistic variables. Rybicki et al. (2014) utilized Burrows' (2002) *Delta* stylometric algorithm to attribute authorship of chapters/passages in two novels co-authored by Conrad and Ford, with specific attention to word frequencies and occurrence patterns. Similarly, Segarra et al. (2016) determined authorship of the *Henry VI* plays by examining the lexical webs formed by adjacent words. Winters (2018) focused on the length, distribution, and repetition of words and sentences in her study that compares the stylistic nuances in different English translations of Natascha Wodin's novels.

Undoubtedly, corpus stylistic studies that emphasize frequency analysis have contributed quantitative insights into stylistic features of texts as well as linguistic idiosyncrasies of their authors. However, it is equally important to recognize that corpus stylistic research focusing on textual patterns and their associated functions provides another dimension to the understanding of style.

3.4.3 Corpus Stylistics as Functions of Textual Patterns

Hunston (2010: 152) defined "patterns in text" as the meaningful repetition of linguistic forms such as words, structures, and sounds. In literary texts, such repetition of linguistic forms is particularly noteworthy because, while creating textual patterns, it also imbues them with potential literary functions. For instance, Louw (1993) demonstrates how the ironic effect in David Lodge's *Small World* is constructed through the collocational pattern "bent on". Fischer-Starcke (2006) illustrates how certain lexico-grammatical patterns formed by the most frequent word sequences can contribute to the characterization of story figures in Jane Austen's *Persuasion.* Culpeper (2009) shows how patterns of "keywords, parts-of-speech, and semantic categories" are linked to character speech in Shakespeare's classic *Romeo and Juliet.*

In some studies, the examination of textual patterns has evolved to consider their functions within a holistic and text-driven perspective, rather than studying them in isolation. These studies often investigate multiple functions of textual patterns collectively, leading to the identification of such literary functions as characterization, fictional world building, and thematic construction. Additionally, these studies frequently employ keywords and/or key clusters as the starting point of investigation. For instance, Mahlberg and McIntyre (2011) explore keywords and their functions as the "building blocks of the fictional world" in Ian Fleming's *Royale Casino*. In their analysis, they propose a keyword classification model that categorizes keywords in fiction into "fictional world signal keywords" and "thematic signal keywords". Mahlberg (2013) examines five-word clusters in Dickens' novels and their local textual functions in the characterization of memorable story figures. These clusters fall on a continuum between contextualizing and highlighting functions related to labels, speech, body parts, narratorial comments, time, and places. Mastropierro and Mahlberg (2017) use keywords as starting points to explore cohesive webs in Lovecraft's *At the Mountains of Madness* and their functions in constructing literary meanings. Similarly, Mastropierro (2018) analyzes keywords and compares their roles in the thematic constructions of "Africa" and "the African" in Conrad's *Heart of Darkness* and its Italian translations. Montoro et al. (2019) compare the differences in syntactic complexity between "serious literature" and "popular fiction", with a specific focus on the "subordinating conjunction markers of syntactic subordination" (p. 296). They find that "serious literature" is not necessarily more complex than "popular fiction" in terms of syntactic structure.

In general, corpus stylistic studies that focus on the examination of textual patterns in literary texts have provided insights into the functional aspects of different stylistic phenomena. This functional perspective complements the formal aspect explored in quantitative-oriented corpus stylistic research.

3.5 A Way to Move Forward

While the majority of corpus stylistic studies have focused solely on non-translated texts, there is an emerging trend in which studies are beginning to include translated texts as well. These studies (e.g., Mahlberg, 2007; Li et al., 2011; Čermáková, 2015, 2018; Mastropierro, 2015, 2018; Mastropierro & Mahlberg 2017) have primarily explored stylistic shifts between source texts (ST) and their corresponding target texts (TT) from such perspectives as semantic prosodies, lexical cohesion, and local textual functions. However, it appears that these studies have overlooked the role of translators in these ST-TT shifting processes. Translation is a human activity that involves not only the product, process, and context, but also the participants (Saldanha & O'Brien, 2014). Therefore, there are reasons to believe that translators, as major participants, play a crucial role in shaping the styles of the TTs and triggering subsequent ST-TT stylistic shifts.

Hence, we argue that incorporating translators into corpus stylistic studies could be a promising way for both corpus stylistic and translator style research to move forward. By focusing on translators, the scope of corpus stylistic research can be expanded, while the employment of corpus stylistic methodologies can provide theoretical and methodological support for the development of translator style research.

For corpus stylistic studies, the inclusion of translator style into the analysis of translated texts could broaden the existing research scope. This could be achieved by shifting the focus from the products (i.e., source and target texts) to the participants involved in the translation process, such as the authors and translators. Since translation is a human activity that occurs within specific sociocultural contexts (Toury, 1980; Saldanha & O'Brien, 2014), a sole examination of the translated texts themselves cannot fully capture the complexities of these human activities. Therefore, when conducting corpus stylistic analyses of translated (literary) texts, it is crucial to expand the research scope to include the participants, the contexts in which the translation takes place, and even the translation process itself.

For translator style research, the integration of corpus stylistic theories and methods into the investigation opens up new possibilities for the field to move forward. As highlighted by De Sutter and Lefer (2020: 6), existing corpus-assisted translation studies, including translator style research, have faced certain limitations such as limited research designs, narrow methodologies, and isolation from other disciplines. Therefore, incorporating corpus stylistic theories and methods into translator style research aligns with De Sutter and Lefer's (2020) new research agenda, which emphasizes multifactorial research designs, methodological pluralism, and interdisciplinarity.

Furthermore, applying corpus stylistic methods to explore translator style offers the following advantages:

1. It facilitates the understanding of a (translated) literary work by connecting linguistic descriptions with literary appreciation (Mahlberg, 2013: 5). This distinguishes the corpus stylistic approach from previous corpus-assisted translator style research (e.g., Baker, 2000; Saldanha, 2011), as it not only examines the formal aspect of language, but also considers the functional aspect.
2. It encourages a quantitative stylistic look at the (translated) literary work in terms of textual functions. Advances in digital humanities and computational linguistics have enabled corpus stylistic studies to utilize computational methods, such as text-mining, to analyze and compare translators' styles. These methods would offer quantitative insights into (translated) texts, facilitating the exploration of translators' functional styles.
3. It provides a relatively comprehensive understanding of translator style through triangulation. By examining translator style from multiple analytical perspectives (e.g., literary function, textual function) and employing various corpus stylistic methods (e.g., cluster analysis, lexico-semantic analysis), researchers gain different viewpoints on the same stylistic phenomenon. This triangulation enhances the reliability of research findings and enriches our comprehension of the examined stylistic phenomenon.

Given these advantages, incorporating corpus stylistic methods into translator style research has the potential to significantly advance both fields, both theoretically and methodologically.

3.6 Summary

This chapter has provided a concise overview of corpus stylistics, highlighting its origins, current status, and future directions. The fusion of corpus linguistics and stylistic research, often referred to as the "corpus turn", has established corpus stylistics as an interdisciplinary field. The wide array of definitions associated with this interdisciplinary field has contributed to a multifaceted understanding of the discipline, albeit at times leading to challenges and misconceptions. Nonetheless, these varying definitions have also empowered researchers to approach stylistic phenomena in (literary) texts from diverse perspectives. Looking ahead, we contend that the inclusion of translator style research within corpus stylistic investigations is important. It serves as a means of providing theoretical and methodological support to translator style research, while simultaneously expanding the research scope of corpus stylistics.

As we conclude this chapter, it is crucial to emphasize its importance as a bridge between the preceding chapter (Chapter 2), which reviews prior studies on translator style, and the forthcoming chapter (Chapter 4), which examines the functional aspect of translator style research.

References

Baker, M. (2000). Towards a methodology for investigating the style of a literary translator. *Target, 12*(2), 241–266.

Biber, D., Conrad, S., & Reppen, R. (1998). *Corpus linguistics: Investigating language structure and use*. Cambridge University Press.

Biber, D., & Reppen, R. (2015). Introduction. In D. Biber & R. Reppen (Eds.), *The Cambridge handbook of English corpus linguistics* (pp. 1–8). Cambridge University Press.

Binongo, G., & Smith, A. (1999). The application of principal component analysis to stylometry. *Literary and Stylistic Computing, 14*(4), 445–65.

Burrows, J. (1997). Style. In: Copeland, E. & McMaster, J. (Eds.) *The Cambridge companion to Jane Austen* , 170–188. Cambridge University Press.

Burrows, J. (2002). Delta: A measure of stylistic difference and a guide to likely authorship. *Literary and Linguistic Computing, 17*(3), 267–87.

Carter, R. (2014). *Language and creativity: The art of common talk*. Routledge.

Čermáková, A. (2015). Repetition in John Irving's novel *A Widow for One Year*: A corpus stylistics approach to literary translation. *International Journal of Corpus Linguistics, 20*(3), 355–77.

Čermáková, A. (2018). Translating children's literature: Some insights from corpus stylistics. *Ilha do Desterro, 71*(1), 117–133.

Conrad, S. (2002). Corpus linguistic approaches for discourse analysis. *Annual Review of Applied Linguistics, 22*, 75–95.

Culpeper, J. (2009). Keyness: Words, parts-of-speech and semantic categories in the character-talk of Shakespeare's *Romeo and Juliet*. *International Journal of Corpus Linguistics, 14*(1), 29–59.

Davies, M. (2015). Corpora: An introduction. In D. Biber & R. Reppen (Eds.), *The Cambridge handbook of English corpus linguistics* (pp. 11–31). Cambridge University Press.

De Sutter, G., & Lefer, M. A. (2020). On the need for a new research agenda for corpus-based translation studies: A multi-methodological, multifactorial and interdisciplinary approach. *Perspectives, 28*(1), 1–23.

Egbert, J. (2012). Style in nineteenth century fiction: A multi-dimensional analysis. *Scientific Study of Literature, 2*(2), 167–98.

Feyaerts, K., & Brône, G. (2005). Expressivity and metonymic inferencing: Stylistic variation in nonliterary language use. *Style, 39*(1), 12–36.

Fischer-Starcke, B. (2006). The phraseology of Jane Austen's *Persuasion*: Phraseological units as carriers of meaning. *ICAME Journal, 30*, 87–104.

Fischer-Starcke, B. (2010). *Corpus linguistics in literary analysis: Jane Austen and her contemporaries*. Continuum.

Fogal, G. G. (2015). Pedagogical stylistics in multiple foreign language and second language contexts: A synthesis of empirical research. *Language and Literature, 24*(1), 54–72.

Ho, Y. (2011). *Corpus stylistics in principles and practice: A stylistic exploration of John Fowles' The Magus*. Continuum.

Hoover, D. L. (2007). Corpus stylistics, stylometry, and the styles of Henry James. *Style, 41*(2), 174–203.

Hoover, D. L., Culpeper, J., & O'Halloran, K. (2014). *Digital literary studies: Corpus approaches to poetry, prose, and drama*. Routledge.

Hunston, S. (2010). How can a corpus be used to explore patterns? In A. O'Keeffe & M. McCarthy (Eds.), *The Routledge handbook of corpus linguistics* (pp. 152–166). Routledge.

Jeffries, L. (2017). *Critical stylistics: The power of English*. Palgrave Macmillan.

Jeffries, L., & McIntyre, D. (2010). *Stylistics*. Cambridge University Press.

Ji, M. (2009). Corpus stylistics in translation studies: Two modern Chinese translations of *Don Quijote*. *Language and Literature, 18*(1), 61–73.

Leech, G., & Short, M. (2007). *Style in fiction: A linguistic introduction to English fictional prose*. Pearson Education.

Li, D., Zhang, C., & Liu, K. (2011). Translation style and ideology: A corpus-assisted analysis of two English translations of *Hongloumeng*. *Literary and Linguistic Computing, 26*(2), 153–66.

Louw, B., & Milojkovic, M. (2016). *Corpus stylistics as contextual prosodic theory and subtext (Vol. 23)*. John Benjamins.

Louw, W. E. (1993). Irony in the text or insincerity in the writer? The diagnostic potential of semantic prosodies. In M. Baker, G. Francis & E. Tognini-Bonelli (Eds.), *Text and technology: In honour of John Sinclair* (pp. 157–174). John Benjamins.

Mahlberg, M. (2007). Corpora and translations studies: Textual function of lexis in Bleak House and in a translation of the novel into German. In V. Intonti, G. Todisco & M. Gatto (Eds.), *La Traduzione. Lo Stato dell'Arte. Translation. The State of the Art*. (pp. 115–135). Longo.

Mahlberg, M. (2013). *Corpus stylistics and Dickens' fiction*. Routledge.

Mahlberg, M. (2015). Literary style and literary texts. In D. Biber & R. Reppen (Eds.), *The Cambridge handbook of English corpus linguistics* (pp. 346–361). Cambridge University Press.

Mahlberg, M., & McIntyre, D. (2011). A case for corpus stylistics: Ian Fleming's *Casino Royale*. *English Text Construction, 4*(2), 204–227.

Mastropierro, L. (2015). '-ly' adverbs in Lovecraf's At the Mountains of Madness and in two Italian translations: A corpus stylistic approach to literary translation. In L. Pontrandolfo (Ed.), *Spazi della Memoria* (pp. 217–241). Edizioni dal Sud.

Mastropierro, L. (2018). *Corpus stylistics in Heart of Darkness and its Italian translations*. Bloomsbury Publishing.

Mastropierro, L. (2019). Book review: Dan McIntyre and Brian Walker (eds), Corpus Stylistics: Theory and Practice. *Language and Literature, 28*(4), 378–381.

Mastropierro, L., & Mahlberg, M. (2017). Key words and translated cohesion in Lovecraft's *At the Mountains of Madness* and one of its Italian translations. *English Text Construction, 10*(1), 78–105.

McCarthy, M., & O'Keeffe, A., et al. (2010). Historical perspective: What are corpora and how have they evolved? In A. O'Keeffe (Ed.), *The Routledge handbook of corpus linguistics* (pp. 3–13). Routledge.

McIntyre, D. (2015). Towards an integrated corpus stylistics. *Topics in Linguistics, 16*(1), 59–68.

McIntyre, D., & Walker, B. (2019). *Corpus stylistics: Theory and practice.* Edinburgh University Press.
Montoro, R., & McIntyre, D. (2019). Subordination as a potential marker of complexity in serious and popular fiction: A corpus stylistic approach to the testing of literary critical claims. *Corpora, 14*(3), 275–299.
Rayson, P. (2015). Computational tools and methods for corpus compilation and analysis. In D. Biber & R. Reppen (Eds.), *The Cambridge handbook of English corpus linguistics* (pp. 32–49). Cambridge University Press.
Rybicki, J., Hoover, D., & Kestemont, M. (2014). Collaborative authorship: Conrad, ford and rolling delta. *Literary and Linguistic Computing, 29*(3), 422–431.
Saldanha, G. (2011). Translator style: Methodological considerations. *The Translator, 17*(1), 25–50.
Saldanha, G., & O'Brien, S. (2014). *Research methodologies in translation studies.* Routledge.
Segarra, S., Eisen, M., Egan, G., & Ribeiro, A. (2016). Attributing the authorship of the Henry VI plays by word adjacency. *Shakespeare Quarterly, 67*(2), 232–256.
Semino, E., & Short, M. (2004). *Corpus stylistics: Speech, writing and thought presentation in a corpus of English writing.* Routledge.
Stockwell, P. (2010). A critical linguistic framework for the analysis of advertisements. *Journal of Pragmatics, 42*(2), 358–374.
Stubbs, M. (1993). British traditions in text analysis: From Firth to Sinclair. In M. Baker, G. Francis & E. Tognini-Bonelli (Eds.), *Text and technology: In honour of John Sinclair* (pp. 157–74). John Benjamins.
Stubbs, M. (2009). The search for units of meaning: Sinclair on empirical semantics. *Applied Linguistics, 30*(1), 115–137.
Tabata, T. (2002). Investigating stylistic variation in Dickens through correspondence analysis of word-class distribution. In T. Saito, J. Nakamura, & S. Yamazaki (Eds.), *English corpus linguistics in Japan* (pp. 165–182). Rodopi.
Teubert, W. (2005). My version of corpus linguistics. *International Journal of Corpus Linguistics, 10*(1), 1–13.
Tognini-Bonelli, E. (2001). *Corpus linguistics at work.* John Benjamins.
Tognini-Bonelli, E. (2010). Theoretical overview of the evolution of corpus linguistics. *The Routledge handbook of corpus linguistics* (pp. 42–56). Routledge.
Toolan, M. (2009). *Narrative progression in the short story: A corpus stylistic approach.* John Benjamins.
Toury, G. (1980). *In search of a theory of translation.* The Porter Institute for Poetics and Semiotics
Winters, M. (2018). The case of Natascha Wodin's autobiographical novels: A corpus-stylistics approach. In Boase-Beier, J., Fisher, L., & Furukawa, H. (Eds.). *The Palgrave handbook of literary translation*, 145–166. Springer Nature.
Wynne, M. (2006). Stylistics: Corpus approaches. *Encyclopedia of Language & Linguistics, 12*, 223–226.

Chapter 4
The Functional Aspect of Translator Style

4.1 Introduction

This chapter provides a theoretical discussion of the functional aspect of translator style based on the insights gained from the previous two chapters. Specifically, this chapter investigates the functional aspect of translator style through the concept of "functional style". The chapter is organized as follows:

Apart from this introductory section, Sect. 4.2 will examine the conceptualization of functional style. In Sect. 4.3, the functional styles that have been conceptualized will be classified into three different categories, forming the foundation for the case studies conducted in Chapters 8, 9, and 10. Section 4.4 will provide a detailed discussion of various methodological aspects related to the analysis of functional style, including the analytical framework, models, and steps. Section 4.5 will conclude the chapter by summarizing the main arguments from the preceding sections and looking forward into the use of the concept of "functional style" in the upcoming case studies.

4.2 Conceptualization of Functional Style

Building upon the discussions in Chapter 3 regarding the potential functions of textual patterns, we introduce a novel concept termed "functional style". In this book, we define a translator's functional style as the distinctive linguistic idiosyncrasies shown by translators as they (re)create functional aspects in target texts. As shown in Fig. 4.1, functional features in texts can vary in terms of scope and type.

Regarding scope, these functional features can be categorized as "global" and "local" features. "Global" features denote universal elements within texts that fulfill general functions, while "local" features pertain to relatively specific elements that

K. Wu and D. Li, *Researching Translator's Functional Style*, New Frontiers in Translation Studies, https://doi.org/10.1007/978-981-95-1221-8_4

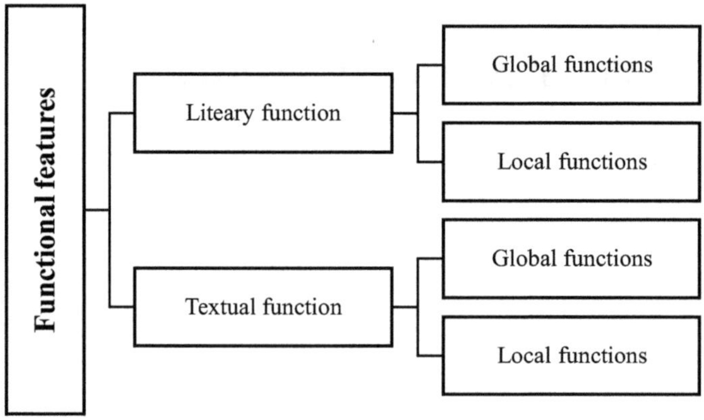

Fig. 4.1 Types and scopes of functional features in texts

also serve functions within texts. Concerning type, functional features can be classified into literary functions and textual functions. Literary functions refer to the diverse purposes or roles that literary elements serve within a literary work, including conveying meaning, evoking emotions, and engaging readers (Reams, 2015: 8). These functions often contribute to the overall aesthetic and artistic qualities of the text. On the other hand, textual functions refer to the specific roles or purposes that various formal features and structures serve within a text (Reams, 2015: 8). These functions play a role in the organization, coherence, and communication of the text.

In terms of literary function, "global" features incorporate, but are not limited to, characterization, thematic reconstruction, and fictional world building. Conversely, "local" features may involve the creation of ironic or humorous effects, expression of viewpoints, presentation of character speech, and so on. Concerning textual function, "global" features could cover textual panorama building, textual coherence, textual cohesiveness, and so on. Meanwhile, "local" features may encompass various formal attributes, such as type-token ratio (TTR), word length dispersion, and average sentence length.

Beyond the definition of functional style and the delineation of the scope and type of functional features, it is crucial to position the study of functional style within the existing translator style research. This positioning provides a more comprehensive understanding of functional style as a concept. The following discussion will elucidate the positioning of functional style studies and establish the connections of this proposed form of translator style with other types of translator style.

As depicted in Fig. 4.2, existing translator style research involves two aspects of language: formal and functional. Research on the formal aspect includes three variants of TT-oriented studies and the first variant of ST-oriented studies (SV-I). Research on the functional aspect comprises the second variant of ST-oriented studies (SV-II) and the proposed functional style studies. A comparison of these proposed functional style studies with the existing TT-oriented and ST-oriented studies reveals some characteristics. Firstly, it does not exclusively align with either TT-oriented or

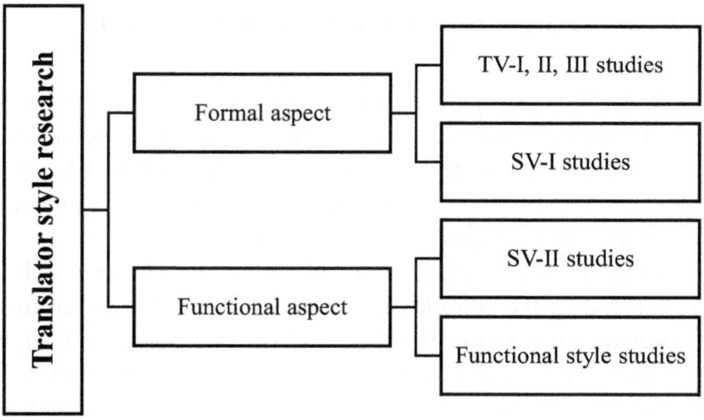

Fig. 4.2 Connections between functional style studies and TT-/ST-oriented studies

ST-oriented studies, although it shares similarities with SV-II studies due to its focus on the functional aspect. Secondly, in contrast to TT-oriented studies that primarily investigate formal linguistic features, the research on functional style places greater emphasis on the functional aspect of language, specifically the potential functions conveyed by these formal linguistic features. Thirdly, it distinguishes itself from SV-II studies by emphasizing "global" functional features found in literary texts. These "global" features comprise multiple textual patterns, in contrast to the relatively "local" functions (e.g., viewpoints, ironic effects, character speech) explored in SV-II studies.

After establishing the working definition of functional style and clarifying its place within the framework of translator style research, it is imperative to move forward with a thorough classification of functional styles. This classification will provide a clear blueprint for the practical application of this newly introduced concept in study.

4.3 Categorization of Functional Style

The book classifies functional styles of translators into three specific forms: "thematic style", "recharacterization style", and "textual-panoramic style". This classification corresponds to three distinct functions that various linguistic forms and patterns can fulfill in literary texts, including thematic reconstruction, recharacterization, and textual panorama building. It is worth stressing that while these three forms are not exhaustive in representing all possible translators' functional styles, they are the most significant and representative types addressed within this book. In the following subsections, we will introduce these three forms of translators' functional styles.

4.3.1 Functional Style as Thematic Reconstruction

According to Wolf (2002: 341), themes are generalizations of "opinions, prejudices, intentions, or ideologies". Themes are inherent in our cognitive structure and are believed to function as meaningful categories that connect lower-level information (van Peer, 2002: 254). In other words, theme is the aboutness of a text, as well as the mental representation of such aboutness in a reader's mind.

In literary context, themes play a crucial role in providing a cohesive thread that assists in organizing the complex semantics of a text. Moreover, themes ensure continuity and establish a sense of identity, allowing readers to navigate through the multiple layers of meaning within the text (Wolf, 2002: 341). Hence, the construction of themes can be seen as an essential consequence of readers' cognitive processing of these layers of meaning. To comprehend the meaning conveyed by written symbols, readers must transform the linear information found in texts into hierarchical structures, in which some elements hold greater importance than others.

The exploration of thematic construction in (literary) texts has been a subject of study in various disciplines, including linguistics, literary studies, psychology, and more recently, computer science. Researchers from these fields have approached the investigation of thematic construction from both product and process perspectives, employing a range of methodologies, such as theoretical approaches (e.g., Coulter & Smith, 2009; Le, 2002; Shen, 2002), experimental and cognitive approaches (e.g., Graesser et al., 2022; McCarthy & Burkett, 2015; Zhang & Hoosain, 2005), and corpus linguistic and computational approaches (Da, 2019; Martindale & West, 2002; Mastropierro, 2018). These studies have deepened our understanding of how themes are constructed in literary texts and the cognitive/psychological mechanisms involved in the process.

For the study of literary translation, these investigations offer insights into the functional styles of translators, particularly concerning thematic reconstruction in translated texts. They shed light on the cognitive and psychological processes involved in readers' comprehension of texts, which in turn might help understand how translators interpret source texts. Additionally, these studies reveal the diverse manifestations of these cognitive and psychological processes in texts. This diversity is useful to the investigation of functional style in translation, as the varied expressions in different translators' target texts not only illustrate reconstructed themes, but also unveil the linguistic idiosyncrasies of translators in thematic reconstruction.

Therefore, this book introduces the concept of "thematic style", which is a specific form of functional style that arises from translators' linguistic idiosyncrasies when they reconstruct original themes in target texts. A more comprehensive exploration of thematic style will be presented in Chapter 8. However, before delving into the thematic style, the following subsection will introduce the concept of "recharacterization style", which represents another distinctive form of functional style.

4.3.2 Functional Style as Recharacterization

In literary studies, a "character" or a "figure" is an individual, whether human or human-like, whose actions can be perceived and predicted (Margolin, 1983: 2). Culpeper (2001) argues that the literary concept of "character" is a textual construct (e.g., words, sentences, paragraphs) and a mental representation of people by readers. Characterization can be broadly defined as the process of portraying or depicting a character in literary works (Reams, 2015: 4). Characterization is crucial to literary works, as it serves to create engaging and relatable characters, advance the plot, convey themes, and evoke emotional responses in readers (Reams, 2015: 7). It contributes to the overall depth, richness, and impact of literary works.

Recognizing the significance of characterization in literary works, it is essential to review previous approaches to characterization before exploring its connection with the present study of functional style. Similar to existing explorations of themes and thematic construction, prior studies on characterization in literature have taken an interdisciplinary approach, incorporating theories and methodologies from various fields such as linguistics (e.g., corpus linguistics), cognitive psychology (e.g., schema theory), and stylistics (e.g., foregrounding theory). For example, Balossi (2014) utilized the corpus linguistic approach to analyze the various methods of characterization in Woolf's *The Waves*. Stockwell and Mahlberg (2015) employed the cognitive poetics/stylistic approach to investigate how readers and authors engage in fictional characterization through mind-modeling. Schubert (2017) used both pragmatic and cognitive semantic approaches to examine the linguistic construction of antiheroes in contemporary fictional television series and their characterization within audience's mind.

These studies have clearly demonstrated that characterization involves both linguistic and cognitive dimensions. Therefore, any investigation into characterization should consider the interplay between linguistic and cognitive aspects. In translator style research, the examination of characterization in translated texts (recharacterization) enables us to analyze how different translators undertake the linguistic reconstruction of characters from source texts and how readers may interpret these reconstructed characters in target texts. The study of recharacterization shares similarities with the exploration of thematic reconstruction in translated texts, as both examine the cognitive and psychological processes underlying the comprehension of textual composition. However, they differ in that recharacterization specifically focuses on the representations of human or people within translated texts, whereas thematic reconstruction pertains to the aboutness or content of the texts.

This book proposes the concept of "recharacterization style" as another form of a translator's functional style. It refers to the linguistic idiosyncrasies that translators show when reconstructing story figures from source texts in target texts. These idiosyncrasies significantly influence how readers interpret these story figures. The book will examine the recharacterization style in Chapter 9. However, before exploring that topic, the subsequent subsection will introduce the concept of "textual-panoramic style", which represents a third form of functional style.

4.3.3 Functional Style as Textual Panorama Building

The book introduces the concept of "textual panorama" as a new concept. Textual panorama is defined as a textual profile based on a set of stylistic indices at various linguistic levels, aiming to provide a comprehensive representation of the text being examined. The purpose of building such a textual panorama is to analyze, from a global and holistic perspective, how a text is structured linguistically at different levels. Textual panorama building, along with thematic construction and characterization, falls under the category of functional features within a text (see Sect. 4.2). However, textual panorama building differs from thematic construction and characterization in that it serves a textual function, while the latter two serve as literary functions.

Explorations of textual panorama are common, although many previous studies may not explicitly use the term "textual panorama" and may have research objectives and designs different from those employed in this book. These previous studies aimed to uncover how textual panorama is constructed in texts and reconstructed in translated texts, with the purpose of revealing the nature of textual function in texts. For instance, Mastropierro (2018) used principal component analysis (PCA) to investigate how different Italian translations of Conrad's *Heart of Darkness* are built upon the most frequent words (MFW) and the most frequent word sequences (MFWs). Wu and Li (2022) employed a set of formal indices (e.g., average word length, moving-average type-token ratio) and MFW/MFWs to study the similarities and differences between translated Chinese *Wuxia* and Western heroic fiction. Sun and Yue (2023) used PCA and N-MFW metrics to explore the translator's (in)visibility from a stylistic perspective.

These studies have shown that the examination of textual panorama can reveal how textual function is realized in (translated) texts, which is helpful in distinguishing one text from another. In literary translation, investigating textual function, specifically textual panorama building in source and target texts, enables us to identify and compare different translators' functional styles. In addition to examining literary functions such as thematic reconstruction and recharacterization, the study of textual functions, particularly textual panorama building, provides an additional perspective on how translators (re)create functional features in translated texts.

Therefore, this book introduces the concept of "textual-panoramic style" as a third form of functional style. It refers to the linguistic idiosyncrasies displayed by a translator when building the textual panorama in target text. The analysis of a translator's functional style in relation to textual panorama building will be conducted in Chapter 10.

4.4 Analysis of Functional Style

Having conceptualized translator's functional style and categorized it into the three different forms, it is now necessary to explore the ways we can analyze such style. This would involve a discussion of the methodological foundations, analytic frameworks, models, and steps needed in the analysis.

4.4.1 Methodological Foundations

The present book takes the Corpus Stylistic Circle and stylometric attribution as the methodological foundations for the investigation of functional style. The following part will provide a short overview of Corpus Stylistic Circle and stylometric attribution, so as to show their relevance to investigating the functional aspect of translator style.

The major concern of the Corpus Stylistic Circle is to link "literary critic's concern aesthetic appreciation with the corpus linguist's concern of linguistic description" (Mahlberg, 2013: 12). In other words, observations of linguistic forms in literary corpora shall be connected to their functions and/or effects as literary appreciation. The Corpus Stylistic Circle derives from Spitzer's (1962) Philological Circle, where linguistic description was assumed to be closely tied to literary application in a mutually motivated and informed manner. In the Philological Circle, the two dimensions (linguistic description and literary application) were considered equally important aspects of a literary text (Spitzer, 1962: 8). Nonetheless, the Corpus Stylistic Circle is more than a simple replicate of the Philological Circle: it adds a third dimension—corpus linguistic description—to this loop (Mahlberg, 2013: 12–13). This means the way we observe linguistic forms has shifted from the relatively "cherry-picking" fashion based on researcher's intuition to observations based on corpora. It is this edge that has endowed corpus stylistics with a potential to go beyond mere linguistic forms and reveal translators' styles by capturing the subtleties in their recreation of literary functions in translation. In this book, this potential is harnessed for the investigation of two specific literary functions: thematic construction and characterization.

However, with its focus on literary functions, the Corpus Stylistic Circle can only reveal one side of translators' functional styles. To unveil the other side, which pertains to textual functions, stylometric attribution becomes a useful tool. Stylometric attribution, dating back to the 19th Century, has found widespread application in identifying the true author of anonymous texts (Rybicki, 2012: 232). This technique is grounded in the belief that there are conscious or unconscious elements of personal style that can help identify the true author of an anonymous text (Rybicki, 2012: 231). To capture these elements of personal style, frequency patterns of the most frequent words (MFW) are often employed as classifiers to distinguish the holistic stylistic features of one author from another. Various types of multivariate statistical analysis, such as principal component analysis (PCA), cluster analysis (CA), and factor analysis (FA), are used to measure the similarities and differences between two texts. Translated texts, like non-translated ones, may also exhibit conscious or unconscious elements of personal style, known as translator style. Hence, stylometric attribution presents a potential method for unveiling the construction of textual panoramas, an important textual function in translated texts.

4.4.2 Analytic Framework

Based on the methodological foundations, the present research designs its own analytic framework (Fig. 4.3) through corpus triangulation, which stresses the importance of "combing multiple sources of data to obtain diverse views on the same phenomenon" (Malamatidou, 2018: 27). As explained in Chapter 1, the focus of this study is on translators' styles within a single piece of translated work. Therefore, the styles examined in our subsequent analysis are limited to four different English translations of *Er Ma*. To elaborate, our research will compare these styles based on the stylistic data acquired from both "literary" and "textual" perspectives, aiming to enhance the validity and reliability of corpus research findings (Denzin, 1989; Malamatidou, 2018).

From the literary perspective, the research will explore these translators' functional styles by analyzing how they recreate the two literary functions, namely

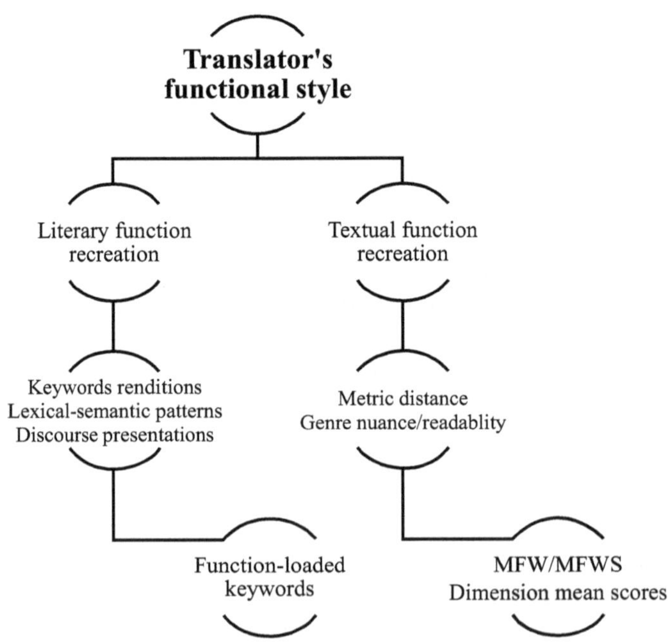

Fig. 4.3 Proposed analytic framework for functional style

thematic construction and characterization. In the process, the study will focus on the ways those translators reconstruct the story theme(s) and recharacterize story figures in translation. From the textual perspective, the study will investigate the translators' functional styles through the ways they build the textual panoramas in target texts. The investigation will concentrate on the MFW/MFWs and the six dimensions proposed by Biber (1988). These linguistic features have proven to be effective textual indicators in previous studies (e.g., Hoover, 2007; Egbert, 2012; Rybicki et al., 2014).

4.4.3 Analytical Models

The theoretical foundations and methodological framework establish the philosophical and operational basis of this research. In alignment with the analytical framework proposed earlier, we have chosen Sinclair's (2004) Extended Units of Meaning and Mahlberg's (2013) Local Textual Functions as the "core" models for examining the interaction between keywords and their contexts in the creation of literary functions. These models will also help us explore how different translators approach these interactions. Additionally, principal component analysis and multidimensional analysis will be employed to assess the construction of textual function by measuring the similarities and differences between the textual panoramas in different translators' target texts. It is worth noting that, although these models are considered the "core", we remain open to incorporating other relevant models, such as those related to discourse presentation, if they prove to be beneficial for our analysis.

4.4.3.1 Extended Units of Meaning

Sinclair (1991, 2004) consistently emphasizes that meaning transcends single words and results from collective efforts of various contextual factors. In other words, the conveyance of meaning transcends the scope of a single word (Stubbs, 2009: 124). Sinclair's model of Extended Units of Meaning posits that a node (a core word or cluster) interacts with its contexts, forming distinct patterns through lexical, grammatical, semantic, and pragmatic relations. These patterns, referred to as "lexical items", encompass four parameters linked to these relations: collocation, colligation, semantic preference, and semantic prosody (Sinclair, 1996: 87–88). In this study, we argue that translators' different handling of these interactions underscores their linguistic idiosyncrasies and thus functional styles. Hence, Sinclair's model is one of the core analytical models in this research.

Local Textual Functions

Originally, Sinclair (1991, 1996, 2004) developed his model to investigate the English language in general, without specific focus on literary contexts. Consequently, his four parameters are not explicitly designed for analyzing literary texts. In literary analysis, the emphasis lies on the literary and aesthetic functions of the text (Mahlberg, 2013: 16–17). This implies that the analysis of a literary text should go beyond mere linguistic interactions and consider the literary and aesthetic purposes underlying these interactions. In response to this, Mahlberg (2013: 17) proposed her model of Local Textual Function, which describes the functional aspects of linguistic items within literary texts and is meant to meet the need of literary analysis. By using this model to examine the linguistic idiosyncrasies of translators in the recreation of literary functions, we can unveil their functional styles. Both Mahlberg's and Sinclair's models will be applied in this study.

Principal Component Analysis

Principal component analysis (PCA), a multivariate statistical analysis technique, is frequently employed in stylometric attribution to assess the overall similarities or differences between texts of comparative features (Manly et al., 2017: 102–103). PCA operates on a set of "n" variables (X_1, X_2, X_n) and combines these variables to generate indices Y (Y_1, Y_2, Y_n), known as principal components. The core concept underlying PCA is to reduce the number of original variables to a smaller set of transformed variables (Manly et al., 2017: 103). In certain quantitative-oriented linguistic and translation studies (e.g., Ji, 2009; Rybicki et al., 2014; Mastropierro, 2018), these variables are often represented by the Most Frequent Words (MFW) and the Most Frequent Word Sequences (MFWS). The frequency patterns of the MFW and/or MFWS are compared to assess the overall similarities or differences between the texts under analysis. Therefore, PCA is well-suited for the present study, as it allows us to measure the extent of diversities or similarities between the textual panoramas of different target texts (TTs) sharing the same source text (ST).

Multidimensional Analysis

The multidimensional analysis (MDA) approach was originally developed by Biber (1988) to compare written and spoken registers in English. It has since been widely used in the analysis of registers, both synchronically and diachronically, across different languages (Xiao, 2009: 421). MDA conducts factor analyses of sixty-seven linguistic features, such as infinitives and third-person pronouns. It has proven effective in studies of world Englishes (e.g., Xiao & Yue, 2009; Shakir & Deuber, 2018), academic discourse (e.g., Crosthwaite & Jiang, 2017; Goulart, 2022), media discourse (e.g., Sardinha & Pinto, 2019; Huang & Ren, 2020), and Internet discourse (e.g., Biber & Egbert, 2016; Sardinha, 2018), among others. More recently, MDA has found application in a few literary translation studies (Diao, 2022), serving as a useful tool for distinguishing the overall stylistic features of one translated text from another. Consequently, MDA is well-suited for this research, as it allows us to measure the overall degree of diversities and similarities between the four translations of *Er Ma*.

4.4.4 Analytic Steps

The analysis of the translator's functional style requires several steps, as outlined below:

Step 1 Involves determining the scope ("global" or "local") and type ("literary" or "textual") of the functional features to be examined. These decisions should align with the specific research objectives and research questions.

Step 2 Consists of selecting appropriate stylistic indices to effectively capture the targeted functional features. These chosen indices are then analyzed within the source text, with a particular focus on understanding how they contribute to the construction of the examined functional features.

Step 3 Requires an investigation of the idiosyncrasies exhibited by different translators as they (re)create the functional features of the source texts within their target texts. These idiosyncrasies can reflect the translators' functional styles, arising from differences between the source text and its target texts, as well as diversities among multiple target texts of the same source text.

Step 4 Involves interpreting previous findings by analyzing possible factors that contribute to stylistic diversities between translators. As translator style research focuses on human agents engaged in translation, it is necessary to examine translational factors (e.g., translators' backgrounds, stances, preferences) and extra-translatorial factors (e.g., patronage, sociocultural influences) that may influence stylistic choices.

Collectively, these steps form a systematic approach to analyze translators' functional styles, covering various scopes and types of functional features presented in texts. This would be useful to understand the functional aspect of translator style in a relatively comprehensive way.

4.5 Summary

This chapter has discussed the functional aspect of translator style, introducing the concept of "translator's functional style". It has conceptualized translator's functional style by providing a definition and situating functional style research within existing corpus-assisted translator style research. The chapter has also classified functional style into three distinct forms: "thematic style", "recharacterization style", and "textual-panoramic style", which involve both literary and textual functions. Methodological considerations related to the analysis of functional style, including foundational methods, the analytical framework, and procedural steps, have also been discussed.

As the first part of the book concludes, it is necessary to stress the interconnectedness of the four chapters in this part. In addition to the introductory chapter (Chapter 1), Chapter 2 provides a brief overview of existing corpus-assisted translator style research, emphasizing one identified research gap highly related to the present study. Subsequently, Chapter 3 explores the theoretical and methodological prospects for bridging this gap through corpus stylistic theories and methods, which lead to the discussion of functional style in the current chapter.

With the theories and methodologies discussed in the first part of this book, the second part will embark on a case study of translator's functional style in the Chinese-English translation of Lao She's novel *Er Ma*. This case study aims to examine the applicability and suitability of the concept of translator's functional style within the specific context of Chinese-English literary translation.

References

Balossi, G. (2014). *A Corpus linguistic approach to literary language and characterization. A corpus linguistic approach to literary language and characterization.* John Benjamins Publishing Company.

Biber, D. (1988). *Variation across speech and writing*. Cambridge University Press.

Biber, D., & Egbert, J. (2016). Register variation on the searchable web: A multi-dimensional analysis. *Journal of English Linguistics*, *44*(2), 95–137.

Coulter, C. A., & Smith, M. L. (2009). The construction zone: Literary elements in narrative research. *Educational Researcher, 38*(8), 577–590.

Crosthwaite, P., & Jiang, K. (2017). Does EAP affect written L2 academic stance? A longitudinal learner corpus study. *System*, *69*, 92–107.

Culpeper, J. (2001). *Language and characterisation: People in plays and other texts*. Longman.

Da, N. Z. (2019). The computational case against computational literary studies. *Critical Inquiry, 45*(3), 601–639.

Denzin, N. K. (1989). *The research act: A theoretical introduction to sociological methods* (3rd ed.). Prentice Hall.

Diao, H. (2022). Homogenized literary co-translation: A hero born and a bond undone. *Across Languages and Cultures*, *23*(1), 92–110.

Egbert, J. (2012). Style in nineteenth century fiction: A multidimensional analysis. *Scientific Study of Literature*, *2*(2), 167–98.

Graesser, A. C., et al. (2022). Reading comprehension and thematic coherence. *Reading Research Quarterly, 57*(2), 445–465.

Goulart, L. (2022). Register variation in understudied academic contexts. *Research in Corpus Linguistics, 10*(2), i–v.

Hoover, D. L. (2007). Corpus stylistics, stylometry, and the styles of Henry James. *Style, 41*(2), 174–203.

Huang, Y., & Ren, W. (2020). A novel multidimensional analysis of writing styles of editorials from China Daily and The New York Times. *Lingua, 235*, 102781.

Ji, M. (2009). Corpus stylistics in translation studies: Two modern Chinese translations of *Don Quijote. Language and Literature, 18*(1), 61–73.

Le, M. (2002). Thematic construction in literary texts. *Literary Studies, 15*(3), 234–251.

Mahlberg, M. (2013). *Corpus stylistics and Dickens' fiction.* Routledge.

Malamatidou, S. (2018). *Corpus triangulation: Combining data and methods in corpus-based translation studies.* Routledge.

Manly, B. F. J., et al. (2017). *Multivariate statistical methods: A primer* (4th ed.). Chapman and Hall.

Margolin, U. (1983). Characterization in narrative: Some theoretical probes. *Neophilologus, 67*(1), 1–14.

Martindale, C., & West, A. N. (2002). Quantitative approaches to the study of literary style. In C. Martindale & A. N. West (Eds.), *The psychology of aesthetics, creativity, and the arts* (pp. 275–294). Cambridge University Press.

Mastropierro, L. (2018). *Corpus stylistics in Heart of Darkness and its Italian translations.* Bloomsbury Publishing.

McCarthy, K. S., & Burkett, C. (2015). Thematic processing in narrative comprehension. *Discourse Processes, 52*(4), 276–303.

Reams, J. (2015). *Characterization in fiction.* San Marcos.

Rybicki, J. (2012). The great mystery of the (almost) invisible translator: Stylometry in translation. In M. Ji & M. P. Oakes (Eds.), *Quantitative methods in corpus-based translation studies: A practical guide to descriptive translation research* (pp. 231–248). John Benjamins Publishing Company.

Rybicki, J., Hoover, D., & Kestemont, M. (2014). Collaborative authorship: Conrad, Ford and Rolling Delta. *Literary and Linguistic Computing, 29*(3), 422–31.

Sardinha, B. (2018). Dimensions of variation across Internet registers. *International Journal of Corpus Linguistics, 23*(2), 125–157.

Sardinha, B., & Pinto, M. (2019). Dimensions of variation across American television registers. *International Journal of Corpus Linguistics, 24*(1), 3–32.

Shakir, M., & Deuber, D. (2018). A multidimensional study of interactive registers in Pakistani and US English. *World Englishes, 37*(4), 607–623.

Schubert, C. (2017). The linguistic construction of antiheroes in contemporary fictional television series. *Language and Literature, 26*(4), 294–314.

Shen, D. (2002). *Thematics in narrative discourse.* Peking University Press.

Sinclair, J. (1991). *Corpus concordance collocation.* Oxford University Press.

Sinclair, J. (1996). The search for units of meaning. *Textus, 9*(1), 75–106.

Sinclair, J. (2004). *Trust the text: Language, corpus and discourse.* Routledge.

Spitzer, L. (1962). Linguistics and Literary History. In *Linguistics and Literary History* (pp. 1–39). New York: Russell & Russell.

Stockwell, P., & Mahlberg, M. (2015). Mind-modelling with corpus stylistics in *David Copperfield. Language and Literature, 24*(2), 129–147.

Stubbs, M. (2009). The search for units of meaning: Sinclair on empirical semantics. *Applied Linguistics, 30*(1), 115–137.

Sun, B., & Yue, M. (2023). The translator's visibility: A stylistic perspective. *Across Languages and Cultures, 24*(1), 52–72.

van Peer, W. (2002). Where do literary themes come from? In W. van Peer (Ed.), *The Quality of Literature* (pp. 253–263). John Benjamins.

Wolf, P. (2002). *Thematics: Interdisciplinary studies.* John Benjamin.

Xiao, R., & Yue, M. (2009). In Baker, P. (Ed.), Using corpora in translation studies: The state of the art. *Contemporary corpus linguistics* (pp. 237–262). Continuum.

Wu, K., & Li, D. (2022). Are translated Chinese Wuxia fiction and western heroic literature similar? A stylometric analysis based on stylistic panoramas. *Digital Scholarship in the Humanities, 37*(4), 1376–1393.

Zhang, X., & Hoosain, R. (2005). Thematic processing in narrative comprehension. *Applied Psychology, 54*(3), 378–395.

Part II
Case Study

Chapter 5
Lao She and His Story of *Er Ma*

5.1 Introduction

Published in 1929, *Er Ma* narrates the journey of a father and son who migrated from China to run a curio shop in London during the early 1920s. In the story, Lao She skillfully juxtaposes the identities of Chinese diaspora and Britons during the early 20th Century, establishing *Er Ma* as a unique work among Lao She's literary repertoire (Jimmerson, 1991: i–ii).

Drawing on the corpus stylistic approach employed by Mastropierro (2018), the current study seeks to bridge corpus analysis with literary criticism. Specifically, this chapter examines the relationship between Lao She's diasporic experiences in London and the two recurring themes of "Diasporic Chinese" and "Local Britons", as identified in previous literary criticism. Section 5.2 introduces Lao She as a writer and explores his experiences in London's Chinese community, shedding light on the potential significance of these themes. Sections 5.3 and 5.4 review previous research on the two themes of "Diasporic Chinese" and "Local Britons". Section 5.5 summarizes the key arguments presented in this chapter, emphasizing the central importance of the two themes in the study.

5.2 Lao She and His Diaspora in London

Lao She, originally named Shu Qing-chun, belonged to a fallen Manchu family and is widely recognized as one of the most influential figures in contemporary Chinese literature (Finkelstein et al., 1984: v; Jimmerson, 1991: i). As a distinguished contemporary Chinese writer (Finkelstein et al., 1984: v; Jimmerson, 1991: i), Lao She received recognition with the honorary title of "People's Artist" for his significant contributions to the development of new Chinese literature (Jimmerson, 1991: iii). Lao She has authored several renowned novels and plays, including *Luotuo Xiangzi*

K. Wu and D. Li, *Researching Translator's Functional Style*, New Frontiers in Translation Studies, https://doi.org/10.1007/978-981-95-1221-8_5

(*The Rickshaw Boy*, 1936), *Er Ma* (*Mr. Ma and Son*, 1929), *Cha Guan* (*Tea House*, 1956), and *Si Shi Tong Tang* (*Four Generations under One Roof*, 1948). These works are characterized by Lao She's distinctive humor and his remarkable command of the Beijing dialect, providing insights into the struggles and challenges faced by socially marginalized lower-class Chinese in the early 20th Century (Jimmerson, 1991: ii). While the majority of Lao She's stories are set in Beijing, his first three novels, *Lao Zhang de Zhe Xue* (*The Philosophy of Lao Zhang*, 1926), *Zhao Zi Yue* (*Sir Chao Said*, 1927), and *Er Ma* (*Mr. Ma and Son*, 1929), were written during his sojourn in London between 1924 and 1930. Notably, *Er Ma* stands out among Lao She's oeuvre for its exploration of themes within the context of 1920s British society, marking a distinct departure from his other works (Finkelstein et al., 1984; Jimmerson, 1991).

Lao She's sojourn constitutes a diasporic experience fraught with British stereotypes and prejudices against the Chinese. As Witchard aptly notes,

> The year when Lao She arrived in London, fear and loathing of the Chinese was fanned not only by reports of 'atrocities' at the output of Britain's Empire, but by the notion of a Yellow Peril at its very heart (Witchard, 2012: 87).

When Lao She stayed at a student hostel near Russell Square, the maid there was reluctant to serve him. On one occasion, he told the maid that he would not come back for dinner, and her response was sarcastic: "Oh, how splendid!" Many years later, Lao She recollected this experience to his friends, stating, "Poor Chinese people are looked down upon wherever they go!" (Hu, 1978: 46). While working as a lecturer at the School of Oriental Studies, University of London, he was surprised that his faculty would rather hire British scholars with limited knowledge of Chinese language and culture than employ Chinese scholars with a good understanding of these subjects as professors of Chinese studies (Witchard, 2012: 68).

Apart from Clement Egerton, with whom he once shared a flat and co-translated the Chinese classic *Jin Ping Mei* (*The Golden Lotus*), Lao She had few local acquaintances in London. Although Lao She never openly mentioned Professor Evans, who assisted him in arranging accommodation, we can discern traces of the man in the fictional depiction of Reverend Evans in *Er Ma*. Reverend Evans is portrayed as a "walking encyclopedia of China" who spent 20 years in the country as a missionary (James, 1980: 7). During sleepless nights, however, Evans fervently prays to God for China to become a British colony, believing that the British Empire could save the Chinese, whom he perceives as a yellow-faced ugly race (James, 1980: 7).

The following will show that these diasporic experiences have significantly contributed to Lao She's creation of the fictional world in *Er Ma*, where all those casts of characters and places in Lao She's personal experiences would resurface as the story prototypes.

5.3 The "Diasporic Chinese" in *Er Ma*

British literary works from the 1920s often perpetuated derogatory stereotypes of the Chinese, characterizing them as "filthy, barbarous, crime-ridden yellow-faced and dark-haired devils" (Beyer, 1980: 182). Consequently, Chinese people in London faced considerable humiliations in various aspects of their lives during this period (Witchard, 2012: 62). Drawing on his personal experiences in London, Lao She skillfully captures this humiliation in his portrayal of Chinese immigrants in 1920s London through the perspective of Britons in *Er Ma* (James, 1980: iii). For instance, in the story, when Mr. Ma presented Chinese tea as a gift to his landlady, Mrs. Wedderburn, her daughter Mary cried out in fear, suggesting that the tea might be poisoned (Dolby, 2013: 72). When Mr. Ma went to purchase an engagement ring for Mrs. Wedderburn, the shopkeeper automatically offered him an inferior one. Upon Mr. Ma's insistence on wanting the best ring in the store, the shopkeeper mistakenly assumed he was Japanese. However, when Mr. Ma clarified that he was Chinese, the shopkeeper regarded him as a thief (Jimmerson, 1991: 312). These fictional scenarios vividly portray the detrimental impact of popular British literature of that time in shaping public stereotypes against the Chinese. In response to this prejudice, Lao She lamented that, in 1920s London, the Japanese enjoyed a much better reputation than the Chinese (Jimmerson, 1991: 375).

In *Er Ma*, Lao She adeptly portrays his protagonists who face formidable external forces, highlighting the unfavorable perception of Chinese minorities during that period (Witchard, 2012: 115). However, the negative images propagated by British stereotypes do not encompass the entirety of the diasporic Chinese experience in this novel. Through his writing, Lao She effectively delineates two contrasting groups of Chinese residing in London. One group, represented by Mr. Ma, comprises older-generation Chinese who staunchly adhere to traditional Chinese culture and values, refusing to accept new ideas of that time. The other group, exemplified by Mr. Ma's son, Ma Wei, and the curio shop assistant, Li Zirong, consists of younger-generation Chinese immigrants who eagerly embrace new ideas and concepts, aspiring to rejuvenate old China socially and culturally (Huang, 2003: 178). People like Mr. Ma hold disdain for businessmen, while harboring dreams of attaining governmental positions. "Mr. Ma longs for refinement and therefore refuses to learn how to manage the curio shop he has inherited" (Hegel, 1982: 299). This stubbornness not only clashes with the ideologies and values prevalent in 1920s Britain, but also directly opposes the vision of the "New Youth" embodied by story characters like Ma Wei and Li Zirong. "They represent a revitalizing generation that believes in Western moral principles such as the pursuit of scientific knowledge, truth-seeking, and diligent work" (Beyer, 1980: 182). In the story, Mr. Ma exhibits no respect for Zirong, dismissing him as a member of the lower class engaged in contemptible jobs. Conversely, his son, Ma Wei, chooses to emulate Li Zirong, working hard and acquiring new skills (Hegel, 1982: 299).

When Lao She wrote *Er Ma*, the world was undergoing tumultuous social transformations, marked by the collision of ideologies, cultures, and worldviews between the East and West (Shen, 1999: 120). In *Er Ma*, Lao She skillfully portrays the entrenched British biases against the Chinese people in London, while also juxtaposing two generations of individuals (both Chinese and British) in a satirical manner, which partly reflected the typical sociocultural backdrop of that time.

5.4 The "Local Britons" in *Er Ma*

Lao She's diasporic experience in London instilled in him mixed feelings towards the British, influencing his portrayal of British characters in his novels. In *Er Ma*, he offers a detailed depiction of British society, standing out for his characterizations of the British as an independent, practical people with a strong sense of integrity and orderliness (Shen, 1999: 115). The story has successfully presented two contrasting groups of Britons.

The first group of Britons were framed by Lao She as ignorant, arrogant, and hypocritic, who hold hostility and prejudice towards China and the Chinese people (Wen, 2000: 125). Due to the immense hostility that media and popular literature displayed towards the Chinese in the 1920s, ordinary Britons were once haunted by Sinophobia (Witchard, 2012: 60–61). In *Er Ma*, these Britons were portrayed as ignorant and arrogant. They had never been to China or cared to learn about the real Chinese, yet they still regarded the Chinese as a barbarous, hideous, and filthy race, with men smoking opium and women binding their feet (Qian, 1999: 113–114). While staying in China, Mrs. Evans, the wife of Reverend Evans, took a contemptuous stance towards the Chinese. She prohibited her two children, Catherine and Paul, from playing with Chinese kids and learning the Chinese language. She believes that they would never grow up as noble and well-bred British citizens if contaminated by these inferior people and their languages. The Britons in the novel were also hypocritical, showing goodwill to help poor Chinese immigrants, while secretly dreaming of subjugating them to British dominance (Xu, 2015: 115). Reverend Evans is a perfect example: while he was willing to help Mr. Ma and his son finds accommodations upon their arrival, he was praying for British colonization of Chinese land.

Another group of Britons in *Er Ma* was framed by Lao She as kind-hearted and upright, characterized by an independent personality with a constant quest for knowledge (Wen, 1997: 125). Catherine Evans, the daughter of Reverend Evans, is a typical character belonging to this group. Even though her mother prohibited her from contacting anything Chinese during their stay in China, Catherine managed to teach herself a little bit of Chinese without her mother's knowledge (Dolby, 2013: 144). She could not see eye to eye with her brother Paul on the narrow-minded patriotism and the outdated tradition of oppression that saw Great Britain as superior to other nations (Dolby, 2013: 235). Instead, she embraced "the radical post-War thinking of Western intellectuals that might provide a model for the New China" (Witchard, 2012: 125). Dr. Simon, a retired university professor, was a regular customer at Mr. Ma's curio shop. He was not only a man devoid of ungrounded prejudices against the Chinese, but also a scholar with keen interests in Chinese culture (Xu, 2015: 115).

Although retired from the University of London at the age of seventy, Dr. Simon was hard-working, conducting research on precious Chinese antiques in his lab (Xu, 2015: 115). Through the portrayal of these Britons in *Er Ma*, Lao She has illustrated the positive side of British characters of that time.

5.5 Summary

This chapter offers a concise account of Lao She's diasporic experience in London and explores two themes that have been identified in previous literary criticism: "Diasporic Chinese" and "Local Britons". It is essential to underscore that Lao She's diasporic experiences have profoundly influenced his subsequent perceptions of the British people and society. These experiences laid the foundation for his literary creation and served as prototypes for his depictions of the British characters and British society in *Er Ma*. Furthermore, it is critical to reiterate that the two themes ("Diasporic Chinese" and "Local Britons") discussed in this chapter will provide the groundwork for the keyword analysis in Chapter 7, and serve as the starting points for exploration of the translators' functional styles in Chapters 8 and 9.

References

Beyer, J. (1980). Reviewed Work(s): *Ma and Son,* a Novel by Lao She by Jean M. James and Lao She. Bulletin of the School of Oriental and African Studies. *University of London, 46*(1), 182–183.

Dolby, W. (2013). *Mr. Ma and Son.* Penguin Classics.

Finkelstein, D., et al. (1984). *The two Mas.* Joint Publishing Co.

Hegel, R. E. (1982). Reviewed Work(s): *Ma and son:* A novel by Lao She by Lao She and Jean M. James. *Chinese Literature: Essays, Articles, Reviews, 4*(2), 299–300.

Hu, K. (1978). Lao She in England. *Renditions: A Chinese-English Translation Magazine,* (10), 46–51.

Huang, Y. (2003). The influence of British culture on Lao She as seen from *Er Ma. Hunan Social Sciences, 2,* 178–179.

James, J. M. (1980). *Ma and son: A novel by Lao She.* Chinese Materials Center Inc.

Jimmerson, J. (1991). *Mr. Ma & son: A sojourn in London.* Foreign Language Press.

Mastropierro, L. (2018). *Corpus stylistics in Heart of Darkness and its Italian translations.* Bloomsbury Publishing.

Qian, Z. G. (1999). Comparison and exploration in diversity: On Lao She's cultural reflections in the novel *Er Ma. Journal of Literature, History and Philosophy, 5,* 113–117.

Shen, Q. L. (1999). A spotlight on Chinese and Western cultures: On Lao She's *Er Ma. Modern Chinese Literature Studies, 1,* 112–125.

Wen, R. M. (2000). The novel *Er Ma* from a cultural criticism perspective (Speech delivered at the International Comparative Literature Conference in the Netherlands, June 1997). *Modern Chinese Literature Studies, 4,* 123–128.

Witchard, A. (2012). *Lao She in London.* Hong Kong University Press.

Xiao, F. (2010). *On the British image in Lao She's writings.* Hunan Normal University.

Xu, Y. H. (2015). The British image in Lao She's *Er Ma. Masterpiece Review, 2,* 115–116.

Chapter 6
Corpora and Methodology

6.1 Introduction

This chapter provides methodological details for the upcoming case studies, including research questions, text collection, corpus compilation, and data analysis. These details offer a comprehensive overview of how corpus stylistics is applied to the examination of the translator's functional style in the Chinese-English translation of *Er Ma*. Section 6.2 introduces the research questions, while Sect. 6.3 outline the source text, target texts, and the reference corpora used for keyword retrieval. Section 6.4 explains the data and outlines the various stages of analysis. Section 6.5 summarizes key points and stresses the implications of applying corpus stylistic methods to investigate functional style.

6.2 Research Questions

The present case study conducts a comparative analysis of the translators' functional styles in the English translations of *Er Ma*. It examines how the translators recreate the two literary functions (i.e., thematic construction, characterization) enacted in the source text in target texts. It also explores how these translators create the textual function of textual panorama building in target texts.

As keywords are building blocks of literary functions (Mahlberg, 2013), exploring how these keywords interact with contexts to create these literary functions and examining how different translators recreate these functions in translation can reveal their functional styles. Similarly, as the most frequent words (MFW), the most frequent word sequences (MFWS), and Biber's (1988) six dimensions are textual classifiers and components of textual functions (Diao, 2022; Rybicki, 2012), examining how these translators construct textual panorama in translation can also unveil their functional styles.

K. Wu and D. Li, *Researching Translator's Functional Style*, New Frontiers in Translation Studies, https://doi.org/10.1007/978-981-95-1221-8_6

Then, we can triangulate the analysis results to gain a relatively comprehensive view of the translators' functional styles as they (re)create the literary and textual functions in the English translations of *Er Ma*. Specifically, the following research questions are raised:

(1) What are the keywords that are immediately relevant to the "Diasporic Chinese" and the "Local Britons" in *Er Ma*?
(2) How do these keywords linguistically interact with their contexts to create the literary functions of thematic construction and characterization in the source text?
(3) To what extent do translators' functional styles diverge or converge in handling these interactions in their English translations of *Er Ma* to recreate the two literary functions?
(4) To what extent do these translators' functional styles differ or converge in creating the textual function of textual panorama building in their English translations of *Er Ma*?
(5) What are the possible factors that contribute to the observed similarities and differences in the translators' functional styles in the English translations of *Er Ma*?

The first research question identifies keywords directly related to the Chinese and Britons in the story. It serves as the starting point for the entire case study, aiming to establish a connection between linguistic forms and literary functions. Corpus stylistics, which emphasizes the relationship between linguistic forms and their functions, underscores the significance of keywords in context (Lambrou, 2013: 204). By identifying the keywords pertinent to the Chinese and Britons in *Er Ma*, it paves the way for further exploration of how the two literary functions (thematic construction and characterization) manifest through these keywords.

The second research question delves into the creation of the two literary functions by examining the interaction between these identified keywords and their contexts in *Er Ma*. Given *Er Ma*'s rich descriptions of the Chinese and Britons (Witchard, 2012: 60), analyzing the connection between these descriptions and the identified keywords enables the examination of lexico-semantic patterns (e.g., extended units of meaning, lexical chains) formed by these keywords. This is important because the study of these lexico-semantic patterns can shed light on the roles played by these keywords in creating the two literary functions in the story.

The third research question investigates the translators' functional styles as they reenact the two literary functions in their translations. It explores the linguistic idiosyncrasies exhibited by these translators in the recreation of the two literary functions, specifically focusing on their treatment of the aforementioned interactions between keywords and their contexts. It is expected that these idiosyncrasies will highlight the translators' functional styles, even though they are confined to the two literary functions of thematic construction and characterization.

The fourth research question explores the translators' functional styles as they shape the textual function of textual panorama building in their translations. It seeks to discern how translators' functional styles may be manifested through the textual function. While translators may show linguistic idiosyncrasies as they recreate literary functions from the source text, they also display certain idiosyncrasies as they construct the textual function in target texts. Therefore, in addition to literary functions, the study also compares the translators' functional styles in terms of the textual function, although it is limited to textual panorama building in this case study.

The final research question contextualizes the answers to the third and fourth research questions. It explores a range of "translatorial" and "extra-translatorial" factors that may contribute to similarities and differences in the translators' functional styles. As a crucial step in corpus-assisted translator style research (Tognini-Bonelli, 2001; Li, 2016), the answers to this research question seek to position the findings of translators' functional styles within broader social, cultural, ideological, and political contexts.

6.3 Texts and Corpora

This section introduces the corpora used in the case study. The corpora comprise the source text, several target texts, and two reference corpora that help identify the required keywords.

6.3.1 The Source Text

As a corpus stylistic study, text collection is the first step in corpus compilation for this research. Simultaneously, as a descriptive translation study, text collection includes both source and target texts. Regarding the source text, the Chinese version of *Er Ma* is readily available online. Its status as a published novel by the late writer guarantees easy and free public access. However, it is crucial to emphasize that the collection of this source text goes beyond a simple "click-and-download" process. The downloaded source text, saved in "txt" format, undergoes meticulous proofreading to verify its accuracy against the hardcopy version, minimizing possible errors. The specific hardcopy utilized for this purpose is "二馬", published by People's Literature Publishing House in 1998. Table 6.1 provides some statistics about the source text.

Table 6.1 Statistics of the source text

	Token	Type	STTR	Sentences
Er Ma (二馬)	75,581	10,350	49.25	6,763

6.3.2 The Reference Corpora

As discussed in Sect. 6.2, the identification of keywords serves as the starting point for the analysis. In this research, the objective is to identify keywords specific to *Er Ma*, rather than those reflecting the general or typical language usage of Lao She or other writers from the same era. To achieve this objective, two Chinese reference corpora, namely RC1 and RC2, will be compiled. Details of these reference corpora and their statistics are presented in Tables 6.2 and 6.3, respectively.

RC1 consists of 14 novels written by Lao She, excluding *Er Ma*. By comparing *Er Ma* with RC1, the study aims to identify keywords characteristic of this specific novel, rather than those representing his general language usage in fiction. On the other hand, RC2 comprises 14 novels written by seven renowned authors, with each author contributing two novels. These novels are contemporaneous (within a decade span) with Lao She. The purpose of RC2 is to identify keywords specific to *Er Ma*, rather than commonly used words by the renowned authors from that period. It's

Table 6.2 List of fiction in RC1 and RC2

	RC1			RC2		
	Author	Fiction	Year	Author	Fiction	Year
1	老舍	鼓書藝人	1949	巴金	家	1933
2	老舍	火葬	1944	巴金	霧雨電	1933–1936
3	老舍	老張的哲學	1928	李劼人	暴風雨前	1936
4	老舍	離婚	1933	李劼人	死水微瀾	1935
5	老舍	駱駝祥子	1939	魯迅	彷徨	1926
6	老舍	貓城記	1933	魯迅	吶喊	1923
7	老舍	牛天賜傳	1936	茅盾	濁	1930
8	老舍	四世同堂	1944–1949	茅盾	子夜	1933
9	老舍	蛻	1938	沈從文	邊城	1936
10	老舍	文博士	1936	沈從文	長河	1938
11	老舍	無名高地有了名	1955	蕭紅	呼和蘭傳	1940
12	老舍	小坡的生日	1934	蕭紅	生死場	1935
13	老舍	趙子曰	1928	蕭乾	籬下集	1936
14	老舍	正紅旗下	1979	蕭乾	夢之穀	1938

Table 6.3 Statistics of RC1 and RC2

	Token	Type	STTR[a]	Sentences[b]
RC1	1,401,178	63,288	50.96	86,303
RC2	990,498	68,728	51.14	65,088

[a]Standardized TTR based on every 1,000 occurrences
[b]Number of sentences

worth mentioning that while efforts have been made to select authors for RC2 in a balanced and representative manner, the lengths of the texts incorporated in RC2 vary. However, this issue can be mitigated by creating separate files for each text instead of merging them into a combined file. This approach allows for better monitoring and control of the influence of an individual text on the analysis results.

Moreover, it is important to proofread all the electronic files in RC1 and RC2 to ensure they are free from errors. Since the texts used in corpus compilation are sourced from the internet, their quality may not be guaranteed. Therefore, the same proofreading procedure applied to the source text (ST) must be repeated for RC1 and RC2. Additionally, paratexts in each of these texts, such as prefaces, author's introductions, chapter labels, appendices, and indexes, will be excluded from both corpora to minimize their impact on the literary analysis.

6.3.3 The Target Texts

To date, there have been four English translations of the novel *Er Ma*. The first translation is titled *Ma and Son: A Novel by Lao She*, translated by M. J. James and published by Chinese Material Center, Inc. in the USA in 1980. The second translation is titled *The Two Mas*, co-translated by K.K. Huang and D. Finkelstein and published by Joint Publishing Co. in Hong Kong in 1984. The third translation is titled *Mr. Ma & Son: A Sojourn in London*, translated by Julie Jimmerson and published by Foreign Language Press in China in 1991. The fourth translation, titled *Mr. Ma and Son*, was translated by William Dolby in 2013. These translations span a significant period of time, with a maximum interval of 33 years. Furthermore, the translators come from diverse professional backgrounds and have different motivations for undertaking the translation, which might result in some stylistic variations in the translation of this novel. Details of the translations and their translators are presented in Table 6.4, and their statistics are provided in Table 6.5.

6.4 Data Analysis

The data analysis in this study consists of five stages, each corresponding to one of the five research questions. Stage 1 involves generating and categorizing keywords specific to *Er Ma*. Stage 2 focuses on examining the interaction between these function-loaded keywords and their contexts. Stage 3 investigates the linguistic idiosyncrasies of the translators in their (re)creation of literary and textual functions in translation. Stage 4 aims to explore underlying factors that contribute to the translators' functional styles. These stages have been designed to effectively address each of the five research questions.

Table 6.4 Translations of *Er Ma* and their translators

Translation	Mode	Year	Publisher	Translator	Nationality	Mother tongue	Profession
Ma and Son: A Novel by Lao She	Single	1980	Chinese Materials Center	M. J. James	US	English	Sinologist
The Two Mas	Collaborative	1984	Joint Publishing HK	K. K. Huang, D. Finkelstein	CHN, US	Chinese, English	Professor, freelance
Mr. Ma & Son: A Sojourn in London	Single	1991	Foreign Language Press	J. Jimmerson	UK	English	Sinologist
Mr. Ma and Son	Single	2013	Penguin Classics	W. Dolby	UK	English	Lecturer

Table 6.5 Statistics of the four translations

	Token	Type	STTR	Sentences
James	95,689	7,048	41.77	10,034
Huang & Finkelstein	109,843	8,152	44.67	2,919
Jimmerson	103,689	8,230	43.40	7,071
Dolby	106,415	8,291	43.81	8,008

6.4.1 Generation and Categorization of Keywords

Stage 1 of this research involves the generation and categorization of keywords from the source text (ST) based on the two preidentified themes, "Diasporic Chinese" and "Local Britons." This stage is crucial as these keywords serve as the bridges between linguistic forms and literary functions. Before the generation and categorization process, it's necessary to segment the ST due to the absence of space between consecutive Chinese words. Once the ST is segmented, two steps are taken to generate and categorize the keywords.

Step 1 Generates two keyword lists by comparing the source text (ST) with RC1 and RC2, respectively. The two reference corpora serve as benchmarks against which keywords in *Er Ma* are identified through comparison. First, the study will compare the ST with RC1 to create a keyword list that includes words unique to *Er Ma*, not found in other novels by Lao She. To achieve this, Jieba (結巴分詞) will be used to segment all running Chinese words in the texts. The resulting outputs will undergo careful proofreading to ensure accuracy. Then, AntConc will be employed to generate the required keyword lists, with a p value of 0.0001 set to include relevant keywords while excluding non-relevant ones. Second, the same procedures will be repeated for the ST-RC2 comparison to generate another keyword list that only includes words specific to *Er Ma*, and not those commonly found in other well-known works from the same period. Finally, overlapping words from both lists will be retained to create a final keyword list that solely contains words completely specific to *Er Ma*.

Step 2 Categorizes the keywords in the final list according to the two themes identified in Chapter 5. This step establishes the connection between linguistic forms and literary functions. First, all function words will be excluded from the final lists as they primarily serve grammatical purposes. This would reduce the final list to a more manageable size. Second, the keywords in the lists will be organized into different subsets under the two identified themes based on Johnson's (2016) model (see Chapter 7). This model not only provides a way to classify relevant keywords into categories, as emphasized by Mahlberg and McIntyre (2011: 207), but also ensures that each keyword holds equal importance in representing fictional themes. Additionally, this model is specifically designed for literary texts, distinguishing it from the models proposed by McEnery (2009) or Scott (2016). It's important to note that the categorization of keywords is a dynamic process, in which any keywords not fitting into existing subsets will lead to the creation of new subsets under the two themes.

6.4.2 From Forms to Functions

Stage 2 examines the interactions between the identified keywords and their contexts. To achieve this, the study employs a combination of Sinclair's (2004) Extended Units of Meaning and Mahlberg's (2013) Local Textual Functions. While Sinclair's model primarily focuses on revealing general lexical patterns in a language, its applicability to the literary context, which emphasizes "specific" rather than "universal" patterns, is limited. Therefore, Mahlberg's model, which emphasizes the local textual function(s) of these patterns, is introduced as a complementary tool in this study. The analysis in this stage comprises three steps:

Step 1 Analyzes the lexico-semantic patterns resulting from these interactions and examining their local textual functions. For this analysis, AntConc will be employed to perform concordance analysis. The node's span will be set at L10:R10, allowing for a context of 10 characters to the left and right of the node. This setting is chosen for this research, as it ensures the inclusion of pertinent contextual information, while excluding extraneous elements that could potentially affect the analysis results.

Step 2 Summarizes the potential literary function(s) carried by these lexico-semantic patterns in *Er Ma*. The repetition of keywords or key clusters, even if they occur infrequently, can indicate functional relevance (Mahlberg,

2013: 62). Therefore, it is necessary to establish connections between the lexico-semantic patterns and their respective literary functions.

Step 3 Focuses on investigating the lexical chains formed by these keywords in the novel and their roles in creating literary functions. A lexical chain refers to the interactions between different lexical items and the whole cohesive effect they create (Mastropierro, 2018: 80). Therefore, it is a highly contextualized linguistic phenomenon, which might play a part in creating literary functions.

6.4.3 Functional Style in Recreating Literary Function

Stage 3 is dedicated to analyzing the translators' functional styles in creating the two literary functions, namely thematic reconstruction and recharacterization. This involves closely examining the linguistic idiosyncrasies shown by the translators when handling the interactions identified in Stage 2. These idiosyncrasies are observed in the shifts between the source text and its target texts, as well as the diversities among these target texts. It is believed that these idiosyncrasies contribute to the recreation of the literary functions in translation and serve as manifestations of the translators' functional styles. This stage consists of two steps:

Step 1 Explores the idiosyncrasies exhibited by the translators, focusing on several aspects. These aspects include how the translators reconstruct the original semantic fields, reestablish the original lexical chains, render the story figure labels, and recreate the original discourse forms in translation. Analyzing each of these aspects provides an understanding of the translators' idiosyncrasies. Combining the results of these analyses yields a comprehensive view of the translators' functional styles as they recreate the two literary functions.

Step 2 Briefly interprets the results obtained in the previous step by highlighting their interpretational effects on the target readership. The case study examines how the similarities and differences in the translators' functional styles may influence the mental constructions of story figures and their identities among target readers.

6.4.4 Functional Style in Creating Textual Function

Stage 4 involves analyzing and comparing the translators' functional styles in creating the textual function of "textual panorama building" in translation. This process is quantitative, where principal component analysis (PCA) and multidimensional analysis (MDA) will be conducted on the four translations. The analysis aims to provide a perspective on the textual functions of the four translations, in addition to the two literary functions. The analysis proceeds as follows:

Step 1 Retrieves parallel word and word sequence lists from each target text (TT) using Intelligent Archive 3.0, which generates n-gram frequency counts.

Step 2 Applies PCA to the parallel word lists of the four translations to identify patterns of similarity and difference. The number of words included in the analysis requires careful consideration, with a focus on the top 200 to 1000 most frequent words (MFW) to represent the majority of tokens in a text (Mastropierro, 2018; Rybicki, 2012).

Step 3 Repeats the analysis in Step 2, but with a shift to word sequences. Only 2-g and 3-g are considered since they represent the most common word sequences in literary texts (Burrows, 2002; Mastropierro, 2018; Rybicki, 2012).

Step 4 Conducts MDA on each of the four translations to identify patterns of similarity and difference. Dimension scores of Biber's (1988) six dimensions are calculated using MAT, and these scores are statistically compared across these translations.

Step 5 Combines and triangulates the results from Steps 2 to 4 to gain insight into how textual panoramas are built in each of the four translations. The textual panoramas are then compared to determine the overall degree of similarity and difference between the translators' target texts.

6.4.5 Interpretation of the Data

The final stage of the study explores underlying factors, both translatorial and extra-translatorial, that may account for the observed similarities and differences in the translators' functional styles. Unlike the previous three stages, the analysis in this final stage adopts an inductive approach, primarily relying on the researcher's observations. It should be noted that this stage does not aim to comprehensively cover all potential factors that could explain the identified stylistic similarities and differences. Instead, it focuses on factors that can provide reasonable explanations for the findings in the previous stages. Given the possibility of numerous latent factors contributing to these stylistic variations, it would be challenging, if not impossible, to include all of them. The analysis in this stage comprises the following two steps:

Step 1 Involves the categorization of all the findings related to the translators' functional styles from the previous stages based on the two comparison modes used in the analysis: source text to target text (ST-TT) and target text to target texts (TT-TT). This step provides a preliminary understanding of the foundations that underpin the observed stylistic similarities and differences.

Step 2 Classifies the potential factors contributing to the translators' functional styles into two categories: "translatorial" and "extra-translatorial" (see Chapter 2). Following this categorization, the study examines possible social, cultural, and ideological factors that may contribute to the findings retrieved from Step 1.

6.4.6 Software Used in Analysis

The software used in the present research includes, but is not limited to, the following: Foxit PDF Editor 12.0, ABBYY FineReader 12.0, AntConc 3.5, Jieba, FactoMineR, Intelligent Archive, and the Multidimensional Analysis Tagger (MAT).

- Foxit PDF Editor is a software with PDF editing functions, employed in this research to clean scanned English translations in PDF for more efficient OCR processes.
- ABBYY FineReader is a software developed to recognize scanned PDF text with a claimed accuracy rate of 97%. This software is used to perform OCR on all the scanned English translations of *Er Ma*.
- AntConc is freeware for corpus analysis and is used in this study to generate word lists and concordance lines for further examination.
- Jieba is a natural language processing package for Chinese based on Python, used to segment all the Chinese texts in the corpora.
- FactoMineR is a statistical package in RStudio, utilized for PCA and results visualization.
- Intelligent Archive is freeware developed by the University of Newcastle (https://c21ch.newcastle.edu.au/ia/). Its primary function in this research is to acquire lists of the Most Frequent Words (MFW) and Most Frequent Word Sequences (MFWS), which serve as data input for PCA.
- The Multidimensional Analysis Tagger (MAT) is software developed by Nini (2019) that replicates Biber's (1988) tagger for analyzing English texts. It generates a grammatically annotated version of the selected corpus, along with statistics for text-type or genre analysis.

6.5 Summary

This chapter delves into the methodological aspects underpinning the forthcoming case study in this research. The research questions serve as guiding principles, directing our investigation, while the data analysis offers practical guidelines for conducting the study. The research questions are structured progressively, with answers to one question informing the subsequent ones. Concurrently, the data analysis provides important specifications for each research step.

Finally, it is paramount to underscore the implications of employing a corpus stylistic approach for exploring the functional styles of literary translators. Utilizing a corpus stylistic framework enables us to transcend the examination of formal linguistic features and accentuates the interconnectedness between linguistic forms and their functions.

References

Biber, D. (1988). *Variation across speech and writing.* Cambridge University Press.

Burrows, J. (2002). 'Delta': A measure of stylistic difference and a guide to likely authorship. *Literary and Linguistic Computing, 17*(3), 267–287.

Diao, Y. (2022). *Multidimensional analysis of translated Chinese: A corpus-based study.* Cambridge University Press.

Johnson, J. H. (2016). A comparable comparison? A corpus stylistic analysis of the Italian translation of Julian Barnes' *Il Senso di una Fine* and the original text *The Sense of an Ending. Language and Literature, 25*(1), 38–53.

Lambrou, M. (2013). Narrative, text and time: Telling the same story twice in the oral narrative discourse of Greek speakers. In M. Lambrou & P. Stockwell (Eds.), *Contemporary stylistics* (pp. 203–215). Continuum.

Lao, S. (1998). *Er Ma.* People's Literature Publishing House.

Li, D. (2016). Translator style: A corpus-assisted approach. In Ji, M., Oakes, M., Li, D., & Hareide, L. (Eds.), *Corpus methodologies explained: An empirical approach to translation studies* (pp. 103–136). Routledge

Mahlberg, M. (2013). *Corpus stylistics and Dickens' fiction.* Routledge.

Mahlberg, M., & McIntyre, D. (2011). A case for corpus stylistics: Ian Fleming's *Casino Royale. English Text Construction, 4*(2), 204–227.

Mastropierro, L. (2018). *Corpus stylistics in Heart of Darkness and its Italian translations.* Bloomsbury Publishing.

McEnery, T. (2009). Keywords and moral panics: Mary Whitehouse and media censorship. In D. Archer (Ed.), *What's in a word-list? Investigating word frequency and keyword extraction* (pp. 93–124). Ashgate.

Rybicki, J. (2012). The great mystery of the (almost) invisible translator: Stylometry in translation. In M. Ji & M. P. Oakes (Eds.), *Quantitative methods in corpus-based translation studies: A practical guide to descriptive translation research* (pp. 231–248). John Benjamins Publishing Company.

Scott, M. (2016). *Wordsmith Tools help.* Lexical analysis software. Retrieved from http://www.lexically.net/downloads/version6/HTML/index. html? getting_started.htm.

Sinclair, J. (2004). *Trust the text: Language, corpus and discourse.* Routledge.

Tognini-Bonelli, E. (2001). *Corpus Linguistics at work.* John Benjamins.

Witchard, A. (2012). *Lao She in London.* Hong Kong University Press.

References

Chapter 7
Keywords in *Er Ma*

7.1 Introduction

In corpus-assisted research, keywords are defined as words statistically characteristic of a corpus when compared with another corpus based on certain norms (Culpeper & Demmen, 2015; McEnery & Hardie, 2011; Scott, 1998). They are notably frequent or rare and often associated with the "aboutness" of this corpus (Laviosa et al., 2016: 31; Scott, 1998: 65). Therefore, identifying keywords closely related to themes could be the starting point for corpus stylistic studies of literary translation (Mahlberg, 2013).

In this study, the generation and categorization of keywords based on the two pre-identified themes (see Chapter 5) establish an initial connection between linguistic forms and literary themes, serving as the first step in investigating translators' functional styles. The establishment of such a connection serves two purposes in this research. Firstly, it offers an alternative perspective that goes beyond the examination of purely linguistic features. Previous translator style research has predominantly focused on formal features of the translated texts (see Chapter 2). In contrast, the present investigation places emphasis on the relationship between linguistic forms and literary themes, thus presenting a different perspective. Secondly, it bridges the interpretation of the source text (e.g., by literary critics) with the translator's reconstruction of such interpretation. Some previous studies on translator style have overlooked the role of source text readers. In response to that, we may consider establishing a link between these readers and the translator, so that we can understand translator's functional style from this perspective.

Section 7.2 provides lists of keywords that are specifically relevant to *Er Ma*. These keywords are generated against the reference corpora to ensure their exclusive association with *Er Ma*. Additionally, this section presents technical details regarding Chinese text segmentation and the determination of keyness levels. In Sect. 7.3, the chosen keyword model for classifying the final list of identified keywords is discussed. The study adopts Johnson's (2016) model to classify the keywords in

K. Wu and D. Li, *Researching Translator's Functional Style*, New Frontiers in Translation Studies, https://doi.org/10.1007/978-981-95-1221-8_7

Er Ma and group them according to the two pre-identified themes. This choice is based on the belief that Johnson's model combines the strengths of previous models proposed by Scott (2000, 2006), McIntyre and Mahlberg (2011), and Mastropierro (2018). Section 7.4 examines the classified keywords, with a particular emphasis on those closely associated with the two themes of "Diasporic Chinese" and "Local Briton". Section 7.5 concludes the chapter by summarizing the findings and highlighting their relevance to the subsequent investigation of translators' functional styles in the upcoming two chapters.

7.2 Keywords Lists

To generate keywords specific to *Er Ma*, the selection of an appropriate reference corpus is crucial, because the reference corpus serves as the norm against which the target corpus (i.e., the source text of *Er Ma*) is compared. Different choices of the reference corpus can directly influence the resulting keyword list. As discussed in Chapter 6, this research uses two reference corpora, RC1 and RC2, to generate separate keyword lists and then compares them to obtain the final list of keywords. The decision to use two reference corpora aims to enhance the reliability of the generated keywords. Keywords that appear in both lists when comparing *Er Ma* with each corpus separately are more likely to be words exclusive to *Er Ma*, rather than reflecting the language usage of either Lao She or other contemporary writers. RC1 consists of all 14 fiction works[1] by Lao She, excluding *Er Ma*, while RC2 includes an additional 14 fiction works[2] by seven well-known authors, with each author contributing two works to the corpus. The inclusion of 14 fiction works in both corpora ensures better consistency and comparability between them.[3] The 14 fiction works in RC2 are temporally synchronous with *Er Ma* (i.e., published within a decade), while their authors were contemporaneous with Lao She, active in China between the 1920s and 1970s.

In addition to the choice of reference corpora, the keyness level is another important consideration in keyword generation. The keyness level determines the potential number of keywords that will be generated in the keyword lists. For this research, the keyness level is determined by setting the p-value of Log likelihood tests in AntConc to 0.0001. This specific level has been chosen based on repeated pilot studies, which have shown that a setting of 0.0001 is least likely to overlook any potential keywords relevant to the two pre-identified themes, while also avoiding the inclusion of words with weaker relevance.

[1] List of the fictions in RC1 is available at Figshare.com (http://dx.doi.org/10.6084/m9.figshare.29572907).

[2] List of the fictions in RC2 is available at Figshare.com (http://dx.doi.org/10.6084/m9.figshare.29572907).

[3] The number of all published fictions by Lao She is 14.

Once the reference corpora have been chosen and the keyness level has been determined, another crucial aspect to consider before generating keywords is the preprocessing and segmentation of the running Chinese characters in *Er Ma* and the two reference corpora in Chinese. To accomplish this, the present study will employ the Jieba package in Python. In the preprocessing step, the Chinese text will undergo the removal of all punctuation marks and redundant spaces. In the segmentation step, a user dictionary[4] needs to be constructed to accurately segment *Er Ma* and the reference corpora. It's worth noting that the default dictionary of Jieba, being unspecific to literary texts, might not be optimal for the segmentation process, since all the Chinese texts in this research belong to the literary genre. Jieba, being an open platform, allows users to create or import their own dictionaries to meet specific requirements for segmenting Chinese characters. In this research, a combination of imported and created segmenting dictionaries will be utilized to align with the specific needs of the study. The imported section of our dictionary consists of a downloaded literary package, while the created part encompasses all the character and place names extracted from both the target and reference corpora. To further enhance the accuracy of segmentation, the output of the segmentations will undergo manual proofreading. This process aims to eliminate unreasonable segmentations to the best extent possible, ensuring the quality of the segmented data.

7.2.1 Keywords and Keywords Lists

The findings from AntConc reveal that a total of 159 keywords are identified in Keywords List 1[5] (Fig. 7.1). Among these keywords, a majority consist of proper nouns closely associated with the two pre-identified themes. For example, character labels such as "老馬" (Old Ma), "馬老先生" (Mr. Ma), "父親" (Father), and "馬則仁" (Ma Zeren) represent the Chinese protagonist, while "小馬" (Mr. Ma Jr.) and "李子榮" (Li Zirong) refer to other Chinese characters in the story. Labels such as "拿破崙", "小狗", "狗", and "狗兒" consistently refer to the dog kept in Mrs. Wendell's house. Nouns like "黃臉"and "大氅" are partly associated with the diasporic Chinese. Similarly, character labels such as "伊牧師", "伊太太", "寡婦", "瑪力", "亞力山大", "保羅", and "凱薩林" pertain to the British protagonists in the story. On the other hand, words such as "洋鬼子" and "外國人" may indicate the fictional portrayal of local Britons. However, it should be noted that since all these keywords are generated based on RC1, they may also include words that are characteristic of Lao She's usage of words in fiction. This is where the comparison between *Er Ma* and RC2 becomes relevant.

Upon comparing *Er Ma* with RC2, the results obtained from AntConc report a total of 254 keywords in Keywords List 2[6] (Fig. 7.2). This number slightly exceeds

[4] Available at Figshare.com (dx.doi.org/10.6084/m9.figshare.29572907).

[5] The complete list is available at Figshare.com (http://dx.doi.org/10.6084/m9.figshare.29572907).

[6] The complete list is available at Figshare.com (http://dx.doi.org/10.6084/m9.figshare.29572907).

Keyword Types: 159 **Keyword Tokens:** 16692 **Search Hits:** 0

Rank	Freq	Keyness	Effect	Keyword
1	756	+ 4057.55	0.0195	马威
2	367	+ 1967.99	0.0095	温都
3	362	+ 1941.16	0.0094	马老先生
4	307	+ 1646.03	0.008	李子荣
5	283	+ 1517.26	0.0074	玛力
6	198	+ 1061.34	0.0052	伊牧师
7	456	+ 941.13	0.0117	中国
8	183	+ 928.55	0.0048	老马
9	174	+ 887.72	0.0045	马先生
10	122	+ 653.85	0.0032	拿破仑
11	117	+ 627.04	0.003	亚力山大
12	93	+ 498.39	0.0024	伊太太
13	84	+ 431.44	0.0022	伦敦

Fig. 7.1 Screenshot of keywords list 1

the number of keywords in Keywords List 1 due to the larger size of RC2 compared to RC1. A closer examination of Keywords List 2 reveals a significant overlap with Keywords List 1, particularly in terms of proper nouns that are highly relevant to character labels, titles, personal accessories, and fictional representations within the story. This could suggest that *Er Ma* incorporates numerous distinctive proper nouns that deviate from the literary language styles of both Lao She and his contemporaries. This deviation can be attributed to the fact that *Er Ma* stands as Lao She's exclusive exploration of the diasporic Chinese experience during his London sojourn (Louie, 2000: 1063). In addition to the shared words, Keywords List 2 also encompasses words that do not appear in Keywords List 1. Except for some Chinese grammatic words such as "能", "沒" "給" or "可是", these non-shared words fall into categories: Chinese words and Western words.

The Chinese words are semantically linked to China and Chinese culture, such as "中文" (Chinese language), "茶葉" (tea leaves), and "綢子" (silk fabric). However, these Chinese words are the minority among the non-shared words, as the majority comprises Western words that are semantically associated with various aspects of language (e.g., 英文, English; 法文, French), people (e.g., 洋鬼子, foreign devil), food (e.g., 火雞, turkey; 牛肉, beef), lifestyle (e.g., 馬戲, circus; 鋼琴, piano), science (e.g., 科學, science; 像片, photograph), and even religion (e.g., 聖經, Bible; 牧師, pastor; 耶誕節, Christmas; 禮拜天, Sunday) in the Western context. While these non-shared keywords in Keywords List 2 may reflect the general language usage of works contemporary to *Er Ma* to some extent, the predominance of Western words in the list also reflects the sociocultural landscape of 1920s China, where learning from the West was a cultural trend (Louie, 2000: 1062).

Keyword Types: 254 **Keyword Tokens:** 20006 **Search Hits:** 0

Rank	Freq	Keyness	Effect	Keyword
1	756	+ 3989.51	0.0195	马威
2	367	+ 1934.97	0.0095	温都
3	362	+ 1908.59	0.0094	马老先生
4	307	+ 1618.4	0.008	李子荣
5	283	+ 1491.8	0.0074	玛力
6	456	+ 1466.6	0.0118	中国
7	198	+ 1043.53	0.0052	伊牧师
8	174	+ 916.99	0.0045	马先生
9	183	+ 791.99	0.0048	老马
10	156	+ 692.21	0.0041	咱们
11	219	+ 676.34	0.0057	儿
12	117	+ 616.52	0.003	亚力山大
13	122	+ 595.32	0.0032	拿破仑

Fig. 7.2 Screenshot of keywords list 2

7.2.2 *List of Shared Keywords*

In comparing Keywords List 1 with Keywords List 2, we find 129 shared keywords, which constitute a substantial portion of both lists. This discovery suggests that what makes *Er Ma* lexically outstanding among Lao She's fiction also sets this work apart lexically from other fiction of the same period. As previously discussed in Chapter 6, identifying *Er Ma*-specific keywords is the initial step in establishing a connection between linguistic forms and literary themes. Therefore, it is crucial to concentrate on the content words within the shared list, as they are thematic relevant and more likely to reflect the two pre-identified themes (see Chapter 5). Among the shared content words, excluding some Chinese grammatical terms, the majority consists of proper nouns associated with character labels (e.g., 馬威, 溫都, 李子榮, 瑪力) and place names (e.g., 中國, 英國, 倫敦, 聖保羅), which reflect specific fictional themes. Additionally, there are other keywords of a more general nature in the shared content words, such as "大氅" (cloak), "黃臉" (yellow-faced), "古玩" (antiques), "煙袋" (tobacco pouch), "戒指" (ring), "呂宋煙" (Lusong cigarette), "布丁" (pudding), and "寡婦" (widow). These words effectively capture the thematic aspects of *Er Ma*, thereby distinguishing the story from other works by Lao She and those by other authors. The content words listed in Table 7.1 serve as our starting points, guiding the selection and categorization of keywords for the following investigations.

Table 7.1 Shared keywords list (content words only)

N	Keyword	N	Keyword	N	Keyword	N	Keyword	N	Keyword
1	馬威	21	鎊	41	禮拜	61	呂宋煙	81	外國人
2	溫都	22	帽子	42	煙袋	62	脖子	82	遞給
3	馬老先生	23	英國人	43	老頭兒	63	大氅	83	叼
4	李子榮	24	英國	44	回國	64	東西	84	自要
5	瑪力	25	華盛頓	45	小狗	65	電影	85	茶壺
6	中國人	26	早飯	46	公園	66	麵包	86	博物院
7	伊牧師	27	西門爵士	47	俗氣	67	布丁	87	牛津
8	中國	28	古玩	48	馬家	68	託盤	88	寡婦
9	老馬	29	父子	49	鼻子	69	社會黨	89	事業
10	馬先生	30	汽車	50	小孩子	70	言語	90	掌櫃的
11	拿破崙	31	母女	51	買賣	71	嘴唇	91	兜兒
12	亞力山大	32	聖誕	52	聖保羅	72	椅子	92	地毯
13	伊太太	33	古玩鋪	53	戒指	73	撅	93	黃臉
14	倫敦	34	先令	54	石碑	74	喬治	94	洋鬼子
15	保羅	35	念書	55	教堂	75	多瑞		
16	凱薩林	36	花兒	56	衣裳	76	歇夏		
17	父親	37	樓下	57	頭髮	77	馬則仁		
18	伊姑娘	38	書房	58	伯父	78	眼鏡		
19	太太	39	樓上	59	吃飯	79	狗		
20	鋪子	40	姑娘	60	裙子	80	圈兒		

7.3 Keywords Classification Models

"For corpus stylistic research that seeks links between literary and linguistic concerns, the classification of keywords can be guided by the search for links with literary critical argument" (Mahlberg, 2014: 384). In the present research, the "literary critical argument" would be the two literary themes pre-identified by literary critics. Hence, categorizing the retrieved keywords into different groups is a crucial step in creating links between linguistic forms and literary themes. To date, several models have been successfully employed to classify keywords in different corpora, including Scott's (2000, 2006) model, Mahlberg and McIntyre's (2011) model, and Johnson's (2016) model.

Scott (2000, 2006) proposes the categorization of keywords into three groups: proper nouns, aboutness keywords, and stylistic keywords. Proper nouns include character labels and place names, whereas Aboutness keywords reflect the content of the text and can help identify what a story is about. Similar to the findings in previous studies by Mahlberg and McIntyre (2011), Mahlberg (2013), and Mastropierro (2018), *Er Ma* also contains a substantial number of proper nouns (e.g., "馬威", "古玩鋪") and aboutness keywords (e.g., "黃臉", "戒指"). The third category is stylistic keywords, which predominantly comprise grammatical words like conjunctions, pronouns, and prepositions. Of these categories, aboutness keywords are most relevant to the present study as they focus on the text's content and are better suited for addressing thematic concerns. However, Scott's model, while suitable for general corpus analysis, may lack the granularity required to effectively categorize thematic elements for the literary analysis at hand. For instance, "中國人" and "英國人" are both aboutness words, but they relate to different themes within *Er Ma*, thus necessitating separate analyses.

Mahlberg and McIntyre (2011) classify keywords into "fictional world signals" and "thematic signals". Fictional world signals are keywords that construct the elements of the fictional world, such as setting and characters. In *Er Ma*, words like "古玩鋪","鋪子", and "教堂" fall into this category. Thematic signals, on the other hand, suggest the underlying themes of the text when they occur alongside other lexical items (Mahlberg & McIntyre, 2011: 209). These keywords are less straightforward and more open to interpretation in terms of contextual meaning. For example, "黃臉" might serve as a thematic signal in *Er Ma*, as it is potentially linked to one of the two pre-identified themes, the "Diasporic Chinese", and can also refer to Mr. Ma or any Chinese minorities in London. Mahlberg and McIntyre (ibid.) further subdivide these two groups of keywords into categories such as "characters", "setting & pros", "temporal indicators", to accommodate various descriptions of fictional worlds and literary themes. In the present study, this model can potentially subdivide the keywords in *Er Ma* into different thematic aspects based on the two pre-identified themes. However, it's important to note that some keywords may blur the boundary between "fictional world signals" and "thematic signals" by serving functions of both categories. For instance, "黃臉" and "洋鬼子" in *Er Ma* might simultaneously function as thematic and fictional world signals. While the two keywords can directly refer to specific characters of "Chinese" or "British" origins, they also convey the images associated with these characters. This overlapping dual function underscores the intricate thematic concerns, which have been extensively discussed by literary critics of *Er Ma* (see Chapter 5). Therefore, in *Er Ma*, the rigid classification of a keyword as either "fictional world" or "thematic" is likely to obscure its underlying thematic connections to the novel.

Johnson (2016) categorizes keywords into "aboutness indicators" and "narrative strategies". The former encompasses plot-related fictional elements (e.g., participants, circumstances, abstract concerns), while the latter deals with points of view (e.g., time references, explanatory discourse markers, negation) in fiction. Johnson's model has the advantage of considering all keywords equally in representing thematic elements in text. This advantage is especially important when we employ this model to thematically sort the keywords in *Er Ma.* Using this model allows for a comprehensive exploration of different aspects related to the two pre-identified themes. Notably, the division of fictional elements in the "aboutness indicator" group does not hinge on whether a keyword functions as a thematic signal or not. This would allow the model to transcend the apparent division between "fictional world" and "thematic signals" in Mahlberg and McIntyre's (2011) model, assigning equal importance to each keyword in representing various facets of fictional themes. However,

Johnson's model could be somewhat "oversized", if we consider every element from both groups. For instance, the "narrative strategies" group, which includes elements like time references and reflexive references (Johnson, 2016: 41), may be of limited relevance to this research, as it primarily focuses on narrative perspective rather than thematic content. Hence, the present study will only consider the "aboutness indicators" group, as it aligns well with the current research focus.

While other models exist, such as Culpeper's (2009) classification into ideational, interpersonal, and textual keywords based on Halliday's functional grammar, and Mahlberg's (2009) grouping into cultural, textual, and computer keywords, they primarily category keywords based on their linguistic rather than thematic functions. Furthermore, Wijitsopon's model (2018), which examines the relationships between words and themes by classifying keywords based on singular and plural forms, may not be readily applicable to languages like Chinese. This is because such languages as Chinese do not entirely adhere to the concept of singular and plural noun forms. Given these considerations, Johnson's model, with a specific focus on the "aboutness indicator" group, is most suitable for the present study. This model is expected to effectively categorize keywords to incorporate various thematic aspects within *Er Ma*, facilitating the subsequent analysis of the translators' functional styles in Chapters 8 and 9.

7.4 Classified Keywords

This section introduces the categorized keywords. Section 7.4.1 will illustrate the categories of keywords, while Sect. 7.4.2 will present the "Chinese Keywords" and "British Keywords" selected from these categories.

7.4.1 Keywords Categories

Following the "aboutness indicator" group in Johnson' model, the keywords in Table 7.1 are classified into four main categories: "participants", "circumstances", "abstract concerns" and "verbal groups". The classification process is meticulous, involving an examination of each keyword (Table 7.1) in the source text of *Er Ma*, using the AntConc concordance tool. Sub-categories are created within each main category by grouping keywords that share contextual meanings. The creation of these keywords sub-categories is a dynamic process: a keyword fallen short of any established sub-categories leads to the creation of a new sub-category. This process repeats itself until the exhaustion of these keywords. The result of this classification is presented in Table 7.2, which includes a fifth category for unclassified keywords. Although these unclassified keywords do not fit into any established sub-categories due to a lack of related contextual meaning, they are not without value.

If more keywords are retrieved, these unclassified keywords may form new subcategories. However, they are excluded from the present analysis of the translators' functional styles, because they are less likely to reveal linguistic idiosyncrasies and thus functional styles.

Table 7.2 Classified keywords in *Er Ma*

Category	Keywords
Participants	
Proper Names	
Character	
Chinese	馬威, 馬則仁, 馬老先生, 老馬, 馬先生, 李子榮
Briton	溫都太太, 瑪力, 伊牧師, 亞力山大, 伊太太, 保羅, 凱薩林, 伊姑娘, 華盛頓, 西門爵士, 喬治, 多瑞
Pet	拿破崙
Political Party	社會黨
Generic Names	
People	父親, 英國人, 中國人, 姑娘, 老頭兒, 小孩子, 伯父,外國人, 寡婦, 掌櫃的, 黃臉, 洋鬼子
Body Part	鼻子, 頭髮, 脖子, 嘴唇
Animal & Plant	花兒, 小狗, 狗
Clothes & Accessories	帽子, 衣裳, 裙子, 大氅, 煙袋, 戒指, 眼鏡, 兜兒
Furniture & Utensil	地毯, 椅子， 託盤， 茶壺
Money & Business	鎊， 先令， 買賣
Meal & Food	早飯, 呂宋煙, 麵包, 布丁
Lifestyle	汽車, 電影
Temporal Indicator	禮拜, 歇夏
Pronominal References	東西
Circumstances	
Place	
Country & City	中國, 倫敦, 英國, 牛津
Local Site	鋪子, 公園, 聖保羅, 教堂, 博物院
Interior Space	樓上, 樓下, 書房
Festival	聖誕
Atmosphere	俗氣, 馬家
Abstract Concerns	父子, 母女, 古玩, 事業, 回國
Verbal Groups	
Body Language	撅著, 遞給, 叼著
Unclassified	念書, 吃飯
Unclassified	言語, 圈兒

7.4.1.1 Participants

As per Johnson's classification (2016: 40), the category of "participants" can be further subdivided into three sub-categories: "proper names", "generic names", and "pronominal references". "Proper names" includes the names of major characters, a pet, and a political party, constituting a significant portion (21.5%) of the keywords in Table 7.1. This proportion differs from previous studies by Mahlberg and McIntyre (2011: 210) and Mastropierro (2018: 97), where proper names accounted for 12% and 4.5% of the total keywords, respectively. This disparity arises due to the distinctive focus of *Er Ma* on two contrasting groups, the "Diasporic Chinese" and the "Local Britons". Furthermore, *Er Ma*'s unique aspect lies in the inclusion of a pet dog named "拿破崙" (Napoleon) and a political party known as "社會黨" (Socialist Party). Concordance evidence shows that "拿破崙", a Pekingese dog residing in Mrs. Wendell's house, is associated with various story figures. Regarding "社會黨", the concordance reveals that it is a British political party with tenuous connections to the Chinese figures in the story.

"Generic names" play a significant role within the "Participants" category and extend across all categories presented in Table 7.2. These generic names cover nine different aspects of the fictional world, including people, body parts, meals, and food (Table 7.2). This level of specificity created by the participants in the fictional world is different from previous research conducted by Mahlberg and McIntyre (2011) and Mastropierro (2018), where generic references to participants have smaller proportions. For instance, Mahlberg and McIntyre (2011) observed that the number of keywords representing "circumstances" outweighed those representing "participants", underscoring the important of fictional settings in the fictional world of Ian Fleming's *Casino Royale*. Similarly, Mastropierro (2018: 97) found that there are more keywords classified as "circumstances" (referred to as "setting & prop") than those classified as "participants" (referred to as "characters") in Conrad's *Heart of Darkness* (Mastropierro, 2018: 98). In contrast, *Er Ma* is different by emphasizing "participants" (i.e., the Chinese and the Britons), along with various closely related items (see Chapter 5).

Approximately half (49%) of the keywords within "Generic Names" are associated with people and clothes & accessories. This observation may once again indicate the thematic prominence of human elements, such as story figures, over other latent themes in *Er Ma*. A closer examination of the concordance lines of keywords within the sub-category of "People" reveals that generic names related to the Chinese, such as "伯父" (uncle) and "黃臉" (yellow face), are often linked to either career success or negativity.

For instance, the keyword "伯父" (the uncle) refers to Ma Wei's deceased uncle, who represents the first generation of Chinese immigrants in Britain and from whom the Mas inherit the curio shop. Concordance evidence suggests that "伯父" is often associated with words like "事業" (career), "英雄" (hero), or "能幹" (capable), creating the impression of a successful businessman. This portrayal is consistent with the emergence of sustainable economic structures within Chinatowns during the early twentieth century, fostering the perception that overseas diasporic Chinese

Fig. 7.3 Concordance of "黄臉"

were contributing to economic success, acknowledged by both insiders and outsiders. This may partly explain why "伯父" is depicted as an "abled career hero".

On the other hand, "黄臉" (the yellow face), as evident in the concordance lines (Fig. 7.3), is predominantly associated with terms such as "討人嫌" (annoying), "打死" (beat to death), "怪物" (monster), "討厭" (disgust), or "抽大煙" (take drugs), projecting an aura of extreme negativity. This negativity may be linked to the prevailing stereotype of the "Yellow Peril" during the late nineteenth Century when the Chinese were often depicted as disruptive and threatening (Mayer, 2013). In contrast, lexical items such as "英國人" (the Briton), "寡婦" (widow), "姑娘" (girl), and "外國人" (foreigner) are frequently associated with aspects like lifestyle, elegance, or power. For instance, concordance lines (Fig. 7.4) featuring "英國人" often co-occur with terms like "規矩" (rules), "香檳" (champagne), "強盛" (robust), "愛花" (fond of flowers), or "厲害" (powerful). Even "寡婦" (Mrs. Wendell), an underprivileged postwar British widow, is largely associated with positive elements such as "結婚" (marriage), "娶" (marry), "鋼琴" (piano), or "股票" (stocks). The present study posits that this stark contrast in fictional representations between the Chinese and the Britons in *Er Ma* may reflect a deep-rooted British prejudice against the Chinese, as perceived through the eyes of Lao She.

7.4.1.2 Circumstances

Following Johnson's model, keywords under "Circumstances" are further divided into "Place", "Festival", and "Atmosphere". The sub-category of "Place" encompasses proper names of countries and cities, interior house spaces, as well as generic references to local sites. In contrast to some previous studies (e.g., Johnson, 2016; Mahlberg & McIntyre, 2011; Mastropierro, 2018), proper place names such as "中國" (China), "英國" (Britain), and "倫敦" (London) make up 33% of the total keywords categorized under "Place". This proportion is notably higher than that found in these previous studies. This indicates the relative importance of these proper place names to the thematic concerns of the story, as they are considered keywords in

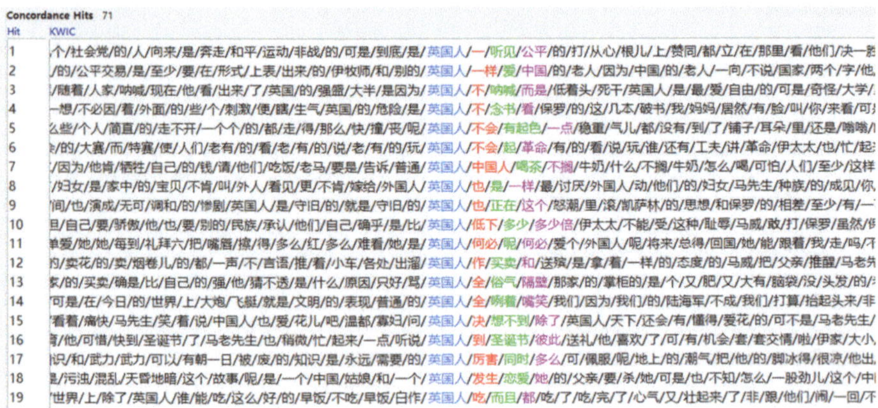

Fig. 7.4 Concordance of "英國人"

AntConc. Keywords associated with interior house spaces, such as "樓上" (upstairs) and "樓下" (downstairs), distinguish this work from previous studies as they were not included as keywords in the latter. We attribute this difference primarily to the fact that many scenes in *Er Ma* take place inside Mrs. Wendell's house.

On the other hand, keywords classified as local sites are more generic and can be interpreted more broadly in relation to the story's themes. For example, "鋪子" is a generic reference roughly equivalent to "shop", but in *Er Ma*, it symbolizes more than just a shop—it represents the "special value" that the diasporic Chinese attached to money and business in the 1920s. The Chinese tended to mix personal favors and family matters with business, and characters like Mr. Ma looked down upon businessmen, believing that "earning some extra cash is outright disgraceful" (Bengtsson, 2015: 24). Concordance lines reveal that when "鋪子" refers to the curio shop run by the Mas, it often co-occurs with negative words such as "賠錢" (loss), "倒了" (bankrupted), "收閉了" (merged by), "賣了" (sold), or "砸了" (smashed). The unfortunate fate associated with the curio shop may, in some way, reflect the doomed consequences of this "special value" for the Chinese protagonist. Similarly, "博物院" refers to the British Museum but carries a deeper meaning within the story. Among its limited 10 concordance lines, almost half of them co-occur with China or the Chinese. The story details inform us that the British Museum is a place where thousands of looted artworks from China are kept (Lao, 1998: 45), partially symbolizing the humiliation suffered by the Chinese during that period.

The sub-categories of "Festival" and "Atmosphere" contain relatively few keywords, but some of them deserve further explanation. For instance, the term "俗氣" (flashy), a negative word in Chinese, is associated with both Chinese and English figures in the story, as indicated by concordance lines. This may partially reflect Lao She's personal experiences in London during the 1920s, revealing his perception of mutual stereotypes and prejudices between the Chinese and Britons (Auerbach, 2009, 2013). Some studies (Jennings, 2007) argue that such stereotypes and prejudices may stem from a mentality of cultural superiority prevalent in both nations, where demeaning other cultures and people is a means to elevate oneself as a "star" under the spotlight. The keyword "聖誕" (Christmas), associated with a major Western festival, presents different atmospheres when it co-occurs with different characters. Concordance lines demonstrate that while this term is predominantly associated with British characters, it is occasionally attached to some Chinese characters, exuding a sense of hecticness. This is supported by its co-occurrence with words such as "忙" (busy with), "跑" (run), or "拼命" (work hard) in some concordance lines. In contrast, when it co-occurs with British characters, it is primarily linked to food and meals, such as "餅" (cake/biscuit), "大餐" (banquet), or "布丁" (pudding). This difference suggests, on one hand, the contrasting attitudes the Chinese and British characters hold towards this major Western festival. On the other hand, the difference may allude to the divergent fates awaiting these two groups during the festivities: the Chinese are preoccupied with survival issues, while the Britons indulge in culinary delights.

7.4.1.3 Abstract Concerns, Verbal Groups, and Unclassified

The sub-category of "Abstract Concerns" comprises keywords that establish a connection between the story's circumstances and more universal themes (Johnson, 2016: 41). Despite this sub-category containing only three keywords, they merit equal attention. "父子" (father and son) and "母女" (mother and daughter) are two words effectively linking the story's circumstances to broader thematic concerns: the experiences of a middle-aged Chinese father and his son as diasporic individuals and the daily life of a British widow and her daughter in the 1920s London. Concordance lines for both "父子" and "母子" reveal glimpses of these experiences and lives.

"父子" sometimes co-occurs with words such as "船票" (ship ticket), "餓死" (starve to death), "護照" (passport), or "巡警局" (police station), indicating the hardships endured by Mr. Ma and his son on their journey to London. Words like "鋪子" (shop), "古玩鋪" (curio shop), or "事業" (career) may symbolize their business endeavors in London, while terms like "不肯" (reluctance), "猜疑" (suspect), and "疑惑" (doubt) represent negative and uncertain aspects, echoing their misfortunes and daily encounters in the city. In contrast, most words that co-occur with "母女" create a different atmosphere, such as "新衣裳" (new dress), "新帽子" (new hat), "汽車" (car), "馬戲" (circus show), and "禮節" (etiquette), alluding to the relatively respectable life of Mrs. Wendell and her daughter Mary in London. As Auerbach (2009: 54) and Bengsston (2015: 5) emphasize, *Er Ma* serves as a direct documentary of the prejudiced Chinese life in early twentieth-century London. In this regard, Lao She (1998: 154) laments in *Er Ma*, "What a weak nation China is, how miserable her people are overseas!"

Lastly, the "Verbal Groups" and "Unclassified" groups include keywords associated with body language and daily life. For instance, keywords classified under "Body Language" consist of three words: "撅" (bend down), "遞給" (pass on to), and "叼" (hold something between lips), which are general body language verbs and, therefore, provide limited thematic and contextual information for further analysis in this study. In the case of "Unclassified" keywords (in both "Verbal Groups" and "Unclassified" categories), words like "回國" (go back to motherland), "圈兒" (loops), and "言語" (speech) are fragments that do not offer much information related to the themes based on their concordance lines. However, concordance lines for "念書" (schooling) and "吃飯" (have a meal) do provide thematic information that deserves further explanation.

In the case of "念書", it frequently co-occurs with "中國" (China), "救國" (save the motherland), "洋鬼子" (foreign devil), or "英國" (Britain). This suggests that China was a troubled nation at that time, and its citizens in Britain needed education to save their motherland. Regarding "吃飯", the accompanying lexical items highlight the contrasting dining cultures between the Chinese and the Britons. When "吃飯" co-occurs with Chinese characters, it is sometimes associated with words like "大聲" (loud), "喝湯" (drink soup), or "筷子" (chopsticks). On the other hand, when it co-occurs with Britons, although less frequent, it is often connected to terms like "規矩" (rules) or "體面" (proper). This contrast not only reflects cultural differences, but also signifies Lao She's perceived prejudice against the dining manners of the Chinese, while elevating those of the Britons. As Kerr and Kuehn (2007: 65) states, "The Chinese food is inedible while the eating habits of the Chinese are barbaric, because they eat with chopsticks instead of normal cutlery". In fact, similar views prevail in *Er Ma*, where diasporic Chinese are frequently referred to as barbaric, dingy, or bothersome in their food choices and dining practices (Lao, 1998: 194).

7.4.2 "Chinese Keywords" and "British Keywords"

The categories of keywords discussed in the previous section establish connections between linguistic forms and literary appreciation. These categories encompass a wide range of elements present in the fictional world of *Er Ma*, covering fundamental components and abstract thematic concerns. However, it is neither practical nor necessary to include all of these keywords in the subsequent analysis. Instead, our focus will be on keywords that facilitate highlighting the translators' functional styles and have strong connections to the two predetermined themes. This decision aligns with one of our research objectives, which is to compare translators' functional styles by examining their linguistic idiosyncrasies. Specifically, we will investigate how they handle the interactions between theme-related keywords and their contexts in the reconstruction of the two themes. The selected keywords will serve as the starting points for comparing these translators' functional styles in Chapters 8 and 9. The following two sections will outline the principles guiding our keyword selection, providing detailed explanations for each choice.

7.4.2.1 The "Chinese Keywords"

The selection of "Chinese keywords" adheres to the principle of prioritizing the translators' functional styles while establishing strong connections to the theme of "Diasporic Chinese" in *Er Ma*. This principle serves as the foundation for identifying keywords to be investigated in the next chapter. The study will select these keywords from Table 7.2 and provide an explanation for each selection.

Starting with the "Proper Names" sub-category under "Participants", five out of the six words under "Chinese Characters" meet the selection criteria and are chosen. These words serve as character labels for two Chinese protagonists, Mr. Ma and Li Zirong, and are directly relevant to the diasporic Chinese theme. Additionally, these two Chinese protagonists have contrasting worldviews and fictional representations (Shen, 1999: 114–115; Wen, 2000: 126). Consequently, the study aims to explore how different translators interpret these different story figures from the source text and linguistically reconstruct them in target texts. This approach is likely to highlight the translators' functional styles. It is worth stressing that this methodological approach differentiates this research from some prior studies of a similar nature (e.g., Mastropierro, 2018; McIntyre & Mahlberg, 2001), which often discard character labels in favor of more inclusive "cover-all" words due to differing research objectives. Nevertheless, this does not imply that this research solely focuses on character labels. It also investigates "cover-all" words relevant to the diasporic Chinese theme.

Therefore, within the "Generic Names" and "Pronominal References" subcategories under "Participants", the terms "中國人" (the Chinese) and "黃臉" (yellow-faced) under are selected. "中國人" and "黃臉" serve as two "cover-all" terms for "the Chinese". An analysis of their lexico-semantic patterns, including extended meanings, lexical chains, and discourse presentations, is likely to unveil the translators' functional styles in target texts. In the remaining keywords within the "Participants" category, most have tenuous connections to the fictional representations of the diasporic Chinese, even if they may appear relevant initially. For example, "大氅" is a traditional Chinese garment, but concordance lines reveal its association with both Chinese and British characters. Similarly, "掌櫃的" (shopkeeper) under "People" seems to be linked to a Chinese shop owner, but concordance evidence indicates its reference to multiple characters with unknown nationalities.

Keywords listed in Table 7.2 outside of the "Participants" category are not selected, as they either contribute less to foregrounding the translators' functional styles or have weak connections to the diasporic Chinese. For instance, the keyword "馬家" (the Mas) is directly relevant to the diasporic Chinese, but it consistently refers to Mr. Ma's family rather than just the Chinese protagonists. Therefore, this keyword might be less helpful in highlighting the translators' styles. Similarly, "回國" (return to the homeland) appears to be connected to the diasporic Chinese as their fate in future, but concordance evidence indicates that this connection is often weak. Consequently, it might be less useful in highlighting the translators' functional styles in the translations.

Finally, the selected keywords for further analysis include "馬則仁", "馬老先生", "老馬", "馬先生", "李子榮", 中國人", and "黃臉". These keywords are associated with two Chinese protagonists with sharp contrasts, as well as the diasporic Chinese as a whole. It is anticipated that these keywords will pave the way for the analysis of the translators' functional styles in Chapters 8 and 9.

7.4.2.2 The "British Keywords"

The selection of keywords for the local Britons follows a similar approach to the previous section. Specifically, within the "Participants" category, the focus is on " 凱薩林", "伊姑娘", "瑪力", and "溫都姑娘", because these words represent the British characters and facilitate a concentrated analysis of the translators' functional styles. Given the substantial number of characters within this category, analyzing all of them would yield fragmented results, making it challenging to prioritize the translators' functional styles. Therefore, we have opted for these four words, which represent two British protagonists displaying sharp contrasts in their views of and attitudes towards the Chinese (Ji, 2009: 71; Wen, 2000: 125). This allows us to effectively investigate how different translators linguistically reconstruct the theme of "Local Britons" and recharacterize these story figures, a window to show their functional styles in translation.

As for the keywords within the "Generic Names" and "Pronominal References" sub-categories under "Participants", we will select the words "英國人" (Briton) and "洋鬼子" (foreign devil). These terms serve as "cover-all" terms for the local Britons and offer the potential to highlight the translators' functional styles. Other keywords in these sub-categories, such as "帽子", "麵包", or "布丁", appear to be equally attached to both the Chinese and British in the story, as indicated by the concordance lines. Therefore, they do not meet our selection criteria and will be excluded.

Regarding the keywords outside the "Participants" category, none of them will be selected, as they have little immediate relevance to the local Britons and provide less assistance in highlighting the translators' functional styles in the subsequent analysis. This decision is based on literal interpretations of their meanings and evidence from their respective concordance lines. For instance, "母女" (mother and daughter) under "Abstract Concerns" is directly related to the local Britons, but it does not serve as a "cover-all" term for them nor depict characters of sharp contrast. Therefore, it is less helpful in highlighting the translators' functional styles. Similarly, "博物院" (museum) could be suitable for emphasizing the translators' functional styles due to its specificity, but it is not exclusively associated with the local Britons, as concordance evidence suggests it is equally linked to the Chinese (cf. 5.4.1.25.4.1.2).

Finally, the selected keywords for further analysis include "凱薩林", "伊姑娘", " 瑪力", "溫都姑娘", "英國人, and "洋鬼子". These words cover two distinct protagonists with sharp contrasts and two "cover-all" terms help build the theme of "Local Britons". This selection allows us to effectively examine and compare the translators' functional styles in Chapters 8 and 9.

7.5 Conclusion

This chapter has identified keywords immediately relevant to the two pre-identified themes in *Er Ma*. Further analysis of these keywords is expected to illuminate the translators' functional styles in the English translations of the story. The use of two reference corpora, RC1 and RC2, in the keyword generation stage ensures that the final list of keywords is exclusively specific to *Er Ma*. This approach helps reduce the impact of extraneous factors on the analysis of the translators' functional styles. In the classification of keywords, Johnson's (2016) model is favored over other possible models due to its equal weighting of each keyword in their role in thematic construction and characterization, a feature that aligns with the research objectives. In the selection of keywords, priority is given to words closely associated with "Diasporic Chinese" and "Local Britons". Since *Er Ma* revolves around these two themes, focusing on keywords related to them provides a better understanding of the translators' functional styles in thematic reconstruction and recharacterization.

It is worth reiterating that these keywords underpin the subsequent analyses in Chapters 8 and 9, facilitating the examination of the translators' functional styles in their recreation of the two literary functions: thematic reconstruction and recharacterization. Thus, the generation, classification, and selection of these theme-related keywords, as discussed in this chapter, establish a fundamental and initial stage for exploring these styles.

References

Auerbach, S. (2009). *Race, law, and the Chinese puzzle in imperial Britain*. Springer Nature.

Auerbach, S. (2013). Margaret Tart, Lao She, and the opium-master's wife: Race and class among Chinese commercial immigrants in London and Australia, 1866–1929. *Comparative Studies in Society and History, 55*(1), 35–64.

Bengtsson, E. (2015). *From China to England: A comparison between Lao She's Er Ma and contemporary travel writings by travelers to China and Europe*. Lund University.

Culpeper, J. (2009). Keyness: Words, parts-of-speech and semantic categories in the character-talk of Shakespeare's Romeo and Juliet. *International Journal of Corpus Linguistics, 14*(1), 29–59.

Culpeper, J., & Demmen, J. (2015). *The Cambridge handbook of English corpus linguistics*. Cambridge University Press.

Jennings, L. (2007). Prejudice. In Ritzer, G. (Ed.), *Blackwell encyclopedia of sociology*. Blackwell Publishing.

Johnson, J. H. (2016). A comparable comparison? A corpus stylistic analysis of the Italian translation of Julian Barnes' *Il Senso di una Fine* and the original text. *The Sense of an Ending. Language and Literature, 25*(1), 38–53.

Kerr, D., & Kuehn, J. (Eds.). (2007). *A century of travels in China: Critical essays on travel writing from the 1840s to the 1940s*. Hong Kong University Press.

Lao, S. (1998). *Er Ma*. People's Literature Publishing House.

Laviosa, S., Pagano, A., Kemppanen, H., & Ji, M. (2016). *Textual and contextual analysis in empirical translation studies*. Springer.

Louie, K. (2000). Constructing Chinese masculinity for the modern world: With particular reference to Lao She's *Two Mas*. *The China Quarterly, 164*, 1062–1078.

Mahlberg, M. (2009). Lexical cohesion: Corpus linguistic theory and its application in English language teaching. In J. Flowerdew & M. Mahlberg (Eds.), *Lexical cohesion and corpus linguistics* (pp. 103–122). John Benjamins.
Mahlberg, M. (2013). *Corpus stylistics and Dickens's fiction*. Routledge.
Mahlberg, M. (2014). Corpus stylistics. In M. Burke (Ed.), *The Routledge handbook of stylistics* (pp. 378–392). Routledge.
Mahlberg, M., & McIntyre, D. (2011). A case for corpus stylistics: Ian Fleming's *Casino Royale. English Text Construction, 4*(2), 204–227.
Mastropierro, L. (2018). *Corpus stylistics in heart of darkness and its Italian translations*. Bloomsbury Publishing.
Mayer, R. (2013). *Serial Fu Manchu: The Chinese supervillain and the spread of yellow peril ideology*. Temple University Press.
McEnery, T., & Hardie, A. (2011). *Corpus linguistics: Method, theory and practice*. Cambridge University Press.
McIntyre, D., & Mahlberg, M. (2011). Keywords and the analysis of literature. In P. Baker (Ed.), *Contemporary corpus linguistics* (pp. 204–226). Continuum.
Scott, M. (1998). *Wordsmith tools*. Lexical Analysis Software.
Scott, M. (2000). Focusing on the text and its key words. In L. Burnard & T. McEnery (Eds.), *Rethinking language pedagogy from a corpus perspective* (pp. 103–122). Peter Lang.
Scott, M. (2006). Key word analysis. In A. Brown (Ed.), *Encyclopedia of language & linguistics* (pp. 615–618). Elsevier.
Wijitsopon, R. (2018). A corpus stylistic study of singular and plural keywords in Jane Austen's Persuasion. *Kemanusiaan: The Asian Journal of Humanities, 25*(2), 1–22.

Chapter 8
Functional Style as Reconstruction of Literary Themes

8.1 Introduction

The two "Chinese keywords" (i.e., "黃臉" and "中國人") and the two "British keywords" (i.e., "英國人", "洋鬼子") selected in Chapter 7 are the starting points of this chapter. These keywords are specific to *Er Ma* and bear close connections to the two themes of "Diasporic Chinese" and "Local Britons" identified in Chapter 5. Therefore, it is expected that they could help foreground translators' functional styles as they reconstruct the two themes in translation. With these keywords, the present chapter examines the translators' functional styles in the four English translations of *Er Ma* through a corpus stylistic analysis that involves both quantitative and qualitative investigations.

The corpus stylistic analysis comprises two stages: the first stage involves analyzing the source text (ST), while the second stage involves analyzing the target texts (TT) and comparing them with the ST. In Sect. 8.2, the focus is on examining the construction of the two themes, namely "Diasporic Chinese" and "Local Britons". Specifically, Sect. 8.2.1 explores the construction of "Diasporic Chinese" by examining the semantic fields shared by the collocates of the two Chinese keywords and analyzing the local textual function attached to these semantic fields. In Sect. 8.2.2, the analysis shifts to the construction of "Local Britons", with an emphasis on identifying the shared semantic fields by the collocates of the two British keywords and analyzing the local textual function associated with these semantic fields.

In Sect. 8.3, the focus shifts to exploring the translators' functional styles through their linguistic idiosyncrasies exhibited in recreating the two themes. Section 8.3.1 investigates the translators' functional styles as they reconstruct the theme of "Diasporic Chinese". This involves examining their renditions of the "Chinese keywords", their reconstructions of the original semantic fields, and their reestablishment of the original lexical chains in the translations. Similarly, in Sect. 8.3.3, the translators' functional styles are examined as they reconstruct the theme of "Local Britons". The analysis in this section also focuses on the renditions of the British keywords, the

K. Wu and D. Li, *Researching Translator's Functional Style*, New Frontiers in Translation Studies, https://doi.org/10.1007/978-981-95-1221-8_8

reconstructions of the original semantic fields, and the reestablishment of the original lexical chains in the translations.

Section 8.4 summarizes the major findings of this chapter, discusses some limitations of the present work, and provides a glimpse into further research in the subsequent chapters.

8.2 Construction of "Diasporic Chinese" and "Local Britons" in *Er Ma*

Attaching literary relevance to a statistical salience entails the identification of "an artistically coherent pattern of choice" at a "particular literary end" (Leech & Short, 2007: 40). This process entails not only detecting such salience, but also conducting discrete investigations into its literary contexts (Mastropierro, 2018: 146). Thus, this section examines the chosen "Chinese Keywords" and "British Keywords" in contexts, exploring how they interact with their contexts to create extended units of meaning in *Er Ma*. This section also generalizes potential local textual functions carried by these extended units of meaning. In this way, the previously established connections between linguistic descriptions and literary appreciations (i.e., literary functions) in Chapter 7 are further explored to uncover the construction of the two themes "Diasporic Chinese" and "Local Britons" in *Er Ma*.

8.2.1 Construction of the Theme "Diasporic Chinese"

This section scrutinizes the construction of the theme "Diasporic Chinese" in the source text. It analyzes the semantic fields shared by the collocates of the two Chinese keywords and explores the local textual function associated with these semantic fields. Section 8.2.1.1 verifies the statistical representativeness of the two Chinese keywords, "黃臉" and "中國人", in the story. Section 8.2.1.2 delves into the construction of the theme by analyzing the collocates and semantic fields they form in the source text. Section 8.2.1.3 investigates the potential local textual functions carried by these collocates and their associated semantic fields.

8.2.1.1 Keywords Statistically Representative of "Diasporic Chinese"

The corpus stylistic analysis of the construction of the "Diasporic Chinese" theme commences by comparing the frequencies of the two Chinese keywords, "黃臉" and "中國人", between *Er Ma* and the two reference corpora (RC1 and RC2). The two keywords are considered general references instead of proper nouns and thus require confirmation of their statistical representativeness in the story. The

Table 8.1 Frequencies of the "Chinese Keywords" in *Er Ma* and the two reference corpora

	Er Ma		RC1		*Er Ma* vs. RC1		RC2		*Er Ma* vs. RC2	
Item	Raw	Norm	Raw	Norm	G^2	Sig	Raw	Norm	G^2	Sig
黃臉	13	0.02	10	0.00	40.25	$p < 0.0001$	5	0.00	46.46	$p < 0.0001$
中國人	235	0.31	328	0.03	559.49	$p < 0.0001$	49	0.01	966.16	$p < 0.0001$

G^2 (Log-likelihood ratio) test is used to assess the statistical significance of the frequency differences between these keywords in *Er Ma* and the reference corpora ($p < 0.0001$). This choice of the G^2-test aims to efficiently evaluate the "goodness-of-fit" of keyword frequencies in different corpora of relatively large sizes. The normalizing (at per thousand words) and analysis of the frequency data are performed by the *Lancaster Log-likelihood and Effect Size Calculator*[1] (hereafter as the calculator) with the results reported in Table 8.1.

Table 8.1 provides a clear contrast in the frequencies of the two keywords across *Er Ma* and the reference corpora. "中國人" (Chinese) is the most frequent word in both *Er Ma* and the reference corpora, with 235 occurrences in the novel, 328 in RC1, and 49 in RC2. In contrast, "黃臉" (yellow face) has lower frequency, appearing 13 times in the novel, 10 times in RC1, and 5 times in RC2. Normalized frequencies indicate relative consistency for "黃臉", with a frequency of 0.02 in the novel and 0.00 in RC1 and RC2. In contrast, "中國人" shows variation in normalized frequency, registering 0.31 in the novel, 0.03 in RC1, and 0.01 in RC2. This aligns with expectations as "中國人" represents a key theme in *Er Ma* and appears frequently in other works by Lao She (Witchard, 2012).

Table 8.1 also demonstrates that the frequency differences of the two keywords between *Er Ma* and the reference corpora are statistically significant. The G^2 value indicates the significance level of these frequency differences (Lancaster Log-likelihood and Effect Size Calculator, 2019). G^2 values above 15.13 correspond to p-values below 0.001, while values below 3.84 indicate p-values above 0.05. The consistently high G^2 values observed in the comparison of the frequencies of the two keywords between *Er Ma* and the reference corpora confirm the statistical significance, signifying substantial deviations in these frequencies. This also confirms that the two keywords are statistically representative of the Chinese people in the story, a crucial precondition for subsequent analyses.

8.2.1.2 "Diasporic Chinese" in Context

In *Er Ma*, the keywords "黃臉" and "中國人" appear 13 and 235 times, respectively, providing general depictions of the diasporic Chinese. Although "黃臉" (the yellow face) has a broader literal meaning compared to "中國人" (the Chinese), it predominantly refers to the Chinese characters in the story. These two words share

[1] Details are available at http://ucrel.lancs.ac.uk/llwizard.html.

Table 8.2 Semantic fields shared by the two Chinese Keywords in the source text

Semantic Fields	**Collocates (L10:R10)**
General Negativity	又黃又腫, 抽大煙, 看不起(8), 不屑於(2), 笑話(7), 罵(8), 不值錢, 不要臉, 丟臉(3), 打怕了, 下賤, 缺點(2), 妓女(3), 髒臭, 弄乾淨, 污濁, 傻蛋, 糊塗, 煮老鼠, 吃老鼠, 吃狗肉, 吃狗, 討厭(8), 可惡, 討人嫌(2), 打死(2)
Treachery, Crime, Peril	陰險詭詐(2), 陰險, 險詐, 卑鄙, 毒藥(5), 毒蛇, 害死人, 害人(4), 造謠言, 私運軍火, 壞事, 殺人, 亂殺, 暗殺, 慘殺, 殺人放火(3), 強盜(2), 強姦, 搶女人, 危險(3), 不安全, 野蠻, 殘忍, 喪掉生命
Dehumanization	沒鼻子(2), 扁鼻子, 狹眼睛, 矮身量, 扁臉, 腫顴骨, 怪物, 東西(2), 玩藝兒(2), 鬼鬼啾啾
Japanese Superiority	日本人(10), 公司, 銀行, 造大炮, 好處, 體面, 主兒, 學鬼子, 含著點怕, 佩服, 奉承

specific semantic fields, contributing to the development of the "Diasporic Chinese" theme. By treating each keyword as a node within a concordance span of L10:R10,[2] this study can analyze their semantic preferences and identify the semantic fields they generate. This analysis reveals contextual information related to the overall portrayal of the diasporic Chinese. Examination of the concordance lines for these two keywords[3] reveals the presence of at least four semantic fields (Table 8.2), which convey a negative tone.

The first semantic field shared by the two keywords are labeled as *General Negativity*. This field is represented by collocates within the L10:R10 range of "黃臉", such as "可惡" (Line 5), "討厭" (Line 1), "又黃又腫" (Line 12), and "抽大煙" (Line 7). Similarly, the collocates of "中國人" within the same range, such as "討厭" (Line 106), "討人嫌" (Line 130), and "髒臭" (Line 222), contribute to this portrayal of negativity. Collectively, these collocates construct a fictional portrayal of the diasporic Chinese as sick, unintelligent, and disgusting human beings. Consider the following two examples:

(1) 馬威也勸過他父親不用帶小狗兒出去, 因為他看見好幾次: 他父親拉著狗在街上或是空地上轉, 一群孩子在後面跟著起哄: "瞧這個老黃臉! 瞧他的臉! <u>又黃又腫</u>!"

(2) 沒到過中國的英國人, 看中國人是陰險詭詐, 長著個討人嫌的黃臉。到過中國的英國人, 看中國人是<u>髒臭</u>, 糊塗的傻蛋。

Example (1) presents Mr. Ma as a sick man with a swollen yellow face, subject to mockery by British children on the streets. Example (2) amplifies the British contempt for the Chinese, suggesting that local Britons, whether or not they have been to China, view the Chinese as either fraudulent crooks or dirty fools.

---

[2] The decision to use L10:R10 in this study, based on repeated pilot studies, ensures the inclusion of essential contextual information while avoiding redundancy. It deviates from previous studies focusing on European languages, which employed L5:R5 settings. Practical considerations regarding the varying information density between Chinese and English translations influenced this decision.

[3] The detailed lists are available at http://dx.doi.org/10.6084/m9.figshare.29572907.

The second semantic field shared by the two keywords are labeled as *Treachery, Crime, Peril*. This field comprises L10: R10 collocates such as "殺人放火" (Line 11), "毒藥" (Line 15), "強盜" (Line 34), and "暗殺" (Line 63) in the concordance lines of "中國人", and "害死人" (Line 7) in those of "黃臉". Collectively, these collocates create a powerful impression that characterizes the diasporic Chinese in *Er Ma* as criminals, engaging in murder, arson, and poisoning, thus endangering the British community. This portrayal is illustrated in the following examples:

(3) 瑪力才接著說: "媽, 不用護著中國人, 他們要是不討人嫌為什麼電影上, 戲裡, 小說上的中國人老是些殺人放火搶女人的呢?"
(4) 中國城要是住著二十個中國人, 他們的記載上一定是五千; 而且這五千黃臉鬼是個個抽大煙, 私運軍火, 害死人把屍首往床底下藏, 強姦婦女不問老少, 和作一切至少該千刀萬剮的事情的。

Example (3) highlights Mary's deeply ingrained bias against the Chinese, who are frequently depicted in films and literature as ruthless criminals committing acts of violence and robbery, as well as assaulting women. Likewise, Example (4), a concordance line of "黃臉", shapes the diasporic Chinese as devilish animals who behead people and rape women.

The third shared semantic field, labeled as *Dehumanization*, intensifies the negative depiction of the diasporic Chinese characters by stripping them of their human qualities. This dehumanization is evident in collocates such as "東西" (Line 2), "沒鼻子" (Line 10), and "怪物" (Line 13) associated with "黃臉", as well as "鬼鬼啾啾" (Line 191), "玩藝兒" (Line 20), and "沒鼻子" (Line 26) associated with "中國人" within the L10:R10 concordance lines. These collocates collectively contribute to a fictional atmosphere in which the Chinese are depicted as repulsive monsters who require colonization by the civilized Britons. Consider the following two examples:

(5) 半夜睡不著的時候, 總是禱告上帝快快的叫中國變成英國的屬國; 他含著熱淚告訴上帝: 中國人要不叫英國人管起來, 這群黃臉黑頭發的東西, 怎麼也升不了天堂!
(6) 外國人心中的中國人是: 矮身量, 帶辮子, 扁臉, 腫顴骨, 沒鼻子, 眼睛是一寸來長的兩道縫兒, 撇著嘴, 唇上掛著迎風而動的小鬍子, 兩條哈吧狗腿, 一走一扭。

Example (5) is a concordance line of "黃臉" with the collocate "東西". It leaves readers with the impression that the Chinese are dehumanized as mere "things". Hence, Reverend Evan, on his sleepless nights, prays for the Britons to rescue and civilize these "things" by subjecting them to British domination. Example (6), a concordance line of "中國人" with the collocate "沒鼻子", presents the readers a hideous representation of the Chinese through the Westerners' eyes: they are short animals without nose and eyes.

The fourth semantic field, labeled as *Japanese Superiority*, diverges from the negativity conveyed in the previous three fields. It revolves around the relatively privileged social status of the Japanese in comparison to the Chinese in *Er Ma*. Examination of the concordance lines of the two keywords reveals adjacent collocate pairs within the L10:R10 span. For instance, in the concordance lines of "黃臉", we find "日本人" (L2, Line 3)—"好處" (R4, Line 3), and in those of "中國人", we find "日本人" (L5, Line 138)—"體面" (L3, Line 138) and "日本人" (R2, Line 205)—"造大炮" (R4, Line 205). These adjacent collocate pairs between the two keywords establish a fictional atmosphere in which the Japanese, despite wearing the same yellow face, are portrayed as a more privileged group than the Chinese. The following examples partly illustrate this point:

(7) 若是他身量高一點, 外國人也許高抬他一下, 叫他聲日本人(凡是黃臉而稍微有點好處的便是日本人)。不幸, 他只有五尺來高,而且兩條短腿確乎是羅圈著一點。
(8) 李子榮算把外國人弄糊塗了: 你說他是日本人吧, 他的臉真不能說是體面。(日本人都是體面的!)說他是中國人吧, 他的黃臉確是洗得晶光; 中國人可有捨得錢買胰子洗臉的?

Example (7) suggests that the Japanese, despite having yellow faces, receive preferential treatment due to their favorable qualities. Example (8) further emphasizes that Chinese, in contrast, lack the economic means to achieve the same level of facial cleanliness and social standing as the Japanese.

8.2.1.3 "Diasporic Chinese" as the "Yellow Peril"

Three of the four shared semantic fields between the keywords "黃臉" and "中國人" are marked by negative stereotypes of the Chinese, while one, *Japanese Superiority*, contrasts with this negativity by elevating the Japanese. We contend that the extended units of meaning formed by these keywords and their collocates across these fields are functionally interconnected in their collective effort to depict the diasporic Chinese as sickly and devilish creatures. These depictions are frequently associated with "Yellow Peril", a racial stereotype that emerged from Germany in the late nineteenth Century as a societal response to the growing fear towards the Asians (Tuchman, 1985).

According to the "Yellow Peril" racial construct, the "yellow-faced" Chinese are portrayed as barbarous and uncivilized hordes that pose a serious threat to Western civilization. Such Sinophobic themes are frequently exploited in some popular British literary works in the late nineteenth and early Twentieth Centuries. Sax Rohmer, the pen name of Arthur Ward, is one of the early British writers who successfully embodies the "Yellow Peril" in one character, Dr. Fu Manchu, who is "a mysterious Chinese doctor with a 'Satan-like face' and a threat to the survival of the entire white race" (Mayer, 2013: 27). Under Rohmer's pen, the Chinese are often portrayed as a race that "wears sometimes a black-eyed pallid face…sometimes a yellow face, but never a face wholly sane and healthy" (Rohmer, 1916: 94–95). Similarly, Thomas Burke (1919) exploits the same "Yellow Peril" theme, depicting how those "yellow-faced" Chinamen sexually ensnare white women and cohabitate with them in London's Limehouse, a scene that strikes fear in the British.

Returning to *Er Ma*, such racial stereotypes in popular literature towards the Chinese are linguistically expressed in three of the four key semantic fields shared by "黃臉" and "中國人": they are portrayed as pallid and unhealthy creatures who are contemptuous (as seen in the semantic field *General Negativity*); as villainous thugs who show no mercy in poisoning, killing, and raping (as shown in the semantic field *Treachery, Crime, Peril*); and as noseless monsters that induce fear (as shown in the semantic field *Dehumanization*). However, the representations of the Chinese in *Er Ma* and some early British popular literature serve different purposes: while Lao She attempts to reveal the "pernicious effects of the media on the lives of Chinese people in London" (Witchard, 2012: 60), the writers of the latter are more interested in "exploiting the dramatic potential" (Witchard, 2012: 60) of the "Yellow Peril" hordes in London.

Nevertheless, compared to the Chinese, the Japanese with the same "yellow face" present a different story in the British perception of that era. The Japanese victory in the Sino-Japanese War of 1894–1895 added another layer to British anxiety over the "Yellow Peril" threat, leading many Britons to believe that the Japanese, armed with Western weapons and tactics, might be capable of defeating the British Empire (Prince, 1987: 2). However, some Britons viewed the Japanese victory differently. They suggest that the rise of Japan in the Far East could potentially represent a future ally against the Russians, rather than a threat (Curzon, 1986: 396). Moreover, the British anxiety over the "Yellow Peril" had predominantly focused on the Chinese, as there were few Japanese immigrants on the British Isles between the 1890s and the 1920s (Stone, 2017). This might have contributed to the "positive relations" between Britain and Japan, culminating in the "first Anglo-Japanese alliance" in 1902 (Stone, 2017: 144). Therefore, we can reasonably argue that British stereotypes of the "Yellow Peril" were directed less towards the Japanese.

In *Er Ma*, this tendency is linguistically manifested by the semantic field of "Japanese superiority" shared by the two keywords ("黃臉" and "中國人"). As discussed in Sect. 8.2.1.2, the Chinese are sometimes compared with the Japanese, with the latter often associated with more positive terms like "體面" and "好處". This may reflect Lao She's perception of Japanese superiority over the Chinese through the British perspective, partially explaining his "harsh indictment of British racism" towards the Chinese (Louie, 2000: 1063).

8.2.2 Construction of the Theme "Local Britons"

This section analyzes the construction of the theme of "Local Britons" in the source text by examining the semantic fields formed by the collocates of the two British keywords. It also investigates the local textual function associated with these semantic fields. Section 8.2.2.1 compares the frequencies of the British keywords with the reference corpora to ensure their statistical representativeness. Section 8.2.2.2 explores the construction of the theme of "Local Britons" through an analysis of the collocates and their semantic fields in the source text. Section 8.2.2.3 examines the potential local textual functions carried by these collocates and their semantic fields.

Table 8.3 Frequencies of the "British Keywords" in *Er Ma* and the two reference corpora

	Er Ma		RC1		*Er Ma* vs. RC1		RC2		*Er Ma* vs. RC2	
Item	Raw	Norm	Raw	Norm	G^2	Sig	Raw	Norm	G^2	Sig
英國人	71	0.09	46	0.00	233.81	$p < 0.0001$	3	0.00	340.96	$p < 0.0001$
洋鬼子	16	0.02	11	0.00	51.62	$p < 0.0001$	35	0.00	24.49	$p < 0.0001$

8.2.2.1 Keywords Statistically Representative of "Local Britons"

Following the methods employed in Sect. 8.2.1.1, the corpus stylistic analysis of the thematic construction of "Local Britons" starts with a frequency comparison of the two British keywords ("英國人" and "洋鬼子") between *Er Ma* and the two reference corpora. We will run the G^2 (Log-likelihood ratio) tests for the same reasons explained in Sect. 8.2.1.1 to find out whether the two British keywords are statistically representative of the Britons in the story. The results obtained through this analysis are summarized in Table 8.3, where statistical significance, G^2 values, and raw/normalized frequencies are presented for each keyword.

In terms of frequency, these British keywords exhibit varying patterns of occurrence across *Er Ma* and the two reference corpora. The term "英國人" (Britons) emerges as relatively prominent within *Er Ma*, with 71 instances and a normalized frequency of 0.09. In contrast, its occurrence in the reference corpora is minimal, featuring only 46 instances (normalized frequency of 0.00) in RC1 and 3 instances (normalized frequency of 0.00) in RC2. Conversely, the keyword "洋鬼子" (foreign devils) is less frequent in *Er Ma*, with 16 occurrences and a normalized frequency of 0.02. However, it is more prevalent in RC1, with 11 instances (normalized frequency of 0.00), and RC2, with 35 instances (normalized frequency of 0.00).

These frequency differences indicate that "英國人" may play a thematic role in Lao She's works, including *Er Ma*. Conversely, "洋鬼子" appears to be of less thematic concern in Lao She's works, including *Er Ma* and RC1, compared to those in RC2. Nevertheless, despite these frequency differences, all comparisons yield G^2 values exceeding the threshold of 15.13.[4] This indicates the statistical significance of the frequency disparities ($p < 0.0001$) when comparing the occurrences of these two keywords between *Er Ma* and the two reference corpora. Thus, it is established that both keywords are statistically representative of the Britons in *Er Ma*, a crucial prerequisite for the subsequent analysis.

[4] Details are available at http://ucrel.lancs.ac.uk/llwizard.html.

8.2.2.2 "Local Britons" in Context

The keywords "英國人" and "洋鬼子" are foundational in the construction of the "Local Britons" theme in *Er Ma*. While "洋鬼子" has the potential to refer to non-Chinese foreigners beyond Britons, it predominantly associates with Britons in the story. As a result, these keywords share common semantic fields in constructing the theme of "Local Britons". By treating these keywords as the nodes, this study generalizes the shared semantic fields by examining the L10:R10 collocates within concordance lines. The analysis of these collocates provides contextual information, which reveals the presence of at least four semantic fields shared by the two keywords (see Table 8.4).

The first semantic field, labeled as *Pride and Prejudice*, portrays the "Local Britons" as arrogant and biased people, particularly towards the diasporic Chinese. This field is exemplified by various representative L10:R10 collocates found in the concordance lines of "英國人", such as "當狗" (Line 27), "討厭" (Line 28), "髒臭" (Line 46), "低下" (Line 38), and "極驕傲" (Line 55). In the case of "洋鬼子", no immediately relevant collocates are discovered within its limited 16 concordance lines. Collectively, these collocates convey a sense of British "pride" and "prejudice". The following examples illustrate some of these collocates in context.

(9) 東方婦女是家中的寶貝, 不肯叫外人看見, 更不肯嫁給外國人, 英國人也是一樣, 最討厭外國人動他們的婦女! 馬先生, 種族的成見, 你我打不破, 更犯不上冒險的破壞! 你我可以永遠作好朋友, 只能作好朋友!"

(10) "你知道, 馬先生, 英國人是一個極驕傲的民族, 看不起嫁外國人的婦人, 討厭娶英國老婆的外國人!"

The pride and prejudice of the Britons in the story are aptly demonstrated by these two examples, in which both cases revolve around a possible cross-national marriage between Mr. Ma and Mrs. Wendell. Example (9) elucidates the British prejudice towards the Chinese through the collocate "成見", illustrating how racial bias plays a role in cross-national marriages. Mrs. Wendell's account implies that the Chinese are perceived as an inferior race in British eyes. Example (10) highlights British pride, with Mrs. Wendell using the collocate "極驕傲" as she rejects Mr. Ma's marriage proposal.

The second semantic field, referred to as *Hypocrisy and Pretension*, sheds light on another characteristic closely associated with the "Local Britons". This field revolves

Table 8.4 Semantic fields shared by the two "British Keywords" in the source text

Semantic Fields	Collocates (L10:R10)
Pride and Prejudice	驕傲 (2), 想不到, 只有, 除了 (2), 成見, 不肯, 看不起 (2)
Hypocrisy and Pretension	形式上, 講究, 愛體面, 講排場, 擺飯, 逞能
Colonialism and Conservatism	管起來, 腳下, 屬地, 守舊 (2)
Rule and Law	公平交易 (2), 公平(2), 平等的, 兩不吃虧, 直說, 直辦, 服從, 秩序 (2), 講規矩, 死心眼兒, 講法律, 律師

around the portrayal of pretentious behavior exhibited by the Britons, which might stem from their pride. L10:R10 collocates such as "講排場" (Line 2), "擺飯" (Line 9), "逞能" (Line 64), and "形式上" (Line 17) in the case of "英國人", and "講究" (Line 5) in the case of "洋鬼子" exemplify this field. These collocates, along with the semantic field they create, convey to readers that the Britons in *Er Ma* excessively emphasize "pretentious" etiquettes. To illustrate this point, let's consider the following two examples.

(11) "唉, 英國人擺飯的時間比吃飯的時間長, 稍微體面一點的人就寧可少吃一口, 不能不把吃飯的地方弄乾淨了! 咱們中國人是真吃, 不管吃的地方好歹。"

(12) 他知道老馬是傻蛋, 傻蛋自然不會寫書。可是不雙方定好, 彼此互助, 伊牧師的良心上不好過, 因為英國人的公平交易, 是至少要在形式上表出來的!

The two provided examples effectively illustrate the pretentious behavior exhibited by the Britons in the story, whether related to table manners or interpersonal interactions. In Example (11), Mr. Ma expresses his frustration with the British "hypocrisy" regarding dining etiquette. The example highlights the excessive time the Britons spent on table settings compared to food consumption. Mr. Ma regards this as "pretentious" British manners, which is beyond his understanding. In contrast, Example (12) offers a narrator's insight into Reverend Evans' inner thoughts, revealing his perception of Mr. Ma as a fool while he maintains fairness on the surface. This demonstrates a form of hypocrisy that is typical of the "Local Britons" in *Er Ma*.

The third semantic field, labeled as *Colonialism and Conservatism*, depicts a colonial mentality of the British, which is sometimes intertwined with conservatism. This field is believed to be a possible consequence of the "British pride" discussed in the first field. Collocates like "戀愛" (Line 8), "管起來" (Line 4), "武力" (Line 33), and "守舊" (Line 18) are observed in the case of "英國人". Within the 16 concordance lines featuring "洋鬼子", no immediately relevant collocates are found. These collocates create an impression that some Britons in the story exhibit a colonial attitude outwardly, while maintaining conservative values inwardly. Consider the following two instances:

(13) 他真愛中國人: 半夜睡不著的時候, 總是禱告上帝快快的叫中國變成英國的屬國; 他含著熱淚告訴上帝: 中國人要不叫英國人管起來, 這群黃臉黑頭發的東西, 怎麼也升不了天堂!

(14) 英國人是守舊的, 就是守舊的英國人也正在這個怒潮裡滾……保羅的呢: 戰爭, 愛國, 連婚姻與宗教的形式都要保存著。

Example (13) portrays Reverend Evans with a professed British colonial mindset towards other nations, highlighting his hypocrisy. He shows love for the Chinese while privately praying for British domination over these "yellow-faced and black-haired" Chinese creatures. In contrast, Example (14) illustrates British conservatism with the recurring use of the collocate "守舊". This conservatism, notably embodied by Paul, a young Englishman in the story, emphasizes a desire to uphold traditional British values in various aspects, including patriotism, marriage, and religion.

The fourth semantic field uncovers an additional characteristic attributed to the "Local Britons": their adherence to rules and laws. This specific trait, distinct from those identified in the previous three fields, is not directly associated with "British pride". Nonetheless, it is portrayed as quintessentially British within the story. We designate this field as *Rule and Law*, featuring several representative L10:R10 collocates, such as "講法律" (Line 13), "公平交易" (Line 17), and "平等" (Line 41) in the concordance lines of "英國人". Correspondingly, within the concordance lines of "洋鬼子", we find collocates like "兩不吃虧" (Line 3) and "死心眼兒" (Line 9). These collocates, along with the semantic field they establish, demonstrate the British respect for rules and laws. Simultaneously, these collocates also seem to hint a completely opposite Chinese cultural practice. This contrast becomes evident in the following two examples, illustrating the cultural dilemmas faced by two Chinese characters in the story.

(15) 李子榮笑也不好, 不笑也不好的直為難。明知道中國人的脾氣是講客氣, 套人情的; 又明知道英國人是<u>直說直辦</u>, 除了辦外交, 沒有轉磨繞圈作文章的。

(16) 馬老先生點了點頭, 其實他心裡說: "洋鬼子真他媽的<u>死心眼兒</u>, 他非把你問得棱兒是棱兒, 角兒是角兒不可!"

Example (15) depicts the dilemma faced by Li Zirong, who grapples with the Chinese culture to prioritize personal connections over strict adherence to rules, in contrast to the British insistence on following established regulations. In this context, the collocate "直說直辦" not only illustrates the British attributes of straightforwardness and rule adherence, but also suggests a different approach commonly found in Chinese culture. Likewise, the collocate "死心眼兒" in Example (16) mirrors a similar dilemma encountered by Mr. Ma, with his strong disapproval for the British "stubbornness". Pragmatically, this British "stubbornness" can be viewed as a direct manifestation of their respect for rules and laws, which is beyond Mr. Ma's comprehension.

8.2.2.3 "Local Britons" as a "Proud and Orderly" Race

Three (viz. *Pride and Prejudice*, *Hypocrisy and Pretension*, *Colonialism and Conservatism*) of the four semantic fields identified in the previous section are functionally related to jointly present the "British pride". In contrast, the fourth field, *Rule and Law*, conveys a sense of "British orderliness". These lexical and semantic patterns collectively establish a local textual function that characterizes the "Local Britons" in *Er Ma* as a "proud" and "orderly" community.

The "Local Britons" are portrayed as a "proud" community that is often associated with arrogance, bias, colonialism, and conservatism. This manifestation of "British pride" is prominently exemplified through various British characters in the story. For instance, during a confrontation between Ma Wei and Paul, Mrs. Evans, Paul's mother, is astounded by Paul's defeat and Ma Wei's audacity to fight a Briton (Lao, 1998: 421). In her perspective, the Britons are inherently superior, noble, and powerful compared to the Chinese, making Ma's confrontation with her son inconceivable (Wen, 2000). In another instance, the "warm-hearted" Reverend Evans, during a sleepless night, prays for British dominance over China (Lao, 1998: 322). This reflects a colonial mindset, which is partly influenced by the pervasive "British pride". Furthermore, Paul's unwavering adherence to traditional ways of religion, marriage, and patriotism underscores the British penchant for preserving their historical traditions, which is also rooted in their pride (Lao, 1998: 621).

The "Local Britons" are also depicted as an "orderly" community that respects rules and upholds the law. This recurring theme is evident whenever the keyword "英國人" is mentioned in the story. For instance, when Ma Wei and Paul engage in a fight, none of the British onlookers attempt to intervene, but instead call for a "fair" duel between the two men (Lao, 1998: 543). In another scenario, when Mary's fiancé, Washington, is involved in an affair with Catherine, Reverend Evans, who is Catherine's father, advises Mary to file a legal suit against the man (Lao, 1998: 589). Even Alexander, a character with a coarse demeanor, is initially described as someone who respects rules. Lao She attributes his later disregard for rules and manners to his prolonged interactions with his Chinese staff (Lao, 1998: 458).

In addition to *Er Ma*, the expressions of British "pride" and "orderliness" also find frequent mention in Lao She's other works. In his prose piece *The Oriental School* (《東方學院》), Lao She laments the British prejudice against Chinese scholars, which results in their unjust denial of academic promotion (Lao, 2018: 204). In the short story *Traveling* (《旅行》), Lao She depicts a British inn's blatant racial discrimination against Chinese guests by denying them check-in. In the prose *The Englishmen* (《英國人》), Lao She comments on the British respect for rules and the law, noting their unwavering commitment to doing what is expected, regardless of personal connections. Personal relationships hold no sway in their business dealings (Lao, 2018: 193). Similar to *Er Ma*, these works often draw connections between British "pride" and "orderliness" and the perceived inferiority of the Chinese.

8.3 Translators' Functional Styles in Reconstructing Literary Themes

The previous section has examined the construction of the two themes, "Diasporic Chinese" and "Local Britons", in the source text. It is revealed that these two themes are linguistically instantiated through the extended units of meaning generated by the theme-related Chinese and British keywords (nodes) and their respective L10: R10 collocates. In the target texts, these themes are reconstructed by different translators under various "translatorial" and "extra-translatorial" influences (to be discussed in Chapter 11). Consequently, it is likely that these translators may use different means in reconstructing the two themes, which are reflected in their linguistic idiosyncrasies (see Chapters 4 and 6). Therefore, this section is dedicated to examining these linguistic idiosyncrasies across the four translations, highlighting and contrasting the translators' functional styles thereby surfaced.

The analytical framework for investigating the translators' linguistic idiosyncrasies (functional styles) in thematic reconstruction is depicted in Fig. 8.1. This analysis focuses on the renditions of the selected "Chinese Keywords" and "British Keywords", as well as the lexico-semantic patterns, such as lexical chains and semantic fields, formed in the translations. These aspects are closely associated with thematic reconstruction and serve as direct reflections of the translators' linguistic idiosyncrasies and, by extension, their functional styles. The renditions of these keywords demonstrate the translators' initial efforts to reconstruct the two themes, while the lexico-semantic patterns show their further endeavors in reconstructing these themes in translation. It's important to note that the analysis of lexico-semantic patterns in this chapter covers two perspectives: lexical chains and semantic fields. The lexical chain represents a cohesive network formed by a keyword throughout the text, whereas the semantic fields are created by grouping L10:R10 collocates of this keyword that share the same semantic preference. By considering both the more lexically-oriented aspect (chains) and the more semantically-oriented aspect (fields), a relatively comprehensive view of the lexico-semantic patterns in translation is presented. The following subsections will illustrate and compare the linguistic idiosyncrasies and functional styles of these translators in thematic reconstruction using this framework.

8.3.1 Renditions of the Function-Loaded Keywords

As outlined in the analytic framework (Fig. 8.1), this section will analyze how the translators render the function-loaded keywords as a part of their initial endeavor in reconstructing the two themes of "Diasporic Chinese" and "Local Britons" in translation.

8.3.1.1 Renditions of the "Chinese Keywords"

In Sect. 8.2.1.1, the study finds that the two Chinese keywords ("黃臉" and "中國人") hold statistical significance in *Er Ma*. Therefore, by comparing how the translators render these two keywords in their target texts (TTs), insights can be gained into their linguistic idiosyncrasies and functional styles. The analysis will begin by summarizing all the translations of these keywords, followed by a statistical comparison of these renditions.

Table 8.5 presents the renditions of the two Chinese keywords by different translators, revealing some notable trends. Firstly, all four English versions employ the two racial slurs "Chinamen" and "Chink" alongside the more standard and neutral reference "Chinese" when translating the keyword "中國人". Secondly, when translating "黃臉" into English, the translators tend to engage in explicitation. While James utilizes four different words to convey "黃臉", the other translators opt for three distinct equivalents to translate the same term.

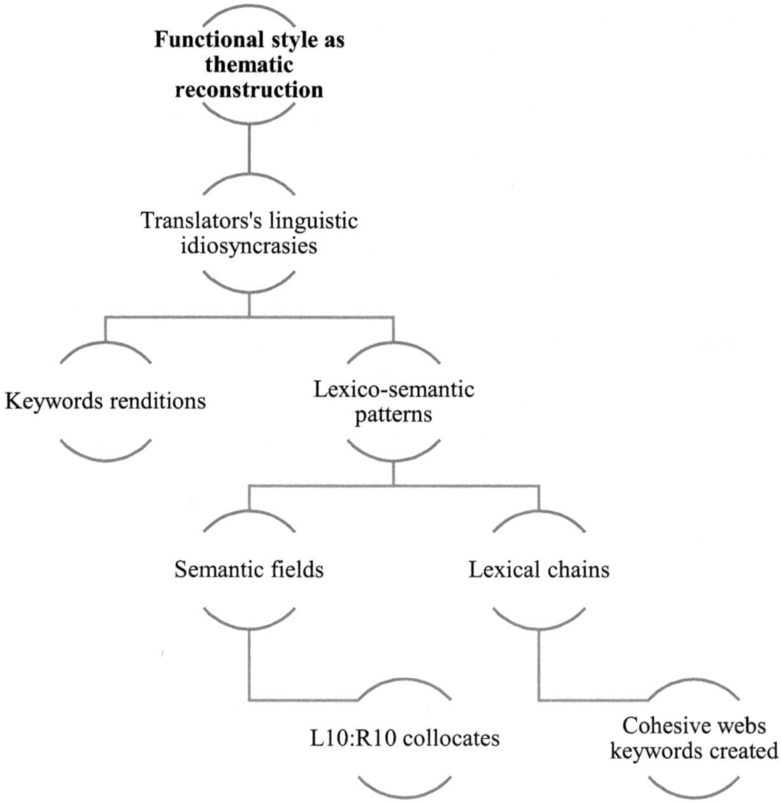

Fig. 8.1 Analytic framework for translators' functional styles as thematic reconstruction

Table 8.5 Translators' renditions of the two "Chinese Keywords"

Item	James	Huang & Finkelstein	Jimmerson	Dolby
黃臉	Yellow face	Yellow face(s)	Yellow face	Yellow face(s)
	Yellow-faced	Yellow-faced	Yellow-faced	Yellow-faced
	Yellow devils	Yellow devils	Yellow devils	Yellow devils
	Yellow-skinned			
中國人	Chinese	Chinese	Chinese	Chinese
	Chinamen	Chinamen	Chinamen	Chinamen
	Chink	Chink	Chink	Chink

To analyze the linguistic idiosyncrasies and functional styles of the translators, a comparison will be conducted based on the renditions presented in Table 8.5. It's important to note that the G^2 tests employed in Sect. 8.2.1.1 were found to be ineffective in revealing these idiosyncrasies, as all comparisons resulted in *p*-values below 0.0001. While this indicates statistical significance, it doesn't sufficiently highlight the translators' linguistic idiosyncrasies and functional styles in their renditions. As

Table 8.6 Renditions of the two "Chinese Keywords" and their frequencies

***Er Ma* (ST)**			**TTs**	**James**		**H. & F.**		**Jimmerson**		**Dolby**		**BNC (fic.)**		**COCA (fic.)**	
ST	Raw	Norm		Raw	Norm	Raw	Norm	Raw	Norm	Raw	Norm	Raw	Norm	Raw	Norm
黃臉	13	**171.19**	Yellow face	4	40.86	5	44.37	3	27.99	3	27.25	13	0.817	22	0.197
			Yellow faces	0	0	1	8.87	0	0	1	9.08	2	0.126	5	0.045
			Yellow-faced	6	61.28	4	35.5	7	65.31	9	81.75	0	0	2	0.018
			Yellow-skinned	1	10.21	0	0	0	0	0	0	1	0.063	7	0.063
			Yellow devils	1	10.21	1	8.87	3	27.99	1	9.08	0	0	1	0.009
			TOTAL	12	**122.57**	11	**97.61**	13	**121.29**	14	**127.16**	16	**1.01**	37	**0.33**
中国人	235	**3094.6**	Chinese	327	3339.94	368	3265.57	341	3181.62	341	3097.3	285	17.914	4756	42.523
			Chinamen	53	541.34	6	53.24	19	177.28	21	190.74	3	0.189	33	0.295
			Chink	6	61.28	5	44.37	5	46.65	5	45.41	62	3.897	276	2.468
			TOTAL	386	**3942.56**	379	**3363.18**	365	**3405.55**	367	**3333.45**	350	**22**	5065	**45.29**

an alternative approach, comparisons will be made using the normalized frequencies (per million) of each item. The fiction subsets from both the BNC (1980s–1993) and COCA (1990–2017)[5] corpora will be chosen as reference corpora to examine the extent of deviation in these renditions from the norm. The choice of these two reference corpora is justified by several factors. Firstly, both corpora encompass translations created during the same time period, ensuring some comparability between them. Secondly, these two reference corpora are widely recognized for their ability to represent distinct genres within the English language. The frequency data for the comparison are provided in Table 8.6.

The data presented in Table 8.6 reveals several key findings. Firstly, all the translators tend to over-translate the two keywords when compared with the two reference corpora. This is supported by the consistent statistical significance observed in pilot studies of these renditions. Secondly, the translators make different frequency choices when translating these keywords compared to the source text. When translating "黃臉" (yellow-faced), they all significantly reduce its frequency in their renditions, with the most significant reduction observed in Dolby's translation (74.28% equivalents of the source text) and the least significant in Huang & Finkelstein's translation (57.02% equivalents of the source text). Conversely, they dramatically increase the frequencies of "中國人" (the Chinese) in their translations, with the most substantial increase in James' translation (127.40% equivalents of the source text) and the least significant increase in Dolby's translation (107.72% equivalents of the source text). Thirdly, the translators make varying decisions regarding the use of "racially charged" vocabulary in their translations of the two Chinese keywords. James' renditions of "中國人" appear to contain the highest proportion (15.28%) of negatively connoted terms, specifically "Chinamen" and "Chink", as indicated by the normalized frequencies. In contrast, Huang & Finkelstein's renditions have the lowest percentage (2.90%)

[5] Details available from https://www.english-corpora.org/.

in this regard. Jimmerson's renditions and Dolby's renditions exhibit percentages of 6.58% and 7.10%, respectively.

These findings, based on normalized frequencies, offer preliminary insights into the linguistic idiosyncrasies and functional styles of these translators in their reconstruction of the "Diasporic Chinese" theme in translation.

8.3.1.2 Renditions of the "British Keywords"

Table 8.7 offers a summary of the English translations of the two British keywords, "英國人" and "洋鬼子", in all four translations. Regarding "英國人", six different renditions are identified: "Englishman", "Englishmen", "(the) English", "The British", "English people", and "English person". Dolby incorporates all six renditions, while Huang & Finkelstein use five of these renditions. In contrast, James' and Jimmerson's versions only include four of these renditions. Notably, the terms "Englishman", "Englishmen", and "The English" (highlighted in gray) are shared by all the translators, while the remaining renditions differ among them.

For the term "洋鬼子", the translators use three identical words in their renditions: "foreign devils", "foreigners", and "devils". These shared renditions offer a preliminary glimpse into the translators' linguistic idiosyncrasies and functional styles when reconstructing the theme "Local Britons". The subsequent analysis will investigate the translators' linguistic idiosyncrasies and functional styles, employing the methods and reference corpora explained in the previous section (Cf. 8.3.1.1). The frequency data for this comparison are provided in Table 8.8.

The table displaying the data of normalized frequencies reveals several significant patterns. Firstly, in comparison to the two reference corpora, the translators consistently over-translate the two British keywords. This aligns with the earlier findings regarding the renditions of the two Chinese keywords, as discussed in Sect. 8.3.1.1. This consistency across the two subsections (Sects. 8.3.1.1 and 8.3.1.2) highlights the translators' linguistic idiosyncrasies and functional styles in rendering these theme-related keywords. Secondly, the translators make varying choices when translating the two Chinese keywords, resulting in notable frequency differences of

Table 8.7 Translators' renditions of the two "British Keywords"

Item	James	Huang & Finkelstein	Jimmerson	Dolby
英國人	English(wo)man	Englishman	Englishman	Englishman
	English(wo)men	Englishmen	Englishmen	Englishmen
	the English	the English	the English	the English
	the British	The British	the British	the British
		English people		English people
				English person
洋鬼子	Foreign devils	Foreign devils	Foreign devils	Foreign devils
	Foreigners	Foreigners	Foreigners	Foreigners
	Devils	Devils	Devils	Devils

Table 8.8 Renditions of the two "British Keywords" and their frequencies

Er Ma (ST)			TTs	James		H. & F.		Jimmerson		Dolby		BNC (fic.)		COCA (fic.)	
ST	Raw	Norm		Raw	Norm	Raw	Norm	Raw	Norm	Raw	Norm	Raw	Norm	Raw	Norm
洋鬼子	16	**210.7**	Foreign devils	13	132.78	15	133.11	12	111.96	21	190.74	2	0.13	25	0.22
			Foreigners	38	388.13	30	266.21	29	270.58	27	245.24	897	56.38	7162	64.03
			Devils	20	204.28	21	186.35	21	195.94	24	217.99	260	16.34	4658	41.65
			TOTAL	71	**725.19**	66	**585.67**	62	**578.48**	72	**653.97**	1159	**72.85**	11845	**105.91**
英国人	73	**961.3**	Englishwoman	3	30.64	0	0.00	0	0.00	0	0.00	43	2.70	197	1.76
			Englishwomen	3	30.64	0	0.00	0	0.00	0	0.00	14	0.88	20	0.18
			Englishman	11	112.35	14	124.23	7	65.31	7	63.58	720	45.26	1558	13.93
			Englishmen	27	275.77	20	177.48	6	55.98	15	136.24	340	21.37	627	5.61
			English people	0	0.00	3	26.62	0	0.00	8	72.66	134	8.42	256	2.29
			English person	0	0.00	0	0.00	0	0.00	1	9.08	15	0.94	42	0.38
			the British	0	0.00	11	97.61	3	27.99	9	81.74	12789	803.87	14675	131.21
			the English	50	510.69	32	283.96	51	475.84	45	454.15	5014	315.16	4356	38.95
			TOTAL	94	**960.10**	80	**709.91**	67	**625.13**	82	**744.80**	19069	**1198.61**	21731	**194.3**

these keywords in relation to the source text. The rendition of "洋鬼子" (foreign devils) by all translators shows a noticeable increase in frequency. James' translation demonstrates the highest increase (344.18% equivalents of the source text), while Dolby's translation exhibits the lowest increase (310.38% equivalents of the source text). In contrast, the frequencies of "英國人" (the English) in the translations experience a slight decrease. Jimmerson's translation shows the most significant decrease (65.03% equivalents of the source text), while James' translation displays the lowest decrease (99.9% equivalents of the source text). Thirdly, there is a notable diversity in the translators' renditions of the keyword "英國人". For instance, James used "Englishwoman" and "Englishwomen" three times each in translation, while the other translators did not incorporate these renditions. Similarly, Dolby employed "English people" 15 times and "English person" 8 times, whereas the other translators, except for Huang & Finkelstein (who used "English people" three times), did not include these renditions.

In summary, the findings from the analysis of normalized frequencies offer initial insights into the translators' linguistic idiosyncrasies and functional styles in the reconstruction of the theme "Local Britons". Subsequent analysis will further explore their functional styles by examining how they reestablish the original lexical chains in their translations.

8.3.2 *Reestablishment of the Original Lexical Chains*

Lexical chains concern how "lexical items relate to each other and to other cohesive devices so that textual continuity is created" (Flowerdew et al., 2009: 1). In this research, the examination of lexical chains is one of the two components of the lexico-semantic pattern, intended to reveal the linguistic idiosyncrasies and functional styles of the translators, as outlined in Fig. 8.1. This section specifically investigates how the translators reestablish the original lexical chains as part of their efforts to reconstruct the themes of "Diasporic Chinese" and "Local Britons" in translation.

8.3.2.1 Reestablishment in the "Diasporic Chinese"

The study hypothesizes that the translators' multiple renditions of the two Chinese keywords (Cf. 8.3.1.1) are likely to disrupt the original lexical chains established by those keywords in the source text (ST). As a result, this disruption of the original lexical chain may highlight the translators' linguistic idiosyncrasies and functional styles. The following analysis explores how the translators' different renditions of a keyword influence the original lexical chains created by the keywords. Special attention will be given to keywords that appear frequently in the texts, as they offer more effective illustrations of these lexical chains.

The subsequent analysis focuses solely on the Chinese keyword "中國人", since it is highly frequent (235 occurrences in the ST) and has at least three different renditions across the four TTs. Although all these translators have maintained the original four semantic fields jointly created by "中國人", and "黃臉", they use multiple English words to render "中國人". This multiplicity weakens the intensity of the original lexical chains created in the ST, where the author employs an identical word throughout the text. Consider the following examples.

(17) **[ST]**

[...] 就是因为那里住着中国人，所以他们要瞧一瞧。就是因为中国是个*弱国*，所以他们随便给那群勤苦耐劳，在异域找饭吃的华人加上一切的*罪名* [...]

心里也同时想到她的朋友约翰：约翰在上海不定多么出锋头呢！他那两只大拳头，一*拳头*还不*捶死*几十个中国人！她的蓝眼珠一层一层的往外发着不同的光彩，约翰是她心目中的英雄！ [...]

家里住着两个中国人，*不好意思*请亲戚朋友来喝茶吃饭；让亲友跟二马一块吃吧？*对不起*亲友，叫客人和一对中国人坐在一桌上吃喝！叫二马单吃吧？又*太麻烦*；自然二马不在乎在那儿吃饭，可是自己为什么*受这份累*呢！算了吧，给他们写信问好，又省事，又四面讨好。况且，在马家父子来了以后，她确是请过两回客，人家不来！她在回信里的字里行间看得出来："我们肯跟两个中国人一块吃饭吗!" [...]

往回说，现在他们正作一个上海的故事，他们在东伦敦找了一群中国人，全是扁鼻子，狭眼睛的*玩艺儿*，你明白我的意思？自然哪，这群人专为成群打伙的起哄，叫影片看着真象中国，所以他们鼻子眼睛的好歹，全没关系；导演的人看这群人和*一群羊*完全没分别：演乡景他们要*一群羊*，照上海就要*一群*中国人，你明白我的意思？[...]

人们都*看不起*中国人吗，*妓女*也不是例外。*妓女*也有她们的自由与骄傲，谁肯招呼人所*不齿*的中国人呢！[...]

普通中国人就*没*有带一镑钱的*资格*，更没有买戒指的胆量；据他想。他正在迟疑不定，温都太太又拉了马老先生一把。两个一齐走出来。[...]

Example (17) demonstrates the establishment of a cohesive lexical chain (indicated by black arrows) by the keyword "中國人" in the ST, where six randomly sampled[6] paragraphs containing this keyword are chosen as text extracts. These paragraphs are arranged in the order they appear in the ST, with the keyword highlighted in yellow and relevant collocates italicized. The entire lexical chain leaves the reader with a unified impression of "negativity" associated with the diasporic Chinese in *Er Ma*. For instance, in the first, fifth, and sixth paragraphs, the keyword is surrounded

[6] The six short paragraphs in this example are randomly sampled, where starting from the first paragraph, every 24th paragraph is chosen out of all the 144 paragraphs that contain this keyword.

by collocates such as "弱国", "罪名", "不齿", and "没…资格", which vividly depict the British contempt for the Chinese. In the second paragraph, the keyword is accompanied by collocates like "拳頭" and "捶死", emphasizing the strong British aversion to the Chinese. The third paragraph, with its three consecutive occurrences of the keyword, evokes a sense of unease towards the Chinese. In the fourth paragraph, the Chinese are portrayed with dehumanizing attributes. Together, these paragraphs contribute to the thematic construction of the "Diasporic Chinese" by presenting a coherent representation of the Chinese in the story.

In the four TTs, the established lexical chain in the ST is disrupted to varying degrees by the translators, who employ different translations, such as "Chinese", "Chinamen", or "Chink" for the keyword "中國人" (see Table 8.5). Consider Examples (18) and (19), where James and Jimmerson use three different words to translate "中國人". While the original negative semantic preferences are retained through the italicized collocates, the semantic fields constructed based on these preferences become hybridized, because they are formed by multiple nodes, namely the three different translations of "中國人". As a result, the cohesion between these translations is reduced compared to the original link in the ST. This disruption not only affects the original lexical chain formed by the single node "中國人", but may also influence readers' interpretation of the TTs.

(18) **[James]**

And all because China's a *weak* nation, every *crime* under the sun is attributed to this community of hard-working Chinese, who are simply seeking their living in a strange and foreign land. […]

What a fine figure John would cut in Shanghai. With those two big fists of his, he could surely thump *dead* a few dozen Chinese with one *punch*. […]

With two Chinese men living in her house, she *no longer* felt comfortable inviting her friends and relatives round to tea. What – have them eat with the Mas? It *wouldn't be* fair, making them eat with Chinese people. She could make the Mas eat on their own, she supposed, but that'd mean too much *bother* for her. Since the Mas' arrival, she'd in fact asked people round twice, but they *hadn't* taken up the invitation. Between the lines of their letters of reply she could read, 'Do you think we're going to sit down to a meal with two Chinese fellows?' […]

They've raked together a crowd of Chinamen from the East End. Flat-nosed, slit-eyed *creatures* the lot. Just for the crowd scenes, of course – for *mobs* and *rioting*, to make the film look like the genuine China. So the quality of their noses and eyes makes no odds. They're *a flock of sheep* as far as the director's concerned. Farm scenes need *a flock of sheep*, and filming Shanghai scenes, you need *a flock of* Chinamen, eh, what! […]

Everybody *despises* the Chinese, and fallen women are no exception to the rule. Even they have their freedom of choice and their pride, and you won't catch any of them going out of their way to attract the attentions of those *subhuman* Chinamen. Why, of course not! […]

As he saw it, an ordinary Chinese fellow *wouldn't have been able to* scrape a pound together, let alone be bold enough to go buying rings. While he stood there wavering, undecided, Mrs. Wedderburn once more grabbed hold of Mr. Ma, and the two of them walked out of the shop together. […]

(19) **[Jimmerson]**

Writers, however, want to have a look merely because Chinamen are living there. Merely because China is a *weak* country, writers can casually, carelessly, lay the blame for all sorts of *crimes* on these hardworking Chinese seeking a living in a foreign land. [...]

He had two bare fists, and in Shanghai didn't he just *pound* dozens of Chink devils to *death* with one of them! Her blue eyes flashed. John was the hero of her heart. [...]

With two Chinamen in the house she felt it *improper* to invite friends and relations to tea or dinner. Could she let them dine with the Mas? Wouldn't she have to *apologize* to them all for making them sit at table with a pair of Chinamen? Should the two Mas eat by themselves? That was too much *trouble*. Of course, the two Mas didn't care where they ate, but why should she wear herself out? Enough, write and ask them how they were and save trouble and get credit for it all around. Furthermore, after the Mas came, she actually had invited people twice and *no one* came! She could read the words between the lines in their *refusals*: Do you think we would be *willing to* dine with Chinamen? [...]

They've got a herd of Chinese extras from east London, all flat-nosed slanty-eyed *pawns*, you know what I mean? Of course, this herd has to have a boss to shout at them to make it really look like China. What their noses and eyes are like isn't really very important. The director thinks there isn't much visible difference between them and *a flock of sheep*. Doing a rustic bit, you need *a flock of sheep*. Doing Shanghai, you need *a herd of* Chinamen, you know what I mean? [...]

Everyone *looks down* on Chinamen. These prostitutes were no exception. They had their own pride and independence. Why should they wait on a Chinaman who was respected by no one? [...]

Ordinary Chinamen *don't have even* one pound to their names, and certainly they haven't the gall to buy rings. While he was trying to make up his mind, Mrs. Wendell pulled at Mr. Ma. The two of them went out. [...]

In Example (18), we can observe how James uses "Chinamen" 8 times (highlighted in gray) and "Chink" once (highlighted in green) as replacements for "Chinese", which is the direct equivalent of "中國人" in English. In this case, the original lexical chain established by "中國人" is entirely disrupted. With these replacements and their accompanying collocates, readers of the target text are more likely to develop persistent racial stereotypes against the Chinese, as implied by the translators' choices. A similar tendency with interpretational impact can also be observed in Jimmerson's case in Example (19), albeit to a lesser degree. In this case, Jimmerson used "Chinamen" 3 times and "Chink" once to replace the otherwise literal translation of "Chinese". As a result, the original lexical chain is partially interrupted, which might evoke a stronger racial sentiment against the Chinese among TT readers.

(20) **[Dolby]**

It's simply because Chinese live there, and they want to take a look—because China is a *weak* country, thus they can casually ascribe a myriad of *odious* names to the industrious, enduring immigrant Chinese who are simply struggling to eke out a living in a strange place.

Her friend John came to mind: he was quite the man in Shanghai, and had *thrashed* a few dozen slimey Chinks to *death*. […]

With two Chinese living in the house she was too *embarrassed* to have friends or family over for tea or dinner. How could she have guests eat together with the Ma's? Why it would be a slight to her guests to *force* them to sit at table with two Chinese! And as for having the Ma's eat alone—well that would just be too *bothersome*. Of course the Ma's didn't really care where they ate, but why should she have to *run* herself *ragged* with all the *fuss* involved! "Never mind," she thought, "I'll just write them and ask how they're doing, it's less *bother* and best all around. Besides, since the Ma's arrival she'd invited people over twice—and they hadn't come! In the letters they wrote declining, she could read what they were thinking right between the lines: "Do you think we *would* dine with Chinamen?! […]

…so they got a bunch of extras in East London—Chinese: a bunch of flat-nosed, slanty- eyed *things*, you know what I mean? Of course the extras will only be in crowd scenes, you know, *fighting* and *rioting* and so on, to make it look like China, so it's not really important what they look like. As far as the director's concerned, these Chinamen aren't any different from *a flock of sheep*—if he were doing a movie set in the countryside he'd use sheep, but this film's in Shanghai so he uses Chinese extras, you see what I mean? […]

Everyone *looked down* on the Chinese —and floozies were no exception. Ladies of the evening had their freedom and pride to look after too, and who of them wanted to deal with universally *despised* Chinamen? […]

[…] most Chinese *didn't have* the standing to carry a pound note on their person-not to mention the pluck to actually go out and buy a ring. While he hesitated, Mrs. Wendell tugged at Mr. Ma and the couple walked out of the shop. […]

(21) **[H & F]**

But because Chinese lived there, tourists wanted to have a look. Because China was a *weak* country, they callously accused industrious Chinese, who had come to a strange land in search of a living, of all sorts of *crimes*. […]

She also remembered her friend John. Who knew what a celebrity he had become in Shanghai? One *blow* from those big firsts of his could *hammer* to *death* dozens of those Chinese *devils*. […]

With two Chinese living in her home, she was *too embarrassed* to invite relatives and friends over for tea or dinner. Were she to make her guests eat with the Mas, she would certainly owe them an *apology* for insisting that they dine at the same table with a couple of Chinese. And it was too much *bother* to make the two Mas eat alone. Of course it wouldn't matter to them where they ate, but why should she cause herself such *trouble*. It was better just to forget about it. When she wanted to find out how her friends and relatives were, she could write to them, which would save time and keep everyone happy. Neither could Mrs. Winter ignore the fact that after the Mas had moved in, she had in fact invited guests on one or two occasions but in each instance the people weren't able to come. She could read between the lines of their replies. "Do you think we'd be *willing to* eat with a couple of Chinese? […]

They're now making a movie about Shanghai and they've found a group of Chinese in East London. They're all flat-nosed, slit-eyed little *things*. Do you get what I mean? Of course, those fellows will be used as extras in the crowd scenes to make the movie look as if it were really filmed in China, so it doesn't matter whether their noses and eyes are good-looking or not. According to the director there's absolutely no difference between that group and *a flock of sheep*. For a scene in the country they need sheep; when it's Shanghai, they need Chinese. Do you get what I mean? […]

For everyone *looked down* on the Chinese, and even prostitutes were no exception. They too were free to do as they pleased, they too had pride, and who would be willing to entertain such *contemptible* people as the Chinese. […]

[…] for the average Chinese was *unlikely* to have even one pound on him and would hardly have the gall to enter a jewellery shop to buy a ring. While he stood there trying to decide what to do, Mrs. Winter gave Mr. Ma senior another tug and the two stomped out of the store […]

Example (20) by Dolby shares some similarities with the previous two examples, as her choice of "Chinamen" partially interrupts the original lexical chain, eliciting racial interpretations from the TT readers. However, these tendencies are less pronounced in her TT compared to the previous examples. This is because more than half (seven-tenths) of the original chain is preserved through the use of "Chinese" in seven instances. While this may partly result in a loss of cohesive focus, Dolby's rendition still maintains a significant portion of the original lexical chain. Conversely, in Example (21), Huang & Finkelstein faithfully reproduced the keyword/node "中國人" in their TT, thereby largely preserving the original lexical chain established by this keyword/node in the ST. This suggests that the interpretational impact their TT has on the target readers could be analogous to that of the ST.

Lastly, it is important to highlight the different linguistic idiosyncrasies exhibited by James and Huang & Finkelstein. In James' translation, there is a noticeable tendency that partially aligns with the arguments by Baker (2011: 216) and Mastropierro (2018: 131): If a translator randomly selects lexical items, they may struggle to establish a coherent lexical chain that is contextually meaningful. James clearly fails to contribute to this lexical chain, as evident in the disjointed translations of "中國人" as "Chinese", "Chinamen", and "Chink". In contrast, Huang & Finkelstein's consistent rendering of "中國人" as "Chinese" successfully aligns with the original lexical chain in the ST.

8.3.2.2 Reestablishment in the "Local Britons"

Following the methodology employed in Sect. 8.3.2.1, this section will concentrate on "英國人", one of the two British keywords, to analyze and compare the translators' linguistic idiosyncrasies in their reestablishment of the original lexical chains. The choice to focus on "英國人" is motivated by two primary considerations. Firstly, it serves as a direct counterpart to "中國人", which was analyzed in the previous subsection (Sect. 8.3.2.1), offering a basis for comparative analysis of the two keywords. Secondly, "英國人" has multiple renditions (e.g., "Englishman", "Englishmen", "English people") in the four TTs, making it an advantageous subject for investigating the translators' interventions in reestablishing the original lexical chains. The different renditions of "英國人" are likely to disrupt the original lexical chain established in the ST, where the same word remains consistent throughout the text. To illustrate this point, the following examples include excerpts from the ST alongside their equivalents in the four TTs.

(22) **[ST]**

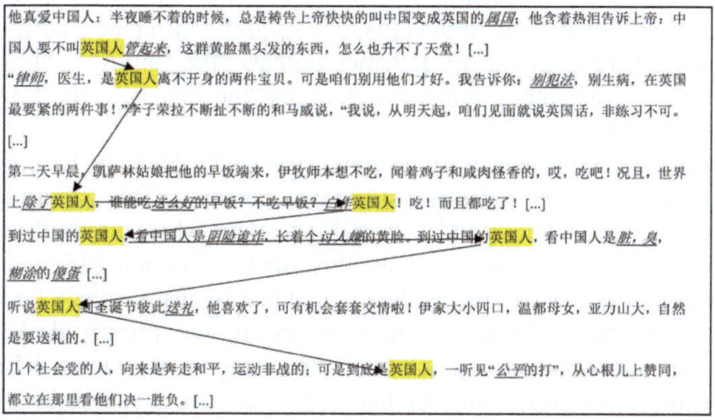

他真爱中国人：半夜睡不着的时候，总是祷告上帝快快的叫中国变成英国的*属国*；他含着热泪告诉上帝：中国人要不叫英国人*管起来*，这群黄脸黑头发的东西，怎么也升不了天堂！[...]

"*律师*，医生，是英国人离不开身的两件宝贝。可是咱们别用他们才好。我告诉你：*别犯法*，别生病，在英国最要紧的两件事！"李子荣拉不断扯不断的和马威说，"我说，从明天起，咱们见面就说英国话，非练习不可。[...]

第二天早晨，凯萨林姑娘把他的早饭端来，伊牧师本想不吃，闻着鸡子和咸肉怪香的，哎，吃吧！况且，世界上*除了*英国人，谁能吃*这么好*的早饭？不吃早饭？*白作*英国人！吃！而且都吃了！[...]

到过中国的英国人，看中国人是*阴险诡诈*，长着个*讨人嫌*的黄脸。到过中国的英国人，看中国人是*脏，臭*，*糊涂*的*傻蛋* [...]

听说英国人到圣诞节彼此*送礼*，他喜欢了，可有机会套套交情啦！伊家大小四口，温都母女，亚力山大，自然是要送礼的。[...]

几个社会党的人，向来是奔走和平，运动非战的；可是到底是英国人，一听见"*公平*的打"，从心根儿上赞同，都立在那里看他们决一胜负。[...]

Example (22) shows how a lexical chain (indicated with the black arrows) is created by the keyword "英國人" in the ST. This example comprises five randomly sampled short paragraphs, with each paragraph being selected based on every 11th paragraph along with the middle paragraph (para.25) out of all 50 paragraphs containing this keyword. The chosen five paragraphs are presented in the sequence they appear in the ST, with the keyword "英國人" highlighted in yellow and its surrounding collocates italicized. Through the keyword and its collocates, a coherent lexical chain is formed across the paragraphs, portraying the "Local Britons" as a "proud", "biased", and "colonial-minded" race. This portrayal is evident upon closer examination of the collocates. For instance, in the first paragraph, the collocates "管起來" and "屬國" highlight their "colonial-mindedness", while in the second paragraph, the collocates "律師" and "別犯法", as well as "公平" in the sixth paragraph, emphasize their commitment to rules and laws. Additionally, the third paragraph exemplifies their "pride" through the collocates "除了", "這麼好", and "白作", while the fourth paragraph reveals their "bias" through the collocates "陰險詭詐", "討人嫌", "髒臭", and "傻蛋".

Moving to the TTs, this original lexical chain is disrupted by all the translators due to their diverse English renditions of the keyword "英國人" (Table 8.7). For instance, both James and Jimmerson employ three different renditions for this specific keyword. In Example (23), James utilizes "the English", "Englishmen", and "Englishman", whereas Jimmerson employs "the British", "the English", and "Englishman" in Example (24).

As a result, the eight instances of the identical node "英國人" in Example (22) are replaced by three different nodes across the two examples. This pattern is similarly observed in the cases of Dolby and Huang & Finkelstein, where they both provide four different translations of this keyword, as illustrated in Example (25) and (26). This disrupts the cohesive web created by the original lexical chain in the ST, even though the original semantic preferences of these nodes are well preserved. Additionally, such disruption is likely to have a potential interpretation effect upon TT readers, as "different cohesive networks in a TT that fail to recreate those of the ST may not trigger the same kind of association in the mind of the target readers" (Baker, 2011: 219; Mastropierro, 2018: 133). In this study, the mental construction of the theme "Local Britons" by TT readers may deviate from that by ST readers, as the disrupted lexical chain is likely to construct a different kind of "Local Britons" compared to the original.

(23) **[James]**

He truly loved the Chinese. At night when he couldn't sleep he always prayed to the Lord to quickly turn China into a British *colony*. With hot tears he said to the Lord, If the Chinese are not *governed* by the English, how will this horde of yellow-faced black-haired creatures ever get to Heaven? […]

"*Lawyers* and doctors are the two treasures Englishmen can't be without. But it's best for us to stay away from them. I'm telling you, *don't break the law* and don't get sick. These are the two most important considerations when you are in England." Li couldn't stop talking. "From tomorrow on, when we meet we must speak English. We must practise. […]

Early the next morning, Catherine brought up his breakfast. Reverend Evans had intended not to eat, but he smelled the grand aroma of bacon and eggs. Yum, eat! After all, can anyone else in the world, *except* the English, eat such a fine breakfast? Not eat breakfast? I would be a *phoney* Englishman! Eat! And eat it all up! […]

Englishmen who have never gone to China think the Chinese are yellow-faced clandestine *schemers* who always arouse *suspicion*. Englishmen who have gone to China regard the Chinese as *filthy, smelly, stupid clods*. […]

Christmas was coming soon. Mr. Ma was a little busier too. He'd heard that at Christmas the English *send presents* around. He was de- lighted. It might be an opportunity to show his feelings! The Evanses, the Wendells, and Alexander, of course, must be given presents. […]

The several socialists who had, heretofore, always urged peace, were pacifists, but at bottom they were Englishmen. When they heard "*fair fight*" they were all for it. They all stood there watching the two of them fight it out to the finish. […]

(24) **[Jimmerson]**

And he genuinely loved the Chinese people. Sometimes in the middle of the night when he couldn't get to sleep, he prayed to God that China would someday be *colonized* by the British; with burning tears in his eyes, he beseeched the Lord: If the Chinese don't let the British *take over*, then all those masses of yellow-faced, black-haired souls will never make it to heaven! […]

"*Lawyers* and doctors are the two most valuable things for the English. But the less we have to deal with them the better. I'm telling you Ma, *don't break the law* and don't get sick—the two most critical things in England!" Li Zirong repeated over and again to Ma: I tell you what, starting from tomorrow we'll only speak in English to each other—it's essential to practice. […]

That next morning Katherine brought him breakfast; he'd decided not to eat anything, but the tasty aroma of the eggs and bacon were too much to resist —"Oh well then, let's have a bite," he thought, "After all, *who else in the world but* the English have such scrumptious breakfasts, and if you don't enjoy breakfast then what's *the point of being* an Englishman!" He downed the whole meal... […]

For the English who've never been to China, Chinamen are *unsightly*, yellow-faced creatures, notoriously *sinister* and *cunning*. For the English who have been to China, the Chinese are a race of *stinking, filthy, empty-headed slobs* […]

Shortly before Christmas, Mr. Ma became somewhat busy himself. He's heard that at Christmas the English *gave* each other *presents*, and he liked the idea, it was a great chance to win some popularity points! There were the Evanses—four there, the two Wendell ladies, and Alexander—naturally he had to give them all presents. […]

There were a few Socialists who were normally staunch champions of peace and non-aggression, but they were in the end English, and as soon as they heard "a *fair fight*." they approved and stood back, waiting to see who would win. […]

The study finds that the extent of disruption in the original lexical chain varied among the translators. This could partly demonstrate their linguistic idiosyncrasies, and thus functional styles. The general trend shows that Jimmerson tends to adhere more closely to the ST by reestablishing a significant part of the original lexical chain, whereas the other translators seem to make less effort in this regard, with Huang & Finkelstein exhibiting the most notable departure. To illustrate, in Example (25), Jimmerson used 9 words to translate the original 8 nodes "英國人", with 6 of them being "(the) English", which are direct equivalents of the original nodes. Consequently, the original lexical chain was largely maintained, creating a cohesive web that closely matched that of the source text. In contrast, in Example (26), Huang & Finkelstein employed 8 words to translate the original nodes, with only two instances of "(the) English". This completely breaks the original chain, as the cohesive web is nowhere to be found.

(25) **[Dolby]**

And yes, he truly loved the Chinese. At midnight, if lying awake unable to sleep, he would invariably pray to God to hurry up and make China a British *dominion*. Eyes filled with hot tears, he would point out to God that if the Chinese were not *taken in hand* by the British, that vast mass of yellow-faced black-haired creatures would never achieve their rightful ascent to the pearly gates. [...]

'*Lawyers* and doctors are two indispensable treasures to the English, but you're better off using neither while you're here. I warn you: *don't break the law*, and don't get sick. The two most vital things when you're in England!' Li Tzu-jung carried on hastily, 'Look here, from tomorrow we'll speak English when we see each other. You've got to practise it. [...]

The next morning, Catherine brought his breakfast up. He hadn't intended to have any, but the eggs and bacon smelt remarkably nice. Ah, better eat up. *Who in the world can possibly* make such a fine breakfast as we English? Not eat breakfast? What leave a crumb. [...]

English people who've never been to China picture the Chinese as *sinister*, *underhand* beings with *disagreeable* yellow faces. And English people who have been to China view the Chinese as *dirty, smelly, bewildered fools* [...]

As Christmas approached, yes, even Mr Ma grew a little busier. He was delighted to hear that the English *gave* one another *presents* at Christmas. What a good opportunity for making friends! Naturally, the four Elys, Mrs Wedderburn and daughter, and Alexander would all have to be given presents. [...]

The handful of socialists among them had always rallied to the cause of peace, always proselytised for harmony. But, all said and done, they were Englishmen, and as soon as they heard the words '*fair fight*', they cheered from the bottom of their hearts, and stood by to watch the pair battle it out. [...]

(26) **[H & F]**

He really loved the Chinese people. When he found himself unable to sleep in the middle of the night, he would always pray to God that China would soon become a *colony* of England. With fervent tears he said to God: "If the Chinese are not *administered* by the British, those yellow-faced, black-haired creatures will never get to heaven, no matter what." [...]

"The *lawyer* and the doctor are an Englishman's two treasures — ones he can never do without. But we're better off not using the services of either," Lee Dze-rung advised. "I'll tell you, the two most important things in England are *not to break the law* and not to get sick." And as if he was unable to terminate the conversation, he continued: "Say, from tomorrow on, let's speak English when we've together. We both need the practice. [...]

Next morning, Katherine brought breakfast to him and although he hadn't planned to eat, he changed his mind when he caught the appetizing aroma of eggs and bacon. "Ah, I'll eat it," he thought to himself. "Who but the English have such delicious breakfasts? What's the point of being English if one passes it up. I'll eat it and I'll eat it all. [...]

To Englishmen who have never been to China, the Chinese are a *treacherous* and *deceitful* race, with yellow faces capable only of arousing *disgust*. To Englishmen who have been there, they are nothing more than *dirty, smelly, stupid fools*. [...]

It was almost Christmas and even Mr. Ma senior was becoming a little busier. He was pleased when he heard that Englishmen *exchanged presents* at Christmas for, indeed, that would give him the opportunity to cultivate his social relations. Of course, he would have to give gifts to the four Edens, the Winters, mother and daughter, and Alexander. [...]

Several Socialists, who previously had been active in the peace movement and who had travelled extensively campaigning against war, were on the scene. But in the final analysis they were Englishmen and as soon as they heard the words "*fair fight*", they gave their hearty approval and stood there watching, letting the fight go on until one person emerged the victor. [...]

The diversity in translation choices between Jimmerson and Huang & Finkelstein might elicit different interpretational effects on target readers, as their renditions of "英國人" carry different implications. Among the four different renditions used by these translators, "the British" may refer to individuals from any part of Great Britain, while "Englishman/Englishmen" specifically denotes those from England. "English people/person" serves as a gender-neutral alternative synonymous with "Englishman/ Englishmen". Consequently, in Jimmerson's case, readers of the translated text are more likely to develop a consistent impression of "英國人" similar to that of the source text readers. This is because Jimmerson consistently employs "(the) English" throughout the paragraphs, despite the presence of three instances of "the British" and "Englishman". In contrast, Huang & Finkelstein's translation is prone to impart a mixed impression of "英國人" to these readers, as they employ four instances of "Englishmen", one instance of "Englishman", one instance of "British", and two instances of "(the) English" in their rendition. This may give TT readers an impression that the translators are suggesting several different types of people in Example (26).

Aside from Jimmerson and Huang & Finkelstein, the remaining two translators show some similarities in their ways to reestablish the original lexical chain in target texts. In Example (23), James chooses three literal equivalents, "(the) English", out of the total 8 words used to translate "英國人". This results in the disruption of the original chain, with only a minor portion being reestablished through the retention of these three literal equivalents. Similarly, in Example (25), Dolby employs three instances of "(the) English" among the 7 words used to translate the original 8 nodes, leading to the disruption of the original lexical chain.

At the same time, the interpretational effects of these two cases on target readers seem to yield a similar outcome to those observed in the cases of Jimmerson and Huang & Finkelstein. TT readers may develop the impression that the original term "英國人" alludes to different types of people in the target texts. For instance, in Example (25), Dolby translates that "if the Chinese were not taken in hand by *the British*" in the first paragraph and then "*English people* who've never been to China picture the Chinese as sinister..." in the fourth paragraph. This seems to convey that the "英國人" who attempt to colonize the Chinese and the "英國人" who despise the Chinese are not the same, because "the British" and "English people" may literally refer to people from different regions. In Example (23), James translates that "If the Chinese are not governed by *the English*..." in the first paragraph and "Lawyers and doctors are the two treasures <u>*Englishmen*</u> can't be without..." in the fourth paragraph. The use of gender-specific language (underlined) in translation suggests that while English people are the colonial masters of the Chinese, it is specifically English men who treasure lawyers and doctors.

Examining the overall picture, it is evident that although all these translators disrupt the original lexical chain with their varied renditions of "英國人", the extent to which they disrupt the original lexical chain differs. Jimmerson and Huang & Finkelstein occupy opposite ends of the spectrum, while James and Dolby exhibit some similarities. This result serves to highlight the linguistic idiosyncrasies of these translators and provides insight into their functional styles.

Table 8.9 Semantic fields shared by the two "Chinese Keywords" in translation (Huang & Finkelstein)

Semantic Fields	Collocates (L10:R10)
General Negativity	bulging, opium (2), despise (3), despicable (2), contempt (3), contemptible, shamelessness, ugly, scum (2), notorious, prostitutes (2), filthy, disgust, disgusting (3), detested, rats, rat-eaters
Treachery, Crime, Peril	treacherous, deceitful, poisoned (2), poison (3), crime, murder (2), murderers, kill, slaughtering, assassins, arson, arsonists, robber, robbery, dangerous, lawless, Godless
Dehumanization	noseless, flat-nosed, slit-eyed, monsters, creatures (2), objects, devils (4), demon-escort
Japanese Superiority	Japanese (9), companies, banks, businesses, artillery, planes, gentleman, pride, fear, admiration, complimentary

8.3.3 Reconstructions of the Original Semantic Fields

This section examines the semantic fields formed by the collocates of the translated Chinese/British keywords—another aspect of the lexico-semantic patterns (see Fig. 8.1) structured by the translators when reconstructing the theme "Diasporic Chinese" and "Local Britons" in translation. The study expects that when these translators reconstruct the original semantic fields in translation, they may show linguistic idiosyncrasies, and thereby their functional styles. The examination of these semantic fields aligns with the corpus stylistic analysis of the Chinese and British keywords discussed in Sect. 8.2. Nevertheless, the investigations in this section differ from those in Sect. 8.2. While Sect. 8.2 aimed at comprehensively analyzing these semantic fields, the focus here is on specific details within these fields, which could effectively highlight the translators' linguistic idiosyncrasies and functional styles.

8.3.3.1 Reconstruction in the "Diasporic Chinese"

The analysis reveals that the translators have preserved the four semantic fields (Tables 8.9, 8.10, 8.11, and 8.12[7]) created by the L10:R10 collocates of the two keywords, as well as the local textual functions enacted in the source text (ST). However, when it comes to the target texts (TTs), their choices of the L10:R10 collocates for the translated keywords vary in terms of the frequencies and semantic intensities. Consequently, the semantic components (subcategories of a semantic field) formed by these collocates and their proportions within each of the four semantic fields differ between the ST and the TTs, as well as among these TTs. The study asserts that such differences could impact how the theme "Diasporic Chinese" is reconstructed in the TTs, thereby serving as indicators of the translators' linguistic idiosyncrasies and functional styles in thematic reconstruction. The following section will examine these differences from both quantitative and qualitative perspectives.

[7] Each semantic component in the tables is highlighted with a color, aligning with the colors assigned to these components as indicated in Table 8.2.

Table 8.10 Semantic fields shared by the two "Chinese Keywords" in translation (James)

Semantic Fields	Collocates (L10:R10)
General Negativity	puffy, opium (3), weak (3), disdain, despised (3), despicable, damned, debased, ugly, broken-down, doormats, vulgar, expelled, dirty, filthy (2), smelly, stupid, disgusting, repulsive (2), detestation, mouse-eating
Treachery, Crime, Peril	schemers, plotters, deceptively, poison (4), poisoners, poisonous, poisoning, murder (2), murderous, slaughtered (3), massacres, assassination, arsonous, munitions, thief, rape, sadistic, cruel, lawless, recklessness, knives, harm
Dehumanization	flat-nosed, slanty-eyed, creatures (2), demons, devil (s) (4), pawns
Japanese Superiority	Japanese (11), banks, companies, enterprises, cannon, airplanes, fear, gentleman, handsome

Table 8.11 Semantic fields shared by the two "Chinese Keywords" in translation (Dolby)

Semantic Fields	Collocates (L10:R10)
General Negativity	puffed, opium (4), despised, despise(s) (2), despising, degraded, uncivil, shamelessness, ugly (2), prostitutes (2), foul, dirty, smelly, fools, rat-eating, disagreeable, detestable, detests, loathsome (3), nasty (4)
Treachery, Crime, Peril	underhand, poisoners, poison (4), sinister (3), murder (3), murderers, murderous, murdering, massacred, arson, arsonists, arms, fire-raising, robbery, rapists, lawless, cruel, barbarian, danger, threatens, horrible
Dehumanization	flat-capped, flat-nosed, slit-eyed, noseless, creatures, objects, monsters, demon, subhuman
Japanese Superiority	Japanese (9), banks, businesses, guns, steamships, aeroplanes, gentleman, flatter, merit, handsome

Table 8.12 Semantic fields shared by the two "Chinese Keywords" in translation (Jimmerson)

Semantic Fields	Collocates (L10:R10)
General Negativity	puffy, opium (3), disdain (3), contempt (2), despised, notoriously, crippled, expelled, rat-eating, stinking, filthy (2), murky, prostitutes, empty-headed, disgusting, unsightly, nasty, detested, dislike
Treachery, Crime, Peril	treachery, treacherous, cunning, sinister (3), poison (4), poisoned, venomous, curse(s) (3), murder (2), arms, robbery, arsonists, murderous, slaughtering, killed, assassins, rape, delinquents, ruthless, fierceness, chaotic, uncivil, riot, knives
Dehumanization	stub-nosed, pancake-faced, flat-nosed, slanty-eyed, skull-capped (2), creatures (2), monsters, objects, devil
Japanese Superiority	Japanese (12), cannons, warships, gentleman, respect, fear

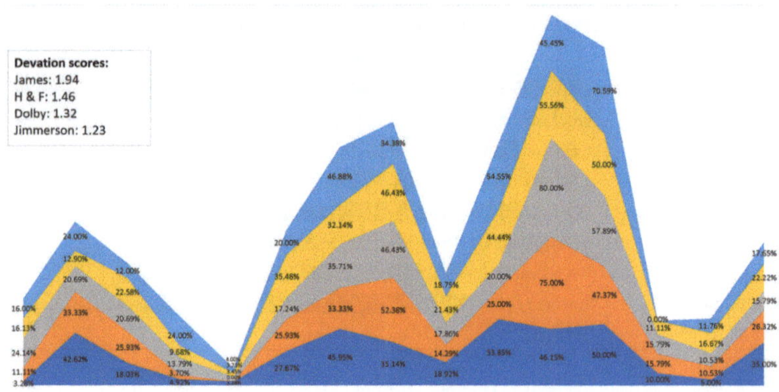

	Sickness	Contempt	Disgrace	Foul	Stupidity	Disgust	Treachery	Crime	Peril	Physicality	Monstrousness	Japanese	Business	Military	Respect
Jimmerson	16.00%	24.00%	12.00%	24.00%	4.00%	20.00%	46.88%	34.38%	18.75%	54.55%	45.45%	70.59%	0.00%	11.76%	17.65%
Dolby	16.13%	12.90%	22.58%	9.68%	3.23%	35.48%	32.14%	46.43%	21.43%	44.44%	55.56%	50.00%	11.11%	16.67%	22.22%
James	24.14%	20.69%	20.69%	13.79%	3.45%	17.24%	35.71%	46.43%	17.86%	20.00%	80.00%	57.89%	15.79%	10.53%	15.79%
H & F	11.11%	33.33%	25.93%	3.70%	0.00%	25.93%	33.33%	52.38%	14.29%	25.00%	75.00%	47.37%	15.79%	10.53%	26.32%
ST	3.28%	42.62%	18.03%	4.92%	3.28%	27.87%	45.95%	35.14%	18.92%	53.85%	46.15%	50.00%	10.00%	5.00%	35.00%

Fig. 8.2 Semantic components and their proportions in the semantic fields ("中國人" and "黃臉")

Quantitatively, these differences are illustrated by the overall proportional deviation of the semantic components[8] across the four semantic fields shared by the two Chinese keywords. The proportional deviation is assessed using a ranking score.[9] The semantic components, along with their labels and proportions within the semantic fields, are depicted in Fig. 8.2.

The analysis reveals that James exhibits the highest deviation (with a deviation score of 1.94) from the original author in her thematic reconstruction of "Diasporic Chinese" in translation. For example, within the field of *Dehumanization*, James shows a 28.85% increase in the "Monstrousness" component, while simultaneously experiencing a 28.85% decrease in the "Physicality" component compared to the ST. These deviations are more noticeable compared to those of other translators for the same components in their respective TTs. In contrast, Jimmerson displays the lowest deviation (with a score of 1.23) from the ST author. For example, in the components of *Treachery, Crime, Peril*, and the "Monstrousness" component of *Dehumanization*, the proportional differences between the ST and Jimmerson's TT range from only 0.17% to 0.93%. On the other hand, the proportional differences between the ST and the remaining three TTs consistently exceed 1%. Regarding the overall proportional deviations of the other translators, the findings indicate that Huang and Finkelstein rank second highest with a deviation score of 1.46, while Dolby follows closely behind with a score of 1.32, slightly above Jimmerson's score. These quantitative findings indicate that Jimmerson's thematic reconstruction of "Diasporic Chinese"

[8] Detailed proportions of each semantic component, as well as overall deviations, are available at http://dx.doi.org/10.6084/m9.figshare.29572907.

[9] The details are available at http://dx.doi.org/10.6084/m9.figshare.29572907.

closely adheres to the ST author, whereas James' reconstruction deviates the most from the ST author.

It's important to emphasize that certain proportional deviations may arise due to necessary translation shifts stemming from inherent linguistic differences between the source language (SL) and target language (TL), or limitations in the chosen collocate span of L10:R10 that might miss certain collocates. However, others can be attributed directly to the translators' idiosyncratic interventions. Both types of deviations have the potential to alter the original thematic construction of the "Diasporic Chinese". Still, it is the translators' idiosyncratic interventions that deserve further investigation, as they are more likely to reveal the translators' functional styles. The following analysis will seek bilingual contextual evidence from the ST and TTs, focusing on notable shifts in semantic intensities of some collocates to trace such alterations resulting from the translators' idiosyncratic interventions.

(27) **[ST]** 設若普通英國人討厭中國人，有錢的英國男女是拿中國人當玩藝兒看。

[James] If ordinary Englishmen dislike the Chinese, rich Englishmen regard the Chinese as *amusing*.

[H & F] If the ordinary Englishman despised Chinese, wealthy English men and women regarded them as mere *objects of amusement*.

[Dolby] If the average English person detests the Chinese, the wealthy, men and women alike, regard the Chinese *objects of amusement*.

[Jimmerson] If you were to say that ordinary classes in English society detested the Chinese, then the wealthy classes on the other hand, saw them as *objects of amusement*.

Example (22) illustrates James's idiosyncratic rendering of a dehumanized portrayal of the diasporic Chinese, which distinguishes her from the other translators and highlights her functional style. The collocate "玩藝兒", which literally means "toy" in Chinese, carries a derogatory connotation towards a person. However, these translators may attempt to mitigate the negative sentiment associated with this collocate by reducing its semantic intensity. This tendency is particularly noticeable in James's case: while the other translators translate the collocate as "objects of amusement", James renders it as "amusing". Consequently, the "contemptible" Chinese individuals in the source text become "entertainers" who amuse the "rich Britons" in James's version, whereas they remain relatively "lifeless" in the versions of the other translators. This linguistic idiosyncrasy displayed by James partly explains her highest deviation score in the TTs, as her translation in this example weakens the dehumanizing effect and sets her apart from the other translators, who mostly preserve the original dehumanizing effect.

(28) **[ST]**…於是中國人就變成世界上最陰險，最污濁，最討厭，最卑鄙的一種兩條腿兒的動物！

[James]...and so the Chinese have been transformed into the most *sinister*, filthy, repulsive, debased creatures on two legs in the whole world!

[H & F] Thus, the Chinese became the most *inscrutably dangerous*, filthy, disgusting, and despicable two-legged creatures in the world.

[Jimmerson] Hence Chinese have been made the most *treacherous* people in the world, the most foul, disgusting, contemptible beasts to walk on two legs!
[Dolby] Thus are the Chinese transformed into the most *sinister,* most foul, most loathsome and most degraded two-legged beasts on earth.

Example (23) exemplifies how the original "treachery" attached to the Chinese is idiosyncratically reconstructed by Huang & Finkelstein in TT, highlighting their functional style. The ST collocate "陰險" is semantically linked to insidiousness, which is largely maintained by James, Jimmerson, and Dolby in their respective TTs through the use of "sinister", "treacherous", and "sinister". In contrast, Huang & Finkelstein opt for "inscrutably dangerous" to translate the same collocate, thereby increasing its semantic intensities by directly employing the term "dangerous". One possible consequence of this increased semantic intensity is a subtle amplification of the "insidiousness" attributed to the Chinese characters in the story. This interpretation is further supported by their idiosyncratic use of "dangerous", which imparts a sense of intimidation compared to the alternative equivalents chosen by the other translators. Consequently, their TT is likely to convey a more menacing impression of the Chinese people to their target readers. Furthermore, this idiosyncrasy of Huang & Finkelstein is also partially reflected in their TT through the second-highest proportional deviation observed in the "Treachery" semantic component among all the four TTs.

(29) **[ST]** 姐姐, 你知道, 我父親那一輩的中國人是被外國人打怕了, 一聽外國人誇獎他們幾句, 他們覺得非常的光榮。
[H & F] Sister, you know that my father's generation of Chinese has been so intimidated by foreigners that just a few words of praise from a Westerner fills them with pride.
[James] Sister, you know the Chinese of my father's generation have been *terrorized* by the foreigners. They hear foreigners praise them and they feel they have been extraordinarily glorified.
[Dolby] You know, Elder Sister, my father's generation's had the *scares* put into them by foreigners, and all they need is to hear those same foreigners bestowing faint praise and they feel tremendously honoured.
[Jimmerson] Sister, you know how his generation of Chinese have been *psychologically crippled* by foreigners—all it takes is a few words of praise from a foreigner and he's overwhelmed, beaming with honor.

Example (24) demonstrates Jimmerson's linguistic idiosyncrasy as she renders an original negative collocate "打怕了". The ST collocate "打怕了" literally means "flinch due to repeated blow" in Chinese. However, in this example, the collocate seems to convey a sense of mental paralysis experienced by the Chinese towards foreigners, likely due to their repeated defeats in the past. Among the translators, Huang & Finkelstein, James, and Dolby translate this paralysis as "intimidated", "terrorized", and "scares", respectively. In contrast, Jimmerson translates it as "psychologically crippled". To some extent, Jimmerson's choice may better preserve the original semantic intensity of the collocate, as "crippled", when combined with "psychologically", suggests a mental breakdown. On the other hand, the translations by the other three translators place a greater emphasis on "fear" rather than this mental breakdown. Consequently, Jimmerson's unique choice partly accounts for the lowest deviation score in her TT, highlighting her linguistic idiosyncrasy and functional style in the translation. For target readers, such idiosyncrasy also tends to bring the ST closer to them, providing them with a clearer understanding of the original mindset attributed to the diasporic Chinese in the story.

(30) **[ST]**沒到過中國的英國人, 看中國人是陰險詭詐, 長著個討人嫌的黃臉。
[H & F] To Englishmen who have never been to China, the Chinese ar**[Jimmerson]**e a treacherous and deceitful race, with yellow faces capable only of arousing *disgust*.
[James]Englishmen who have never gone to China think the Chinese are yellow-faced clandestine schemers who always arouse *suspicion*.
[Dolby] English people who've never been to China picture the Chinese as sinister, underhand beings with *disagreeable* yellow faces.
For the English who've never been to China, Chinamen are *unsightly*, yellow-faced creatures, notoriously sinister and cunning.

Example (25) shows how different translations of a negative ST collocate, associated with the Chinese, stylistically differentiate Dolby and Jimmerson from James and Huang & Finkelstein in terms of semantic intensity. The ST collocate "討人嫌" literally means "repulsive", conveying an unfavorable impression of the Britons towards the Chinese in the story. Huang & Finkelstein and James respectively translate this collocate as "disgust" and "suspicion", while Dolby and Jimmerson take a different approach by rendering it as "disagreeable" and "unsightly", respectively. Consequently, the semantic intensities conveyed by the collocates in Dolby's and Jimmerson's translations are slightly weaker than those in James' and Huang & Finkelstein's translations, but closer to the original. Specifically, "disagreeable" or "unsightly" suggests an unpleasant or unfavorable English impression of the Chinese, capturing the original semantic intensity of the collocate. In contrast, "disgust" or "suspicion" either enhances this intensity or diverges from the original pragmatic meaning of the collocate. This difference highlights the idiosyncrasy shared by Dolby and Jimmerson in translation—a greater preservation of the original portrayals of the Chinese in the story, which is also reflected in their relatively low scores of overall proportional deviations (Fig. 8.2).

8.3.3.2 Reconstruction in the "Local Britons"

This section examines these translators' linguistic idiosyncrasies and functional styles by examining the ways they rebuild the original semantic fields in reconstructing the "Local Britons" theme. The rebuilt semantic field, along with its diverse semantic components, constitutes another aspect of the lexico-semantic patterns that will be examined within the framework outlined in Fig. 8.1. To ensure the comparability of our findings of the translators' functions styles across sections, we will employ the same strategy as previously outlined in Sect. 8.3.3.1.

Table 8.13 Semantic fields shared by the two "British Keywords" in translation (James)

Semantic Fields	Collocates (L10:R10)
Pride and Prejudice	proud, better (2), honorable, never, only (3), except, abominate, dislike, sneer
Hypocrisy and Pretension	form, appearances, boastful, prate
Colonialism and Conservatism	colony, governed, feet, conservative (2)
Rule and Law	fair (2), equal, rules (2), obedience, lawyers, law (2)

Table 8.14 Semantic fields shared by the two "British Keywords" in translation (Huang & Finkelstein)

Semantic Fields	Collocates (L10:R10)
Pride and Prejudice	proud, alone, impossible, prejudices, smirks, despised, disgust
Hypocrisy and Pretension	dignified, meticulous, show, show-off
Colonialism and Conservatism	administered, conservative
Rule and Law	fair, fairness, equal, mutuality, directness, pragmatism, obedience, lawyer, law

Table 8.15 Semantic fields shared by the two "British Keywords" in translation (Jimmerson)

Semantic Fields	Collocates (L10:R10)
Pride and Prejudice	proud, only, disdain, detest
Hypocrisy and Pretension	arranging, ostentation, showing-off, fussy
Colonialism and Conservatism	colonized, conservative, reticent
Rule and Law	fair (4), reciprocity, equality, straightforward, utilitarianism, rules (2), order (2), obedience, lawyers

In their endeavor to reconstruct the theme of "Local Britons" in target texts, the translators exhibit noteworthy trends that warrant discussion. Firstly, they consistently preserve the four semantic fields associated with "Local Britons" (as shown in Tables 8.13, 8.14, 8.15, and 8.16[10]) and the corresponding local textual function discussed in Sect. 8.2.2.3. This tendency remains consistent throughout the semantic field analyses conducted in this study. Secondly, the translators display a certain degree of consistency in their approaches to reconstructing the "Local Britons" theme. However, despite this consistency, their linguistic idiosyncrasies in such reconstruction exhibit variations from both quantitative and qualitative perspectives. These idiosyncrasies offer some insights into their functional styles.

To differentiate the translators' linguistic idiosyncrasies and functional styles, we employ the overall proportional deviation score[11] as a quantitative measure. This score quantifies the extent to which the translators deviate from the source text in terms of semantic components, as indicated by labels and proportions in Fig. 8.3, when reconstructing the themes. The calculation method for this score remains

[10] Each semantic component in the tables is highlighted with a color, aligning with the colors assigned to these components as indicated in Table 8.4.

[11] Detailed proportions of each semantic component, as well as overall deviations, are available at http://dx.doi.org/10.6084/m9.figshare.29572907.

Table 8.16 Semantic fields shared by the two "British Keywords" in translation (Dolby)

Semantic Fields	Collocates (L10:R10)
Pride and Prejudice	proud, only, alone, never, detests, belittle, sneers
Hypocrisy and Pretension	manners, presenting, show-off
Colonialism and Conservatism	dominion, feet, conservative
Rule and Law	fair (2), equal, fifty-fifty, straightforward, utilitarianism, discipline, rules, obedience, lawyers

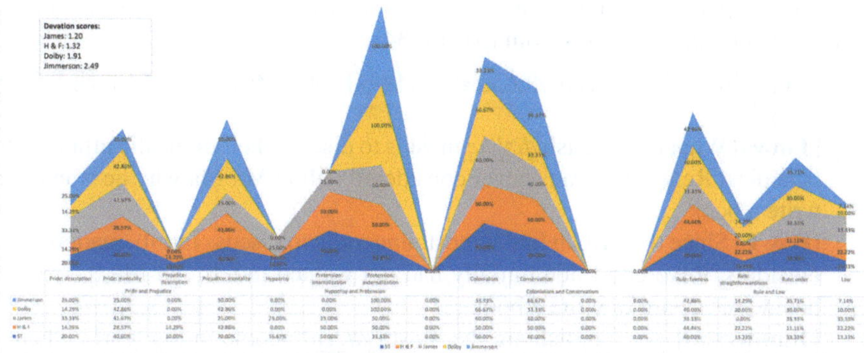

Fig. 8.3 Semantic components and their proportions in the semantic fields ("英國人" and "洋鬼子")

consistent throughout the entire research in this book to ensure uniform analysis results.

The findings presented in Fig. 8.3 reveal that, concerning the thematic construction of "Local Britons", Jimmerson exhibits the highest score (2.49), while James has the lowest (1.20). For example, Jimmerson increases the proportion of "Pretension: externalization" under the category of *Hypocrisy and Pretension* from the original 33.00% to 100%, at the expense of other semantic components within the same field. Similarly, she reduces the proportion of "Colonialism" under the category of *Colonialism and Conservatism* from 60.00% to 33.33%, representing the highest level of deviation among these translators for this component. In contrast, James maintains the original ratios of the two semantic components under *Colonialism and Conservatism* at 60.00% and 40.00%, respectively. Meanwhile, James slightly increases the percentage of "Pride: mentality" under *Pride and Prejudice* from 40.00% to 41.67%, demonstrating a deviation level significantly lower than that of the other translators for the same component. Regarding the deviation scores of the remaining translators, Dolby has the second highest score (1.91), and Huang & Finkelstein have the third highest (1.32).

Overall, the patterns of proportional deviation in the linguistic idiosyncrasies of these translators when reconstructing the theme "Local Britons" differ from those observed in their reconstructions of the theme "Diasporic Chinese". This partially reveals the different strategies employed by the translators in reconstructing the two themes, indicating their divergent perspectives on these two themes within the story.

Similar to the findings concerning the "Diasporic Chinese", the results discussed above may stem from the chosen collocate span of L10:R10, the translators' intervention, or a combination of both factors. However, it is the translators' intervention that warrants further investigation, as it unveils their linguistic idiosyncrasies and functional styles. In the following analysis, specific examples from the source and target texts will be examined to provide contextual evidence for such intervention. The translators' intervention might have the potential to alter the original semantic fields and components, resulting in a modified reconstruction of the "Local Britons" theme. Consider the examples from (31) to (34).

(31) **[ST]** 英國人最不喜歡和旁人談家事，伊牧師本來不想告訴老馬，他為什麼要寫書。

[James] What the English *dislike* most is to discuss their domestic affairs with outsiders. Reverend Evans never considered telling Mr. Ma why he wanted to write a book …

[H & F] Since the British find it most *repugnant* to discuss family matters with outsiders, Reverend Eden initially had not wanted to tell Old Ma the reason behind his desire to write a book ...

[Jimmerson] The English are the most *reticent* people in the world when it comes to talking about their family affairs, and the Reverend hadn't intended to tell Mr. Ma the real reason why he wanted to do the book project…

[Dolby] The English are *reluctant* to talk about their domestic affairs with outsiders, and the Reverend Ely had originally had no intention of telling the elder Ma his reason for wanting to write a book.

Example (31) presents a facet of Jimmerson's linguistic idiosyncrasies (functional styles) and their potential interpretational effects on the target readers. The collocate "不喜歡" in the ST line suggests "dislike" in its literal sense, but also conveys the British reluctance to share their family affairs with outsiders. In the TTs, the translators have made different choices. Jimmerson translates the collocate as "reticent", which, according to the *Cambridge Dictionary*[12] online (hereafter as *the Dictionary*), implies an "unwillingness" to express one's feelings or thoughts. While this choice may seem semantically different from the original, it effectively captures the original meaning by pragmatically implying the reluctance to "speak out one's mind". Conversely, the choices made by the other translators are less effective in capturing the same sense. For instance, Dolby's choice of "reluctance" may indicate a similar "unwillingness", but it has a broader semantic scope and is not specifically focused on expressing one's feelings or thoughts, according to the *Dictionary*. James and Huang & Finkelstein respective uses "dislike" and "repugnant" are associated with negative vehemence. As a result, target readers are more likely to form varied impressions of the "Local Britons". In the cases of both Jimmerson and Dolby, the original representation of the "Local Britons" as a "conservative" group is more likely to

[12] https://dictionary.cambridge.org/dictionary/english/.

be conveyed to the readers. In the cases of James and Huang & Finkelstein, these readers are inclined to perceive the "Local Britons" as more assertive.

(32) **[ST]** "你要是不叫我幫助你, 我也就不求你了! 你知道, 英國人的辦法是八兩半斤, 誰也不要吃虧的! 我不能白求你!"
[James] "I wasn't just asking you to help me for nothing. I can do something for you, *too*".
[H & F] "I can't just ask you to help me without doing something for you *in return*" ...
[Jimmerson] You know how the English are about *fair* exchange—nobody gets taken advantage of! You can't expect me to ask you a favor without being able to offer something in return!"
[Dolby]"If you won't let me help you, I won't ask you to help me. You know the English way – *fifty-fifty*, with neither party losing on the deal. I can't ask you to do it for nothing".

Example (32) highlights Dolby's linguistic idiosyncrasies in the rendition of the collocate "半斤八兩" and the consequent interpretational effects on target readers. "半斤八兩" is a Chinese idiom that literally means "seven kilos and eight grams" and metaphorically implies "much the same". However, in the ST line, it alludes to the British practice of "fair-play". Dolby translates it as "fifty-fifty", which not only preserves the original metaphor, but also maintains a focus on "number", thus faithfully conveying the concept of British "fairness" to target readers. In contrast, Jimmerson renders the same collocate as "fair", disregarding the original "number-based" metaphor. Consequently, her target readers, although able to grasp the original British "fairness", miss out on the metaphorical cognitive process experienced by the readers of the ST and Dolby's TT. Regarding James and Huang & Finkelstein, they omit the keyword "英國人" and replace it with "too" and "in return", respectively. As a result, their target readers are more likely to develop a different impression of the original "Local Britons", because the originally implied fairness is downplayed, as there is no direct reference to the Britons to establish the connection.

(33) **[ST]** 他含著熱淚告訴上帝: 中國人要不叫英國人管起來, 這群黃臉黑頭發的東西, 怎麼也升不了天堂!
[James] With hot tears he said to the Lord, If the Chinese are not *governed* by the English, how will this horde of yellow-faced black-haired creatures ever get to Heaven?
[H & F] With fervent tears he said to God: "If the Chinese are not *administered* by the British, those yellow-faced, black-haired creatures will never get to heaven, no matter what".
[Jimmerson] If the Chinese don't let the British *take over*, then all those masses of yellow-faced, black-haired souls will never make it to heaven!
[Dolby] Eyes filled with hot tears, he would point out to God that if the Chinese were not *taken in hand* by the British, that vast mass of yellow-faced black-haired creatures would never achieve their rightful ascent to the pearly gates.

Example (33) demonstrates James' linguistic idiosyncrasies in representing the colonial mindset associated with the "Local Britons" and the resulting interpretational effects on target readers. The original line employs the collocate "管起來", which literally means to "govern" or "control". In James' case, her rendition of the collocate as "governed" faithfully reproduces the original meaning, transferring this colonial mindset to her target readers. This partly aligns with the lowest deviation score observed in her TT. On the other hand, Huang & Finkelstein render the collocate as "administered", which, according to the *Dictionary*, carries a broader meaning than "governed" due to an additional implication of "management" or "arrangement". Consequently, readers of Huang & Finkelstein's version are more likely to develop a positive perception of this colonial mindset. In contrast, Jimmerson and Dolby translate the same collocate as "take over" and "taken in hand", respectively. The *Dictionary* suggests that these metaphorical phrases are semantically linked to "responsibility" and "improvement". As a result, readers of Jimmerson's TT and Dolby's TT may be inclined to glorify this British colonial mindset in the story.

(34) **[ST]** 英國人本來是<u>最講</u>規矩的, 亞力山大少年的時候也是規矩禮道一點不差; 自從到中國作買賣, 他覺得對中國人不屑于講禮貌 ……

[James] Actually, the English are the ones who <u>*preach*</u> the most about good form. When young, Alexander did not deviate at all from the rules of etiquette. But after he went to China to trade, it wasn't worth bothering about proper form when dealing with the Chinese.

[H & F] In his youth Alexander had been as well-mannered as any Englishman, who were generally <u>*meticulous*</u> on matters of etiquette. But being in China as a businessman left him with the feeling that there was no need to be polite to Chinese.

[Jimmerson] Generally speaking the English are most <u>*particular*</u> about observing rules of propriety, and in Alexander's younger days he too abided to proper etiquette. But ever since he'd gone to do business in China, he had grown too loath to uphold standards of politeness in his dealings with Chinese…

[Dolby] The English actually <u>*give*</u> a great deal of <u>*attention to*</u> manners, and as a young man Alexander had possessed flawless manners and etiquette. But when he went to China, he felt that being polite to the Chinese wasn't worth the bother ...

Example (34) illustrates Huang & Finkelstein's linguistic idiosyncrasies and the resulting interpretational effects on target readers. The ST line focuses on British etiquette and uses the collocate "最講", which literally means "care most about" (etiquettes). The different renditions of this collocate by the translators in the four TT lines reveal two contrasting reconstructions of the "Local Britons": one being assertive and the other reserved. In the cases of James, Jimmerson, and Dolby, their translations employ terms such as "preach", "particular", and "give…attention to", respectively, leading to a more assertive reconstruction of the "Local Britons" regarding their concern for etiquettes. This is likely to provide their target readers with an original understanding of the British obsession with etiquettes. Conversely, Huang & Finkelstein opt for the translation "meticulous", which, according to the *Dictionary*, conveys a sense of being "careful" or "discreet". Consequently, this rendition suggests a more reserved attitude towards the obsession with etiquettes and is likely to prompt an alternative interpretation among target readers: the "Local Britons" are simply being cautious about etiquettes rather than being obsessed with them.

8.4 Conclusion

This chapter explored the translators' functional styles in their English translations of *Er Ma* through the linguistic idiosyncrasies they show in reconstructing the two themes of "Diasporic Chinese" and "Local Britons". The exploration was conducted using the analytical framework presented in Fig. 8.1, which covers three key aspects: keyword rendition, reestablishment of lexical chains, and reconstruction of semantic fields.

In terms of keyword rendition, all the translators provided multiple renditions for both "Chinese Keywords" and "British Keywords". Consequently, there were variations in the frequencies of these renditions in the TTs compared to the ST and the reference corpora.

Regarding the reestablishment of lexical chains, the translators adopted varied approaches when reconstructing the two themes. For "Diasporic Chinese", James disrupted the original lexical chain, while Huang & Finkelstein maintained the chain through their literal rendition of "中國人" as "Chinese". Conversely, when reconstructing the theme of "Local Britons", Jimmerson preserved the original lexical chain by consistently translating "英國人" as "(the) English", while Huang & Finkelstein broke this chain by providing multiple renditions for the same word.

Concerning the reconstruction of semantic fields, the translators exhibited diverse approaches for the two themes. In the case of "Diasporic Chinese", Jimmerson made the least effort to alter the original proportions of semantic components, while Huang & Finkelstein and James showed the greatest efforts in the same regard. However, the situation reversed when it came to "Local Britons". Jimmerson appeared to invest the most effort in modifying the original proportions of various semantic components, whereas James and Huang & Finkelstein exhibited the least effort in this aspect.

It's important to note that the findings in this chapter have some limitations. Firstly, the discussion of the translators' functional styles is presented solely from the perspective of thematic reconstruction. Secondly, the interpretation of the reconstructed themes in the translations is limited to their potential effects on the target readership. However, these limitations will be addressed in the subsequent chapters. Chapter 9 will present findings on the translators' functional styles in terms of the recharacterization of story figures, and Chapter 11 will discuss underlying factors that could account for the translators' functional styles.

References

Baker, M. (2011). *In other words: A coursebook on translation* (2nd ed.). Routledge.

Burke, T. (1919). *Out and about London.* Henry Holt and Company.

Curzon, G. N. (1986). *Problems of the far East.* Archibald Constable and Company.

Flowerdew, J., & Mahlberg, M. (Eds.). (2009). *Lexical cohesion and corpus linguistics* (Vol. 17). John Benjamins Publishing.

Lao, S. (1998). *Er Ma.* People's Literature Publishing House.

Leech, G. N., & Short, M. (2007). *Style in fiction: A linguistic introduction to English fictional prose* (No. 13). Pearson Education.

Louie, K. (2000). Constructing Chinese masculinity for the modern world: With particular reference to Lao She's the *Two Mas. The China Quarterly, 164*, 1062–1078.

Mastropierro, L. (2018). *Corpus stylistics in heart of darkness and its Italian translations.* Bloomsbury Publishing.

Mayer, R. (2013). *Serial Fu Manchu: The Chinese supervillain and the spread of yellow peril ideology.* Temple University Press.

Prince, G. (1987). *The yellow peril in Britain, 1890 to 1920.* McGill University.

Rohmer, S. (1916). *The return of Dr. Fu-Manchu.* A. L. Burt Company.

Stone, N. (2017). The yellow peril in Britain. In *Proceedings of International Academic Conferences* (No. 5007633). International Institute of Social and Economic Sciences.

Tuchman, B. W. (1985). *The Zimmermann telegram.* Random House Trade Paperbacks.

Wen, R. M. (2000). The novel *Er Ma* from a cultural criticism perspective (Speech delivered at the International Comparative Literature Conference in the Netherlands, June 1997). *Modern Chinese Literature Studies, 4*, 123–128.

Witchard, A. (2012). *Lao She in London.* Hong Kong University Press.

Chapter 9
Functional Style as Recharacterization of Story Figures

9.1 Introduction

This chapter investigates the characterization and recharacterization of story figures in *Er Ma* and its four English translations, utilizing the same methods as Chapter 8 to ensure comparability of the analysis results. The chapter commences with five "Chinese Keywords" serving as labels for two Chinese figures ("馬則仁", "馬老先生", "老馬", "馬先生", and "李子榮"), and four "British Keywords" representing labels for two British figures ("凱薩林", "伊姑娘", "瑪力", and "溫都姑娘") previously selected in Chapter 7. These keywords are expected to facilitate the investigation of the translators' functional styles for the reasons explained in Chapter 7.

Section 9.2 will investigate the characterization of Chinese and British figures in *Er Ma*, with Sect. 9.2.1 focusing on Chinese figures and Sect. 9.2.2 concentrating on British figures. Section 9.3 will explore the translators' functional styles by scrutinizing their linguistic idiosyncrasies in recharacterizing these story figures. This section will be subdivided into three subsections: Section 9.3.1 will examine the translators' reestablishment of the original lexical chains, Sect. 9.3.2 will analyze their reconstructions of the original semantic fields, and Sect. 9.3.3 will center on their recreations of the original discourse presentation. Furthermore, the potential interpretational effects of these recharacterizations on target readers will be discussed. Section 9.4 will present a conclusion based on the findings from the previous sections and look forward to the research in the subsequent chapters.

9.2 Characterization of Story Figures in *Er Ma*

To examine the connections established in Chapter 7 between linguistic descriptions and literary functions, this section focuses on exploring the lexico-semantic patterns generated by the chosen figure labels. It also aims to generalize the potential local

K. Wu and D. Li, *Researching Translator's Functional Style*, New Frontiers in Translation Studies, https://doi.org/10.1007/978-981-95-1221-8_9

textual functions that these patterns enact. To ensure consistency and comparability of analysis results, the collocate span in this chapter will be maintained at L10:R10, aligning with the setting used in Chapter 8.

9.2.1 Characterization of Chinese Figures

The method employed for investigating the characterization of story figures is akin to the one used in the examination of thematic construction (see Chapter 8). As outlined in Chapter 7, the five chosen Chinese keywords ("馬則仁", "馬老先生", "老馬", "馬先生", "李子榮") represent two Chinese figures of sharp contrast. A further analysis of these words in translation is expected to show these translators' functional styles as they recharacterize these story figures. In the following section, we will focus on "Mr. Ma" and "Li Zirong", two contrasting Chinese figures represented by the five keywords, to investigate how these Chinese figures are characterized in the story context.

9.2.1.1 Chinese Figures in Context

The four labels, "馬則仁", "馬老先生", "老馬", and "馬先生", appear 9, 365, 183,[1] and 169 times, respectively, in the source text (ST). Collectively, these labels refer to one of the protagonists, Mr. Ma, in the story. These labels, along with the expanded units of meaning they represent, contribute to the characterization of this individual in the story. By treating each label as the node within the L10:R10[2] concordance span, we can examine their semantic preferences and identify the semantic fields they create. These fields are expected to contain some contextual information associated with the portrayal of Mr. Ma. Analyzing the concordance lines[3] for each label, it becomes evident that there are at least three shared semantic fields. These fields incorporate various collocates (as shown in Table 9.1) that convey a predominantly negative prosody.

The first semantic field, labeled as *Gloom and Shame*, depicts Mr. Ma as an unfortunate character burdened with various miseries and misfortunes in his life. This portrayal is evident through collocations such as "病人" (patient) and "死不了" (cannot die) within the concordance lines of "馬先生". Additionally, expressions like "淒涼" and "慘澹" (bleak), "丟臉" (shameful), and "教訓" (lesson) appear in

[1] In the story, the term "老馬" is used to refer to both Mr. Ma and Ma Wei. However, in the context mentioned here, the term "老馬" specifically pertains to Mr. Ma.

[2] The decision to use L10:R10 in this study, based on repeated pilot studies, ensures the inclusion of essential contextual information while avoiding redundancy. It deviates from previous studies focusing on European languages, which employed L5:R5 settings. Practical considerations regarding the varying information density between Chinese and English translations influenced this decision.

[3] The detailed lists are available at dx.doi.org/10.6084/m9.figshare.29572907.

Table 9.1 Semantic fields shared by the figure labels in the source text (Mr. Ma)

Semantic Fields	Collocates (L10:R10)
Gloom and Shame	病人(2), 有病, 病(6), 死不了(3), 死了(3), 餓不死, 餓死(2), 撞死, 摔死(3), 半生不死, 一命嗚呼, 淒涼, 慘澹(2), 悲哀, 委屈(3), 不舒坦(2), 教訓(3), 看不起(4), 沒出息(2), 丟臉, 好吃懶做, 傻蛋(4), 傻(2), 糊塗(4), 俗氣(2), 討厭(2), 喝醉(3), 灌醉(2), 清閒, 閒人
Career and Business	賠錢(3), 賠償(2), 砸毀, 歇業, 賣了, 窮營業, 官運(2), 買賣(12), 事業, 古玩(2), 鋪子(15), 貨物(2),買賣人(3), 作官(5), 股東, 掌櫃的(5), 工錢(2), 錢(8), 價錢, 看賬,
Love, Marriage, Women	愛上(2), 看上, 愛情, 嫁, 娶(2), 婚姻, 戒指(14), 妻子(3), 溫都寡婦(10), 寡婦(3), 婦人(8), 婦女(4)

the concordance lines of "馬老先生". Similarly, "傻蛋" (fool), "看不起" (look down upon), and "野蠻人" (barbarian) are present in the concordance lines of "老馬", while "一命嗚呼" (dying), "好吃懶做" (lazy and gluttonous), and "沒出息" (hopeless) are found in the lines related to "馬則仁". Please consider the following examples:

(1) "死是死不了啦, 還是不舒服!"一想起自己是病人, 馬先生心裡安慰多了: 誰不可憐有病的人!回來,李子榮都得來瞧我!
(2) 伊牧師始終沒看起馬先生, 他叫老馬寫書, 純是為好叫老馬幫他的忙!他知道老馬是傻蛋, 傻蛋自然不會寫書。

Example (1) shows a concordance line of "馬先生", highlighting various elements contributing to his misery through such collocates as "病人" (patient), "死" (death), and "可憐" (wretched). Additionally, this example reveals Mr. Ma's contradictory stance, combining self-paralysis with arrogance, suggesting the inevitable failure of his life in London. Example (2) presents a concordance line of "老馬", showcasing Reverend Evans' overt disdain for Mr. Ma. This sentiment is evident in the L10:R10 collocate "傻蛋" (fool), as well as other words like "沒看起" (look down upon) and "不會" (incompetent).

The second semantic field, labeled as *Business and Career*, portrays Mr. Ma as a failure in business and career. The portrayal is exemplified by some L10:R10 collocates in the concordance lines of different labels. For instance, in the concordance lines of "馬先生", collocates like "賠錢" (losing money) (Line 147) and "窮營業" (poor business) (Line 31) can be found. Similarly, in the concordance lines of "馬老先生", collocates like "作官" (holding a government position) (Line 334) and "買賣" (buying and selling) (Line 324) illustrate this portrayal. The concordance lines of "老馬" include collocates such as "砸毀" (ruined) (Line 37) and "作官" (holding a government position) (Line 70, 146), while the concordance lines of "馬則仁" feature the collocate "買賣人" (trader) (Line 3). The following two concordance lines represent excerpts of "馬先生" and "老馬" respectively, providing the characterization of Mr. Ma as a "failure" in business, and an "addict" to government jobs.

(3) 馬先生真為了難! 事實是簡單的: 買賣賠錢, 得想主意。可是馬先生, 真正中國人, 就不肯這麼想, 洋鬼子才這麼想呢; 李子榮也這麼想, 黃臉的洋鬼子!

(4) 可惜老馬只想回國, 而不明白國家是什麼東西。可惜老馬只想作官, 而不知道作官的責任。可惜老馬愛他的兒子, 而不懂得怎麼教育他。

Example (3) presents a naive view taken by Mr. Ma, which, coupled with his stubbornness and narrow-mindedness, explains the reasons for his lack of success in the curio business. Example (4) highlights Mr. Ma's persistent aspirations of becoming a government official in China, despite his ignorance regarding many aspects such as the concept of nationhood, the responsibilities of an official, and even proper parenting.

The third semantic field pertains to another significant aspect of Mr. Ma's life, which we refer to as *Love, Marriage, Women.* In *Er Ma*, a pivotal plot revolves around Mr. Ma's proposal to Mrs. Wendell, a widow, which fully showcases the British bias towards the Chinese (Wen, 2000: 125). This field is characterized by some L10:R10 collocates, such as "戒指" (ring) (Line 38, 110) and "婦女" (women) (Line 64) in the concordance lines of "馬先生"; "妻子" (wife) (Line 253) and "戒指" (Line 256, 304, 331, 340, 355) in the lines of "馬老先生"; "戒指" (Line 97), "愛上" (fall in love with) (Line 136), "看上" (take a liking to) (Line 169), and "寡婦" (widow) (Line 169) in those of "老馬"; "溫都寡婦" (Mrs. Wendell) (Line 9) in those of "馬則仁". It is clear that, when it comes to love and marriage, the preferred collocates for the four labels associated with Mr. Ma are "戒子" (ring) and Mrs. Wendell (the widow). However, even these collocates, which are connected to love and marriage, serve to illustrate the deep-seated British prejudice against the diasporic Chinese during that era. The following examples provide further illustration:

(5) 馬老先生要看戒指, 夥計給他拿來一盒子小姑娘戴著玩的小銅圈, 全是四個便士一隻。馬老先生要看貴一點的, 夥計看了他一眼, 又拿出一盒鍍銀的來, 三個先令兩隻。老馬先生還要貴的, 夥計笑得很不自然的說:"再貴的可就過一鎊錢了!"

(6) 英國普通人以為一個人愛花愛狗愛兒女便是好丈夫。 瑪力的意思是:溫都太太愛上老馬啦。溫都寡婦沒言語, 半惱半笑的瞪了她女兒一眼。

Example (5) illustrates a concordance line of "馬老先生", in which a British shop assistant at a jewelry store assumes that Mr. Ma, being Chinese, would not be able to afford a wedding ring (as indicated by the L10:R10 collocate "戒指") priced higher than one pound. This example highlights the implicit bias and prejudice against Mr. Ma based on his Chinese ethnicity. Example (6) depicts a concordance line of "老馬", subtly conveying Mrs. Wendell's underlying self-disapproval for falling in love with Mr. Ma. This becomes evident when the author uses the expression "半惱半笑" (smiling annoyance) to depict Mrs. Wendell's mixed emotions as her daughter hints at her romantic affection towards Mr. Ma.

Analyzing the collocates found within the L10:R10 span of the four labels reveals a predominantly negative portrayal of Mr. Ma in the story. Moreover, the three shared semantic fields associated with these labels contribute to the characterization of Mr. Ma as a traditional and conservative Chinese figure, who embraces a defeatist mindset in response to his misfortunes in London. In contrast, Li Zirong, Mr. Ma's curio shop assistant and another Chinese protagonist, is portrayed in a completely different manner, as shown by the following semantic fields.

The keyword "李子榮", which directly labels Li Zirong, appears 308 times in the ST. Using "李子榮" as the node, we can examine its concordance lines within the span of L10:R10 to generalize the semantic fields (preferences) associated with this story figure. The results reveal at least four semantic fields that contribute to the characterization of Li Zirong in the story, with many collocates within these fields carrying positive connotations. A detailed overview of these semantic fields is provided in Table 9.2.

The first semantic field is *Diligence and Workaholism*, illustrated by collocates like "拼命的" (Line 86), "忙" (Line 118, 192, 300) and "收拾" (Line 251). These L10:R10 collocates collectively create a portrayal of Li Zirong as a different type of diasporic Chinese in London: hardworking, diligent, and tireless – a workaholic. Here are some examples:

(7) 貨物在聖誕前一個月到了倫敦, 他和李子榮<u>拼命的</u>幹:點綴門面, 定價碼, 印說明書……整整的一天准幹七點鐘。

(8) "叫我老李, 別先生先生的!"李子榮笑著說。他已經把貨架子的一部分<u>收拾</u>乾淨了, 也洗了臉,黃臉蛋上光潤了許多。

Example (7) presents a concordance line that includes the collocate "拼命的". It depicts Li Zirong as a workaholic, working long hours every day, engaging in strenuous physical labor to prepare the curio shop for Christmas. Example (8), on the other hand, highlights Li Zirong's diligence, as he efficiently cleans stock shelves while attending to customers, showcasing his multitasking capabilities.

The second semantic field, labeled as *Resourcefulness and Confidence*, portrays Li Zirong as a clever and self-assured man. This characterization is evident through L10:R10 collocates such as "神氣" (Line 98), "張羅" (Line 246), "自信的" (Line 253) and "出主意" (Line 300). These collocates collectively depict Li Zirong as resourceful and confident, in addition to his diligence and workaholism. Here are two examples:

(9) 自從李子榮<u>出主意</u>預備聖誕大減價,馬威和李子榮(他天天抓著工夫來幫忙) 忙得手腳朝天, 可是不許老馬動手。

(10) 世事是繁雜的, 誰能都想得到呢!但是李子榮是<u>自信的</u>人, 他非常的恨自己。

Table 9.2 Semantic fields shared by the figure labels in the source text (李子榮)

Semantic Fields	Collocates (L10:R10)
Dash, Diligence, Workaholism	拼命的, 拼命, 趕緊, 飛跑(2), 跑(8), 跑過來, 趕過來, 沒工夫(2), 抓著工夫, 忙(4), 窮忙(2), 操心(2), 打著精神, 自告奮勇, 幫忙, 收拾(3), 清理, 幹(4), 念書(5), 貨物(2), 嘮叨
Resourcefulness and Confidence	出主意, 主意(3), 張羅(2), 勸, 辯護, 假裝, 故意, 機靈, 會辦事, 懂行, 挺胸脯, 自信的, 自傲, 神氣(2), 掙錢(2), 做生意, 大減價, 豪傑(2)
Practicality and Utility	不講面子, 別客氣, 注重事實, 不必妄想, 不應, 會做飯, 作衣裳, 洗衣裳, 破衣(2), 舊衣, 送禮(4)
Attached Negativity	俗氣 (4), 沒皮沒臉, 神經病, 洋鬼子 (2)

Example (9) and (10) represent two concordance lines containing the collocates "出主意" and "自信的", respectively. Example (9) highlights Li Zirong's business acumen through his proposal for a pre-Christmas promotion in the shop. This upcoming promotion kept both him and Ma Wei occupied, working long hours every day, ultimately resulting in increased business for the shop. Example (10), however, is an internal monologue of Li Zirong in which Lao She (the narrator) conveys Li's mixed feelings—he is a confident man, yet he somehow harbors self-doubt.

The third semantic field, labeled as *Practicality and Utility*, captures one of the key attributes of Li Zirong. This field is closely intertwined with the other two fields, as it is believed that Li Zirong's practical nature underpins his diligence and resourcefulness. Given his economically disadvantaged background, earning a living in a foreign land necessitates hard work and astute thinking. Moreover, his practicality extends to various facets of his life. He staunchly upholds that a "gift" should be both cost-effective and long-lasting, and maintains conservative beliefs regarding the practicality of an "uneducated wife". These aspects are exemplified by collocates such as "送禮" (giving gifts), "做飯" (cooking), and "作衣裳" (making clothes). Here are two examples to illustrate these points:

(11) 馬威主張到節送禮是該當的, 李子榮說送禮不應花錢太多。馬威說買東西就得要好的, 李子榮說他的破表已經帶了三年, 實在沒買好表的必要。

(12) "你不信?我不冤你,真的!母親給定的!"李子榮的臉都紅勻了:"二十一歲,會做飯, 作衣裳, 長得還不賴!"

Example (11) and (12) are concordance lines that include some of these collocates. Example (11) underscores Li Zirong's practical approach to selecting holiday gifts: he opts for durable yet cost-effective items, akin to the watch he has worn for three years. Example (12) sheds light on Li's criteria for choosing a wife—an undereducated woman willing to undertake household chores for him.

The fourth semantic field, labeled as *Attached Negativity*, diverges from the previous three fields as it highlights the "negative" aspects associated with Li Zirong. This field portrays Mr. Ma's negative impression of Li Zirong. It is characterized by collocates such as "俗氣" (tacky), "沒皮沒臉" (shameless), and "洋鬼子" (foreign devil), which largely comprise traditional and conservative Chinese stereotypes imposed on this progressive Chinese youth. The following examples illustrate the point:

(13) 沒法跟這樣人打交待, 他滿不顧面子! 我沒法子!...... 瞧李子榮, 沒皮沒臉! 你叫他走, 他說法律吧, 交情吧, 扯蛋! ......沒法子! ......沒面子!

(14) 馬先生繞著圈兒想, 越想自己的理由越充足, 越想越離事實遠, 越離事實遠越覺得自己是真正好中國人—李子榮是黃臉洋鬼子!

Examples (13) and (14) portray Mr. Ma's disdain and feelings of powerlessness regarding Li Zirong, a progressive Chinese figure in the story. This kind of negative sentiments attached to Li Zirong could demonstrate the self-limiting mindset of some traditional and conservative Chinese individuals, represented by Mr. Ma, who refuse to accept new values and ideas.

9.2.1.2 A "Self-paralytic" Man Versus a "Self-made" Man

The present research argues that the extended units of meaning formed by the keywords and their L10:R10 collocates across the four semantic fields of Mr. Ma are functionally connected to the portrayal of an old-school Chinese *wenren* (scholars), characterized by self-paralyzing attitudes towards life. In contrast, the extended units of meaning associated with "李子榮" jointly serve a local textual function by introducing a progressive Chinese youth who is self-reliant and eager to embrace his new life in a foreign land.

Mr. Ma, a morally reprehensible Chinese protagonist, adopts a self-paralyzing stance towards his diasporic life in London. Several aspects of his life contribute to this self-paralysis. He disdains physical labor and places too much pride in traditional scholarly pursuits. He claims to exercise self-restraint, but frequently seeks companionship with women. He is ambitious about his London life, but daydreams about joining bureaucracy back to China (Louie, 2000:1068). Mr. Ma demonstrates a lack of practical understanding of his life in London, resulting in a disconnection from his circumstances. Similar viewpoints are expressed by Lao She himself when discussing Mr. Ma: he is neither virtuous nor wicked; he is deeply attached to China's cultural past, leading to a sense of pride and self-esteem; he is uncertain about his future, which makes him indolent and immobilized (Kong, 2005: 63). Such characterizations of Mr. Ma are linguistically manifested through the four key semantic fields associated with him, presenting readers with an old-style Chinese *wenren*, self-paralyzing but proud (Louie, 2000:1067; Wen, 2000: 126).

Li Zirong, in stark contrast, emerges as a "counter-balance" character to Mr. Ma (Louie, 2000: 1068). He is a self-made progressive individual who abandons the traditional role of the Chinese *wenren* and instead embraces Western values. He is diligent and works tirelessly in the curio shop. He demonstrates resourcefulness in planning holiday business promotions and protecting the shop from mobs. Above all, he is a practical man who values utility, even in his choice of a wife. Simultaneously, he aspires to prioritize business over bureaucracy, understanding that business and finance are crucial to building a robust nation (Wang, 1999: 20). He diligently acquires knowledge from various sources, understanding that knowledge might be a way for the revival of the Chinese nation. Linguistically, the semantic fields formed by the L10:R10 collocates of the node "李子榮" collectively serve a local textual function that consistently characterizes Li Zirong as a progressive new-generation Chinese youth (Wang, 1999: 20; Wen, 2000:126).

9.2.2 Characterization of British Figures

The analysis of the characterization of the British figures follows a similar methodology that has been used to examine the characterization of the Chinese figures. As explained in Chapter 7, the four selected keywords ("凱薩林", "伊姑娘", "瑪

力", "溫都姑娘") represent two contrasting British figures. By examining the renditions of these British keywords, the study aims to unveil the translators' functional styles as they recharacterize these story figures. The forthcoming discussion will focus specifically on "Catherine" and "Mary", two contrasting British protagonists represented by the aforementioned keywords. The objective is to explore how these British figures are characterized in the story.

9.2.2.1 British Figures in Context

Catherine is a distinctive story figure who embodies the "idealized" Briton in Lao She's narrative (Ma, 2004:56; Qian, 1999: 115; Xiao, 2010: 53). Throughout the story, she is most frequently referred to as "凱薩林" or "伊姑娘", with both labels occurring 51 times in the ST. These two labels collectively contribute to a partial characterization of Catherine through the shared semantic fields created by their L10:R10 collocates in the ST (see Table 9.3).

A notable semantic field associated with Catherine revolves around her "spirit of learning", which we refer to as *Knowledge and Study*. In the story, Catherine, along with Sir Simon, distinguishes herself from other British figures (Ma, 2004: 56; Qian, 1999: 115; Ji, 2009: 71). Her perspective on acquiring new knowledge is portrayed as more open-minded and progressive. This distinction is partially exemplified in the ST through collocates such as "書籍" (books, Line 18), "自由" (freedom, Line 40), and "知識" (knowledge, Line 47) in the concordance lines of "凱薩林". Similarly, the concordance lines of "伊姑娘" feature "念書" (reading, Line 3, 9, 32, 33, 50). Consider the following examples:

(15) "馬威! "伊姑娘拉住馬威的手: "馬威!好好的念書, 不用管別的! 我知道你的苦處, 你受的刺激! 可是空暴燥一回, 能把中國就變好了嗎?不能!

(16) 人生, 據我看, 只有兩件快活事: 用自己的知識, 和得知識!" 說到這裡, 凱薩林又微微的一笑。

Example (15) illustrates Catherine's embodiment of the "spirit of learning" as she advises Ma Wei to seek new knowledge instead of dwelling on China's troubles. This demonstrates Catherine's conviction that knowledge is important in addressing the challenges faced by the Chinese nation. In Example (16), Catherine's unwavering statement further reinforces her belief in the joy and fulfillment derived from knowledge. These instances, coupled with Catherine's forward-thinking perspectives portrayed in the story, distinguish her from those more "conventional" British characters like Mrs. Wendell and Paul. Lao She imbues Catherine with an idealized sense of progressiveness that aligns with his own aspirations (Ji, 2009: 71; Ma, 2004: 58).

Table 9.3 Semantic fields shared by the figure labels in the source text (Catherine)

Semantic Fields	Collocates (L10:R10)
Knowledge and Study	知識 (2), 念書 (7), 念點書, 多學一點, 書房, 學校, 書籍
Tolerance and Respect	你教我, 中國話 (2), 背著, 救中國

Another significant semantic field associated with Catherine pertains to her unbiased attitude towards the Chinese people and their language. This field, referred to as *Tolerance and Respect*, is less overt but discernible through some L10:R10 collocates found in the concordance lines of the two figure labels. Examples of these collocates include "你教我" (teach me, Line 26) and "中國話" (Chinese language, Line 45) in the concordance lines of "凱薩林", and "中國話" (Chinese language, Line 25) in those of "伊姑娘". The following examples further illustrate this field.

(17) 凱薩林是在中國的外國學校念書的, 而且背著母親學了不少中國話, 拿著字典也能念淺近的中國書。

(18) "馬威, 你教我半點鐘, 我教你半點鐘。我把這本雜誌上的一段翻成中國話, 你逐句給我改。你打算念什麼?"

Example (17) presents a concordance line featuring the collocate "中國話". It illustrates Catherine's unbiased attitude towards the Chinese language. This stance becomes particularly evident with the additional collocate "背著", indicating Catherine's determination to learn Chinese despite the discouragement from her mother. In Example (18), Catherine's unbiased stance is demonstrated through her interest in translating a magazine from English into Chinese. The collocate "你教我" once again highlights her commitment to learning the Chinese language with the mutual assistance of Ma Wei.

Mary, in sharp contrast to Catherine, embodies a more conventional British figure in the story. She is directly referenced by the labels "瑪力" and "溫都姑娘", which occur 280 and 43 times, respectively, in the ST. The L10:R10 collocates surrounding these labels give rise to three noticeable semantic fields (see Table 9.4) that characterize Mary as a shallow and sentimental woman with deep-rooted prejudices against the Chinese. The study will term these three fields as *Sentiments*, *Shallowness*, and *Prejudice*, respectively. This interpretation aligns with some literary criticism that characterized Mary as "secular", "sentimental", "shallow", "mediocre", and "prejudiced" (Wen, 2000: 125; Zhu, 2007: 15). In the semantic field of *Shallowness*, some notable collocates include "報紙上" (in the newspapers, Line 160) and "不會" (doesn't understand, Line 216), "不懂的" (don't understand, Line 273) in the concordance lines of "瑪力", as well as "小說式的" (novel-like, Line 2) and "毒藥" (poison, Line 29, 31) in those of "溫都姑娘". The following examples provide some contextual illustrations of these collocates.

Table 9.4 Semantic fields shared by the figure labels in the source text (Mary)

Semantic Fields	Collocates (L10:R10)
Sentiments	別哭, 哭起來, 抽達, 顫（著）(2), 淚珠, 眼淚 (3), 含著淚, 哭喪著臉, 報委屈, 傷心, 失望, 怪笑, 唏的一笑, 噗哧一笑, 酸酸的一笑, 撒著嬌兒, 樂
Shallowness	報紙上(3), 報紙, 電影(2), 小說(3), 不會, 不懂的, 驕傲, 小說式的, 亂七八糟
Prejudice	不該, 不肯, 不用, 不可能的事, 拒絕, 毒藥 (3), 殺人放火, 討人嫌, 挨打的貨, 警告(2)

(19) 瑪力姑娘的經濟和倫理的關係是由報紙上看來的，她的討厭中國人也全是由報紙上，電影上看來的，其實她對於經濟與中國人的知識,全不是她自己揣摸出來的。
(20) 溫都姑娘這個警告是有歷史的，是含著點近於宗教信仰的：回回不吃豬肉,誰都知道;中國人用毒藥害人—一種信仰!

Example (19) shows Mary's shallowness through the collocate "報紙上". It reveals that her limited comprehension of Chinese culture and her aversion to Chinese people stem not from personal experiences, but rather from information acquired through newspapers. Example (20) further exemplifies this shallowness with the collocate "毒藥". Mary instinctively warns her mother about the Chinese being treacherous and using poison, a belief rooted in historical portrayals prevalent in popular British literature.

If we consider Mary's shallowness as a possible underlying cause, her deep-seated prejudices towards the Chinese might be the resulting consequences. Another significant semantic field that emerges from the L10:R10 collocates associated with Mary's labels is *Prejudice*, which appears to dominate this British figure throughout the story. Some notable collocates within this field include "不該" (Line 24, 58), "討人嫌" (Line 251), "不可能的事" (Line 25), and "不肯" (Line 29) in the concordance lines of "瑪力"; and "毒藥" (Line 21, 31), "打死" (Line 30), and "挨打的貨" (Line 18) in those of "溫都姑娘". Consider the following two examples.

(21) 瑪力忽然把手抽出去,站起來,說:"你我?不可能的事!""為什麼?我是個中國人?愛情是沒有國界的,中國人就那麼不值錢,連愛情都被剝奪了嗎!
(22) "誰叫你把房租給中國人呢!" 溫都姑娘把報紙扔在一邊……溫都姑娘看著他,笑了,好象是說:"中國人,挨打的貨!就不會生氣!"

Example (21) highlights Mary's deep-seated prejudice towards the Chinese with the collocate "不可能的事", which clearly demonstrates her rejection of Ma Wei's love because of his Chinese identity. Example (22) further exemplifies this prejudice. Mary holds her mother responsible for renting rooms to the Chinese, as she considers them to be "losers" undeserved of anything. This blatant racism reflects Mary's biased perspective and reinforces her entrenched prejudices throughout the story.

The third semantic field that characterizes Mary is her sentimental disposition, which is evident through her frequent displays of tears and laughter. Referred to as *Sentiments*, this semantic field is represented by collocates such as "含著淚" (Line 33), "淚珠" (Line 49), and "怪笑" (Line 144) in the concordance lines of "瑪力", as well as "撒著嬌兒" (Line 9) in those of "溫都姑娘". Consider the following two examples:

(23) "媽!媽!"瑪力含著淚說,兩個眼珠好象帶著朝露的藍葡萄珠兒:"好幾天沒看見他了,給他寫信,也沒回信。我得找他去,我得問問他!媽,我現在恨他!"她倒在母親的懷裡,嗚嗚的哭起來。
(24) "哈哈!哈哈!"瑪力還是怪笑,臉上通紅,笑了幾聲,把頭伏在鋼琴上哭起來。

Example (23) shows Mary's sentimentality through the collocate "含著淚", which describes her shedding tears while experiencing the disappointment of receiving no replies from her boyfriend. Example (24) depicts Mary's emotional state with the collocate "怪笑", indicating a hysterical laughter that eventually bursts into tears. These examples demonstrate Mary's intense emotions, particularly in the context of her troubled romantic relationship with her boyfriend.

9.2.2.2 A "Progressive" Lady Versus a "Narrow-Minded" Girl

The L10: R10 collocates of these figures' labels and the extended units of meaning they create are interrelated to serve a local textual function, presenting us with two contrasting types of Britons with opposing worldviews (Ji, 2009: 71). The first type is liberal-minded, embracing a progressive outlook on the postwar new world, where old and new values of morality, religion, and politics are in constant conflict. The second type appears to be stuck in the past, clinging desperately to the old values in a changing world. Catherine and Mary represent these two contrasting types of Britons, with Catherine embodying the "progressive" lady and Mary representing the "narrow-minded" girl.

Catherine represents the first type of Briton, who is an idealized figure under Lao She's pen. Her progressiveness is well demonstrated by her attitudes towards life and the diasporic Chinese. In life, she knows what she truly wants and thus earns herself a dignified and meaningful living (Lao She, 1998: 626). In the story, she pursues her love by moving to live with her boyfriend without hesitation—a rather fearless move at that time. She craves knowledge, believing that knowledge is true happiness in life (Lao She, 1998: 489)—a rare thought among the British ladies in the story. When facing the diasporic Chinese, her stance is liberal and open-minded: she gives them unbiased respect and values their cultures. Linguistically, such progressiveness of Catherine is instantiated through the semantic fields shared by the collocates attached to the two labels ("凱薩林" and "伊姑娘"). Together, these lexico-semantic patterns characterize this "progressive" lady, who is liberal and tolerant, free from narrow-minded prejudices (Ji, 2009: 71; Wen, 2000: 127; Zhu, 2007: 15).

Mary represents the second type of Britons in the story: narrow-minded and biased. She is narrow-minded as she clings steadfastly to values that come from newspapers and films. She believes that fashion means being the latest, even at the cost of fitness—a philosophy she applies to her daily clothing (Xiao, 2010: 36). She argues that the Chinese are no more generous than the Britons when it comes to money—a theory she learns from newspapers (Qian, 1999: 116). Meanwhile, she is biased—a personal trait stemming from her narrow-mindedness. She loathes the Chinese, as she instinctively believes they are insidious and degraded. She sees the Chinese as insidious devils who often poison people and low-life losers constantly beaten by other nations (Xiao, 2010: 51). Consequently, she rebuffs the fervent courtship from Ma Wei, regarding him instinctively as an "insidious" and "degraded" Chinese. Linguistically, such narrow-mindedness of Mary is effectively conveyed through the semantic fields shared by the L10:R10 collocates of the two labels ("瑪力" and "溫都姑娘") in the source text.

9.2.3 *Translators' Functional Styles in Recharacterizing Story Figures*

This section examines the translators' functional styles in their recharacterization of the story figures in the four translations. To enhance comparability with the results in Chapter 8, we also will focus on the linguistic idiosyncrasies these translators show in recharacterizing the figures. The framework (Fig. 9.1) used for investigating these linguistic idiosyncrasies closely resembles the one employed in Chapter 8, with some minor adjustments made due to practical considerations, as explained below.

In accordance with the framework, this study will analyze the translators' linguistic idiosyncrasies and thus functional styles by examining their renditions of figure labels, reconstructions of the original lexico-semantic patterns, and handling of discourse presentation in translation. Lexico-semantic patterns are included in the

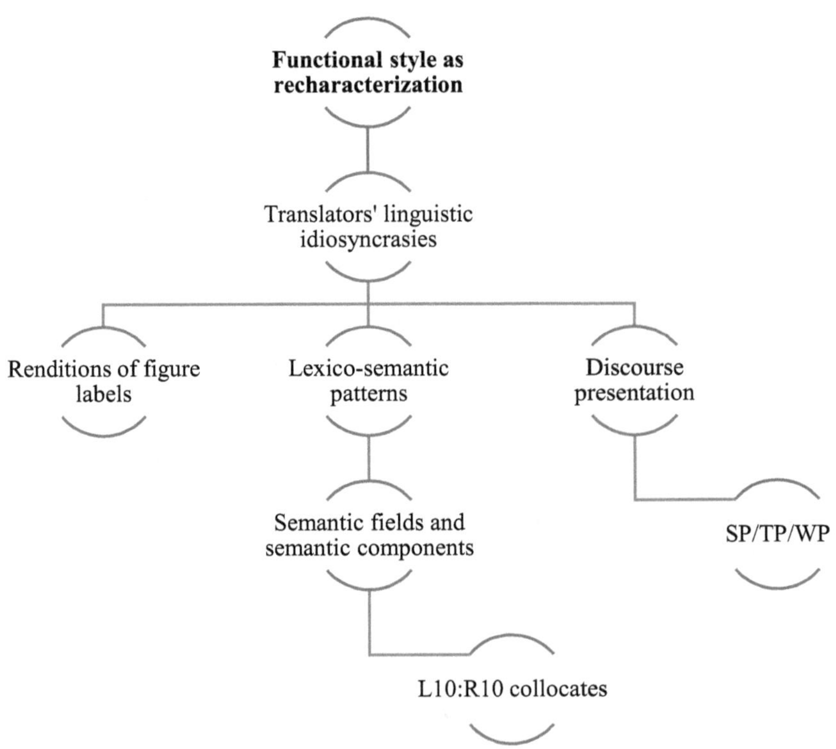

Fig. 9.1 Analytic framework for translators' functional styles as recharacterization

framework for the same reasons elaborated in Chapter 8 (Cf. 8.3). Discourse presentation is newly integrated into the framework because of its demonstrated potential in revealing translator style (Huang, 2015: 57–77). Furthermore, the study posits that discourse presentation is connected to the characterization in literary texts, as it is closely associated with story figures and plots, even though it does not strictly fall under the category of lexico-semantic patterns. In the following three sections from 9.3.1 to 9.3.3, the study will explore and compare the linguistic idiosyncrasies and functional styles of these translators based on this framework.

9.2.4 Renditions of Figure Labels

In line with the analytic framework outlined in Fig. 9.1, this section will examine how the translators render the labels of story figures as part of their effort to recharacterize these figures in translation.

Tables 9.5 and 9.6 summarize the translators' renditions of the labels for the Chinese and British figures in the story. These tables show a greater degree of diversity in the translations of Chinese figure labels compared to the translations of British figure labels. Firstly, as depicted in Table 9.5, the translations of Chinese figure labels exhibit a considerable degree of variation among the translators. They offer 11 distinct renditions for Mr. Ma (e.g., Old Ma, Old Mr. Ma, The Elder Ma) and four different renditions for Li Zirong (i.e., Li Tzu-rung, Lee Dze-rung, Li Zirong, Li). Secondly, as shown in Table 9.6, the translations of the British figure labels demonstrate a notable lack of diversity. The translators provide only 10 renditions (e.g., Catherine, Katherine, Miss Wendell) for the labels of the two British figures, with many of these renditions (e.g., Catherine/Katherine, Miss Evans/Miss Eden/ Miss Ely, Miss Wendell/Miss Winter/Miss Wedderburn) appearing to be influenced by the translators' personal preferences (see Chapter 11 for explanation).

Therefore, analyzing the renditions of the labels for the Chinese figures is more effective in capturing the translators' linguistic idiosyncrasies and functional styles in recharacterizing these story figures. The following analysis will focus specifically

Table 9.5 Renditions of the labels for Chinese figures

Item	James	Huang & Finkelstein	Jimmerson	Dolby
李子榮	Li Tzu-jung / Li	Lee Dze-rung	Li Zirong / Li	Li Tzu-jung / Li
老馬	Old Ma	Old Ma	Old Ma	Old Ma
馬老先生		Old Mr. Ma / Mr. Ma Senior	The Elder Ma	The Elder Ma
馬先生	Mr. Ma	Mr. Ma	Mr. Ma	Mr. Ma
馬則仁	Ma Tse-jen	Ma Dze-ren	Ma Zeren	Ma Tse-jen
				Ma old chap/lad/mate

Table 9.6 Renditions of the labels for British figures

Item	James	Huang & Finkelstein	Jimmerson	Dolby
凱薩林	Catherine/Kate	Katherine/Kate	Katherine/Kate	Catherine
伊姑娘	Miss Evans	Miss Eden	Miss Evans	Miss Ely
瑪力	Mary	Mary	Mary	Mary
溫都姑娘	Miss Wendell	Miss Winter	Miss Wendell	Miss Wedderburn

on the translators' renditions of these Chinese figure labels, which reveal several noteworthy patterns.

Firstly, Jimmerson (1991) predominantly employs Mandarin phonetic transcription for the renditions of the labels, whereas other translators utilize either Wade-Giles romanization (e.g., Li Tzu-jung) or the Yale Spelling System (e.g., Lee Dze-rung).[4] Secondly, James (1980) tends to simplify or omit the translation of Mr. Ma's four labels, retaining only "Mr. Ma", "Old Ma", and "Ma Tse-jen". In contrast, Dolby (2013) and Huang & Finkelstein (1984) present more intricate renditions of these labels by offering additional equivalents. Thirdly, Dolby's renditions show some integration of the other translators' work: her translation of "李子榮" aligns with James' rendition, while her renditions of Mr. Ma's four labels bear similarity to those by Huang & Finkelstein and Jimmerson. Various factors might have contributed to these patterns, including translation motivations, personal preferences, and post-translational influence, which will be discussed in more detail in Chapter 11.

9.2.5 Reconstructions of the Original Semantic Fields

This section delves into the translators' linguistic idiosyncrasies and functional styles by examining how they restructure the original semantic fields. The reconstructed semantic field, including its various semantic components, is another facet of the lexico-semantic patterns (see Fig. 9.1) these translators use to recharacterize the story figures. We will explore how the Chinese figures (Sect. 9.3.2.1) and the British figures (Sect. 9.3.2.2) are recharacterized by these translators, aligning with the analyses conducted in Sect. 9.2.1.1 and Sect. 9.2.2.1. To ensure comparability, we will continue to employ the same strategy used in Chapter 8. This strategy prioritizes the examination of specific details (e.g., figure labels) that effectively capture the translators' linguistic idiosyncrasies, rather than attempting to cover all details.

[4] Results based on http://pank.org/pinyin/, a platform for converting different Chinese phonetic systems.

Table 9.7 Semantic fields shared by the figure label attached to "李子榮" in translation (Huang & Finkelstein)

Semantic Fields (Li)	Collocates (L10:R10)
Dash, Diligence, Workaholism	hurriedly, rushed (5), busy, exuberant, strenuous, eagerly, vigorously (2), feverishly, forcibly (2), forcefully (2), zealot, passionate, passionately, efforts, undertook, work (3), studied (2), progress
Resourcefulness and Confidence	figure, decided (2), idea, suggestions, suggest, suggested (3), advised (3), advice, exhorted, observed, thinking (2), thinker, argued (3), managed, arrangement, intentionally, pretend, self-confident, pride, valor, carefully
Practicality and Utility	frankly, blunt (2), cook, sew, old, broken
Attached Negativity	vulgar (4), shameless, absurd, dishonesty, devil, exasperated, agitated

Table 9.8 Semantic fields shared by the figure label attached to "李子榮" in translation (James)

Semantic Fields (Li)	Collocates (L10:R10)
Dash, Diligence, Workaholism	hurried (3), hurrying, hastened, rapidly, busy, tired, frantically, crazy, vigor, ardent, hard (3), work (2), blather
Resourcefulness and Confidence	plan (2), decision, decisive, idea(s) (3), propose, thoughtful, pretend, clever, useful, confidence (2), self-confident, fearless (2), straightened, smugly, proudly, snorted, hero (3), risk
Practicality and Utility	straightforward, straightforwardly, frank, cook, sew, broken (2), old (2)
Attached Negativity	vulgar (5), dirty, damned, detestable, rascal, devil

9.2.5.1 Reconstruction Based on Chinese Figures

Preliminary findings indicate that the translators have largely retained the original seven semantic fields and their associated local textual functions present in the source text (ST) (Cf. 9.2.1.2). However, they exhibit linguistic idiosyncrasies in their selection of L10:R10 collocates for the translated labels (keywords) of the figures. This is particularly evident in the case of "李子榮", where the translators employ different collocates to accompany the translated labels in their target texts (TTs). Consequently, the semantic components, which are subcategories within each of the four semantic fields related to "李子榮" (Tables 9.7, 9.8, 9.9 and 9.10[5]), vary between the TTs and differ from the ST. These TT-TT variations and ST-TT shifts are believed to partially alter the characterization of the man (李子榮) in the TTs. Our preliminary study also reveals that variations and shifts in the case of "Mr. Ma" are less significant in altering such characterization, thus providing limited insight into the translators' functional styles. Therefore, our subsequent investigations will focus exclusively on "李子榮", excluding "Mr. Ma", and will employ both quantitative and qualitative approaches.

[5] Each semantic component in the tables is highlighted with a color, aligning with the colors assigned to these components as indicated in Table 9.2.

Table 9.9 Semantic fields shared by the figure label attached to "李子榮" in translation (Dolby)

Semantic Fields (Li)	Collocates (L10:R10)
Dash, Diligence, Workaholism	hurried (2), dashed, hastily (2), rolled-up (2), enthusiastic, volunteered, resolved, studying (3), work (2), working, tried, help (3), packing (2), wrapped (2), wrapping (3), cleaning (2), cleared, tidying (2), soiled, business (5)
Resourcefulness and Confidence	suggested, suggesting, suggestions, advised, proposed, pretended, deliberately, witty, able, self-confident, resolutions, gutsy, godsend
Practicality and Utility	down-to-earth (2), bluntly, shouldn't (2), cooking, sewing, shabby (2), battered, commerce
Attached Negativity	vulgar (2), ill-bred, obnoxious, brazen, shameless, ludicrous, dumbly, devil (2)

Table 9.10 Semantic fields shared by the figure label attached to "李子榮" in translation (Jimmerson)

Semantic Fields (Li)	Collocates (L10:R10)
Dash, Diligence, Workaholism	ran (4), rushed (2), racing, busy, rolled-up, madmen, animated (2), volunteered, wrapping (3), packing, worked, clean, study, studies, progress
Resourcefulness and Confidence	capable, suggestions, suggested, advice, idea(s) (4), figure, plan (3), lecture, lecturing, reasoning, pretended, intentionally, wit, educated, self-assured, proud, hero, business (7)
Practicality and Utility	straightforward, candid (2), blunt, cook, sew, broken-down (2), lasted, tattered, modern
Attached Negativity	vulgar, unrefined, uncouth, looney, shameless, mean, poor, devil (2)

Quantitatively, the alterations in characterization can be demonstrated through the overall proportional deviation of the semantic components[6] across the four semantic fields related to "李子榮". This deviation reflects the extent of changes made. The deviation is scored and ranked accordingly,[7] while the semantic components, their labels, and proportions within the semantic fields are presented in Fig. 9.2. The analysis results show that, of all these translators, Huang and Finkelstein make the most significant changes (the deviation score[8] is 1.45) in the overall proportions of different semantic components across the four semantic fields. The most notable deviation occurs in the semantic component "Idea" within the semantic field of *Resourcefulness and Confidence*, where Huang and Finkelstein substantially increase the component ratio from 33.33% in the ST to 72.41% in their TT (Fig. 9.2). This deviation level of 39.08% is considerably higher than the maximum deviation observed in the same component in the TTs of other translators (maximum of 14.95% by Jimmerson). In contrast, Jimmerson appears to make the least effort in altering the proportions of these semantic components across the fields, with a deviation score of 1.03. This is

[6] The details are available at dx.doi.org/10.6084/m9.figshare.29572907.

[7] The details are available at dx.doi.org/10.6084/m9.figshare.29572907.

[8] The calculation method and process are available at dx.doi.org/10.6084/m9.figshare.29572907.

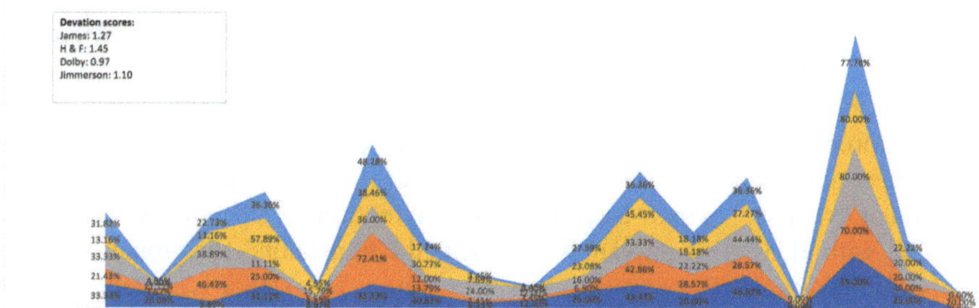

	Dash	Hecticness	Vigor	Work & Study	Others	Idea	Cleverness	Confidence	Arrogance	Others	Straightforwardness	Maritial Utility	Personal Utility	Others	Impressions	Representations	Mood
	Dash, Diligence, Workaholism					Resourcefulness and Confidence					Practicality and Utility				General Negativity		
Jimmerson	31.82%	4.55%	22.73%	36.36%	4.55%	48.28%	17.24%	3.45%	3.45%	27.59%	36.36%	18.18%	36.36%	9.09%	77.78%	22.22%	0.00%
Dolby	13.16%	0.00%	13.16%	57.89%	15.79%	38.46%	30.77%	7.69%	0.00%	23.08%	45.45%	18.18%	27.27%	9.09%	80.00%	20.00%	0.00%
James	33.33%	11.11%	38.89%	11.11%	5.56%	36.00%	12.00%	24.00%	12.00%	16.00%	33.33%	22.22%	44.44%	0.00%	80.00%	20.00%	0.00%
H & F	21.43%	3.57%	46.43%	25.00%	3.57%	72.41%	13.79%	3.45%	3.45%	6.90%	42.86%	28.57%	28.57%	0.00%	70.00%	10.00%	20.00%
ST	33.33%	20.00%	8.89%	31.11%	6.67%	33.33%	20.83%	8.33%	12.50%	25.00%	33.33%	20.00%	46.67%	0.00%	75.00%	25.00%	0.00%

Fig. 9.2 Semantic components and their proportions in the semantic fields ("李子榮")

particularly evident in the component of "Hecticness" within the field of *Dash, Diligence, Workaholism*, where Jimmerson reduces the component ratio from 20.00% in the ST to 4.55% in her TT.

Dolby and James, on the other hand, exhibit deviational levels of different semantic components that fall between those of Huang & Finkelstein and Jimmerson, with deviation scores of 1.63 and 1.11, respectively. Dolby's significant deviations are evident in the "Work and Study" component within the field of *Dash, Diligence, Workaholism.* She increases the ratio of "Work & Study" from 31.11% in the ST to 57.89% in her TT, while completely eliminating the proportion of "Hecticness" (20.00% in the ST) from her translation. Similarly, James' deviations are noteworthy in the "Vigor" component within *Dash, Diligence, Workaholism*, as she raises the proportion from 8.89% in the ST to 38.89% in her TT.

The quantitative results reveal the divergence among these translators as they recharacterize "李子榮" in target texts, thereby shedding light on their linguistic idiosyncrasies and functional styles through the recharacterization. To gain deeper insights into these linguistic idiosyncrasies and functional styles across the translators, qualitative evidence will be presented through bilingual contextual examples. Consider the following examples:

(25) **[ST]** 好, 你去吃飯吧, 替我謝謝馬老先生!多吃點呀!" 李子榮笑起來了。
[H & F] Alright, time for you to go and eat. Thank Mr. Ma senior for me. Eat hearty". <u>*exhorted*</u> Lee Dze-rung, beginning to chuckle.
[James] All right, you go have lunch and give my thanks to your father. Eat lots!" Li began to laugh.
[Jimmerson] I'll let you go to dinner, please give my thanks to your father, and by the way —make sure you eat up!" Li chuckled.
[Dolby] Off you go and have your meal, and give Mr. Ma my thanks. And eat a bit more now!' Li Tzu-jung started laughing.

Example (25) illustrates the linguistic idiosyncrasy of Huang & Finkelstein, wherein they enhance the "Idea" component within the field of *Resourcefulness and Confidence* by introducing the term "exhorted" into their translation. This choice of "exhorted" is exclusive to their translation and is not found in the source text or the other three translations. This unique usage of "exhorted" partly contributes to their highest deviation score. Consequently, this exclusive choice alters the characterization of "李子榮" in their translation, portraying him as a persuasive individual brimming with ideas. This alteration highlights the translators' functional style and reveals their favorable stance towards this story figure. This stance is evident not only through the proportional increase of the "Idea" component, but also through a similar increase in the "Vigor" component in the semantic field of *Dash, Diligence, Workaholism.* Additionally, this stance involves the replacement of certain negative words (e.g., "神經病") in the source text with more neutral words (e.g., "exasperated" and "agitated") in the semantic field of *Attached Negativity* in the translation.

(26) **[ST]**李子榮向來是什麼事<u>不怕</u>, 今天可有點退縮, 臉上通紅, 不知道怎樣才好。

[James] Formerly <u>*fearless*</u>, Li was a little hesitant. His entire face was red and he didn't know what to do.

[H & F] Lee Dze-rung had <u>*never*</u> before been <u>*intimidated*</u> by anything, but on that day for the first time he felt a little apprehensive.

[Jimmerson] Li had <u>*never*</u> been <u>*afraid*</u> of anything, but today he seemed to cower a bit; he kept blushing and wondering what to do.

[Dolby] Li Tzu-jung was <u>*never*</u> at a <u>*loss*</u> for words, but today he seemed timid and bashful, and his face was bright red.

Example (26) demonstrates how James emphasizes the "Confidence" component in the field of *Resourcefulness and Confidence* through her use of the collocate "fearless". This choice differs from the other translators, who use quasi-equivalents like "never…intimidated", "never…afraid", and "never…loss". James' direct portrayal of self-confidence in the man (李子榮) solidifies the representation of the figure's self-assurance in the translation, leaving readers with a more personified and positive impression of the man. This direct depiction highlights James' linguistic idiosyncrasy and functional style in recharacterizing the story figure.

(27) **[ST]** "不容易? 天下沒有容易的事!" 李子榮咚的一聲站起來, 頗有點<u>自傲的神氣</u>。

[James] "Not easy? There's nothing easy anywhere on earth!" Li snorted rather <u>*proudly*</u> as he stood up.

[H & F] "Not easy? Nothing in this world is easy", Lee Dze-rung emphasized with a thump as he stood up, exuding a great sense of <u>*pride*</u> in himself.

[Jimmerson] "Easy? Nothing on this earth is easy!" Li Zirong got up with a forceful thud, looking quite <u>*proud.*</u>

[Dolby] 'Not easy? Nothing comes easy in this world.' Li Tzu-jung plonked his feet heavily as he stood up, wearing a decided look of <u>*self-satisfaction.*</u>

Example (27) illustrates Dolby's linguistic idiosyncrasy through the omission of the "Arrogant" component within the semantic field of *Resourcefulness and Confidence.* While other translators use words such as "proudly", "pride", or "proud" to translate "自傲的神氣" in the ST, Dolby opts for the term "self-satisfaction". This choice by Dolby effectively diminishes the arrogance associated with 李子榮, partially altering the characterization of the story figure in the TT, and thus highlighting his functional style. Such idiosyncrasy may also influence the interpretation of target readers, who are more likely to develop a favorable impression of 李子榮 due to the replacement of negative "Arrogant" components with milder descriptions like "self-satisfaction" in this example.

(28) **[ST]** 貨物在聖誕前一個月到了倫敦,他和李子榮拼命的幹: 點綴門面, 定價碼, 印說明書……

[James] The goods had arrived in November. He and Li *worked as hard* as they could, deciding on prices, getting a catalog printed and decorating the door.

[H & F] The merchandise arrived in London a month before Christmas. He and Lee Dze-rung *worked feverishly* to decorate the window, put price tags on the goods, print explanatory notes . . .

[Jimmerson] When the Christmas stock arrived in London in November, he and Li Zirong *worked like madmen*, decorating the display windows, pricing the new goods, printing up brochures ...

[Dolby] The goods that Wang Ming-ch'uan had obtained for them reached London just before Christmas, and he and Li Tzu-jung set to *work with a vengeance*, decorating the shopfront, pricing things, printing the catalogue . . .

Example (28) illustrates how Jimmerson intensifies the "Vigor" component in the field of *Dash, Diligence, Workaholism* through her use of the collocate "madmen". This unique usage distinguishes her from the other translators and the ST author. "Madmen" in her TT seems to invigorate "李子榮", who is always devoted to his work in the curio shop. In contrast, such vigor and workaholism of the man are presented with the verb "幹" in the ST and re-represented with adverbs or phrases like "hard", "feverishly", and "with a vengeance" in the other three TTs. This linguistic idiosyncrasy of Jimmerson highlights her functional style in this particular example.

9.2.5.2 Reconstruction Based on British Figures

The results in this subsection, similar to those in the previous subsection (Sect. 9.3.2.1), demonstrate a consistent trend among the translators. They maintain all the original fields of the labels, preserving the local textual functions enacted in the source text (ST) within their target texts (TTs). However, the variation in the number of L10:R10 collocates, each carrying distinct pragmatic implications, in their reconstructions of the original semantic fields can potentially change the patterns of the original semantic components within these field. This highlights the linguistic

Table 9.11 Semantic fields shared by the figure label attached to Mary in translation (James)

Semantic Fields	Collocates (L10:R10)
Sentiments	cry, snuffled, trembling, trembled (2), tears (3), tearful, hysterically, wildly, flushed (2), frightened, grinned (2), grinning, laughed (4), giggled, happy (2), happier
Shallowness	newspaper(s) (2), film(s) (2), fiction, proud
Prejudice	refused, Chinamen, Chinaman, poison (3), murder, ravish, warning

Table 9.12 Semantic fields shared by the figure label attached to Mary in translation (Huang & Finkelstein)

Semantic Fields	Collocates (L10:R10)
Sentiments	cry, sobbed, sobbing, crying, trembled, trembling, teardrops, tears (2), flushed (2), disappointment, heartbroken, uneasiness, laugh, laughter, laughing, giggling, grin, sneered (2), unhappy, happy, cheerful
Shallowness	movie (2), novels, newspaper, proud, spoiled
Prejudice	unwilling, Chinaman, poison (2), revulsion, scum, warned

Table 9.13 Semantic fields shared by the figure label attached to Mary in translation (Jimmerson)

Semantic Fields	Collocates (L10:R10)
Sentiments	cry, sobbed, trembling, trembled, snorted, moist, tears (3), flushed (3), hysterical, hysterically, disappointment, irritated, tizzy, vexed, sniggered, grinned, laugh, laughter, happy
Shallowness	fiction, dream, pampered, proud, facetious, styles, wildcat
Prejudice	Chinamen, poison, murdering, abducting

idiosyncrasies and functional styles of these translators during the recharacterization process.

Such idiosyncrasies and styles are especially clear in the translation of the two labels related to Mary, one of the two British story figures explored in Sect. 9.2. Results show that there are notable shifts between the ST and the TTs in the semantic components under the three semantic fields (Tables 9.11, 9.12, 9.13 and 9.14[9]) created by the two labels of Mary. In contrast, similar shifts are less pronounced in the case of Catherine (with the two labels "凱薩林" and "伊姑娘")—the other British story figure discussed in Sect. 9.2. With the primary objective of tracing the translators' linguistic idiosyncrasies and functional styles, our focus will solely be on the two labels related to Mary, as the shifts in semantic components are more likely to show these idiosyncrasies and styles. As with the analysis in the previous subsection, the exploration of these translators' linguistic idiosyncrasies and functional styles in the present chapter will be approached from both quantitative and qualitative perspectives.

[9] Each semantic component in the tables is highlighted with a color, aligning with the colors assigned to these components as indicated in Table 9.4.

Table 9.14 Semantic fields shared by the figure label attached to Mary in translation (Dolby)

Semantic Fields	Collocates (L10:R10)
Sentiments	trembled, wail, cry, sobbed, tears (3), teardrops, wetly, red, flushed, hysterically, manic, grief, disappointment, startled, resentful, laughter, laughing, giggles, giggled, happiness, happy (2), jolly
Shallowness	film (s) (3), novels (2), plays, books, newspaper (3), proud (2), romantic
Prejudice	Chinamen, poison (2), cringing, bad, murderers, arsonists, rapists

Quantitatively, these linguistic idiosyncrasies (functional styles) are partially reflected in the overall proportional deviations (Fig. 9.3[10]) of the semantic components[11] within the three semantic fields. The calculation method aligns with the one used in the previous subsection, ensuring a consistent and comparable analysis. The results indicate that the greatest deviation is observed in Jimmerson's TT, with a deviation score of 2.39, while the weakest deviation is found in Huang and Finkelstein's TT, scoring 1.17. For Jimmerson, the most significant contributing factor to this deviation lies in the "Stereotyping" component of *Prejudice.* Jimmerson increases the proportion of this semantic component from the original 46.15% to 100% (a ratio of 53.85%), eliminating the other components within the original semantic field. Even the "Inner feeling" component under *Sentiments*, which has the smallest contribution to the deviation, exhibits a proportional increase of 2.39% (from 15% to 17.39%) in her TT, a moderate increase compared to the other translators' TTs. In Huang & Finkelstein's TT, the "Stereotyping" component under *Prejudice* also contributes the most to the overall proportional deviation, with an increase ratio of 25.27%, elevating it from the original 46.15% to 71.42% in the TT. Conversely, the "Body language" component under *Sentiments* does not contribute to the same deviation.

The overall proportional deviations in James' TT and Dolby's TT fall between those of Jimmerson's TT and Huang & Finkelstein's TT. In James' case, the component that contributes the most to the deviation is still "Stereotyping" under *Prejudice*, with an increase ratio of 31.62% (from the original 46.15–77.77%). On the other hand, the smallest contributing components in James' case are "Facial express" and "Happiness", both with an increase ratio of 2% (from 30 to 32% and from 10 to 12%, respectively). In Dolby's case, "Stereotyping" under *Prejudice* once again emerges as the component with the greatest contribution to the overall proportional deviation, with an increase ratio of 53.85%. Conversely, "Inner feeling" under *Sentiments* exhibits the smallest contribution, with a limited ratio of 1%. Between the two translators, the overall proportional deviation in Dolby's TT is higher than that in James' TT, as indicated by their deviation scores of 1.77 and 1.38, respectively.

A noteworthy pattern emerges when comparing the quantitative findings presented above with those from the previous subsection (Sect. 9.3.2.1). Huang and Finkelstein exert the greatest effort in altering the overall proportions of semantic components across different fields as they recharacterize the Chinese figures. However, their level

[10] The detailed calculations are available at 4e dx.doi.org/10.6084/m9.figshare.29572907.

[11] The details of these proportions are available at dx.doi.org/10.6084/m9.figshare.29572907.

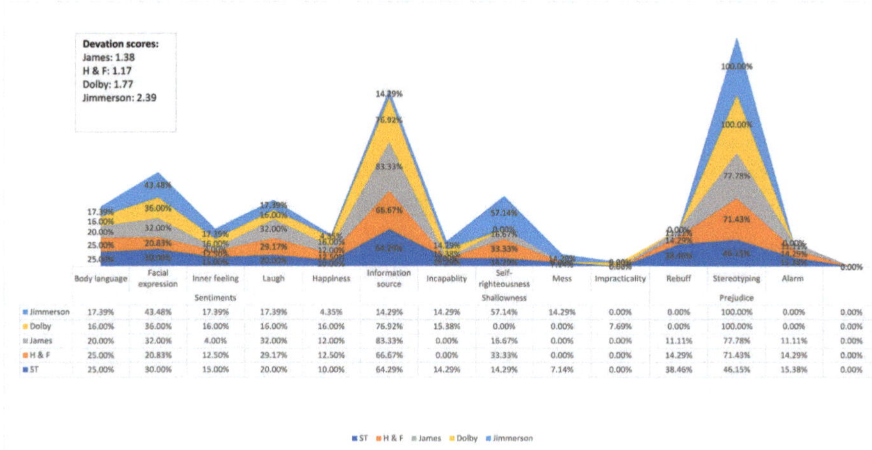

	Body language	Facial expression	Inner feeling	Laugh	Happiness	Information source	Incapablity	Self-righteousness	Mess	Impracticality	Rebuff	Stereotyping	Alarm	
			Sentiments					Shallowness				Prejudice		
Jimmerson	17.39%	43.48%	17.39%	17.39%	4.35%	14.29%	14.29%	57.14%	14.29%	0.00%	0.00%	100.00%	0.00%	0.00%
Dolby	16.00%	36.00%	16.00%	16.00%	16.00%	76.92%	15.38%	0.00%	0.00%	7.69%	0.00%	100.00%	0.00%	0.00%
James	20.00%	32.00%	4.00%	32.00%	12.00%	83.33%	0.00%	16.67%	0.00%	0.00%	11.11%	77.78%	11.11%	0.00%
H & F	25.00%	20.83%	12.50%	29.17%	12.50%	66.67%	0.00%	33.33%	0.00%	0.00%	14.29%	71.43%	14.29%	0.00%
ST	25.00%	30.00%	15.00%	20.00%	10.00%	64.29%	14.29%	14.29%	7.14%	0.00%	38.46%	46.15%	15.38%	0.00%

Fig. 9.3 Semantic components and their proportions in the semantic fields ("Mary")

of effort decreases significantly when recharacterizing the British figures. Conversely, Jimmerson demonstrates minimal effort in shifting these proportions when recharacterizing the Chinese figures, but exerts maximum effort when recharacterizing the British figures. On the other hand, James and Dolby consistently invest similar efforts in such shifts across both the Chinese and British story figures. The potential factors contributing to this pattern are diverse and will be discussed in Chapter 11. For now, we will employ the same method as in the previous subsection, focusing solely on examining the potential effects these shifts and deviations may have on the perception of the British figure "Mary" by target readers.

A more qualitative perspective is taken to study the effects of these shifts/deviations, with some ST-TT examples cited as contextual evidence to trace how these shifts/deviations highlight these translators' linguistic idiosyncrasies and functional styles. Consider the following examples:

(29) **[ST]** "哈哈! 哈哈!" 瑪力還是<u>怪笑</u>, 臉上通紅, 笑了幾聲, 把頭伏在鋼琴上哭起來。
[James] Mary <u>*laughed hysterically*</u> her face turning red. After the outburst she leaned her head on the piano and wept.
[H & F] "Haha, haha", Mary went on, her face entirely flushed as she continued <u>*laughing in that queer way*</u>. But after a few such outbursts she rested her head against the piano and broke out sobbing.
[Jimmerson] "Hah hah, Hah hah!" Mary <u>*rattled on hysterically*</u>, and put her head on the piano top and started weeping.
[Dolby] 'Ha ha! Ha ha!' Mary was still <u>*laughing hysterically*</u>, and her face was bright red. Then, after a few more laughs, she laid her head on the piano and began to cry.

Example (29) shows how Huang and Finkelstein demonstrate their linguistic idiosyncrasies and functional styles through a distinct portrayal of Mary's laughter compared to the other translators. They opt for a literal rendering of the collocate "怪笑" (underlined and italicized) as "laughing in that queer way", deviating pragmatically from the original description of Mary's sudden emotional outburst. Consequently, this seemingly faithful and intervention-free recharacterization of the figure, despite partly attesting the lowest deviation score of their TT, may produce a veered perceptive effect on the target readers. These readers are prone to associate this "queer way" with "unnaturalness", instead of an uncontrolled emotional outbreak. Contrarily, the rest three translators turn away from the literal way by rendering "怪笑" unanimously as laugh/rattle "hysterically". Since "hysterically" connotes an uncontrolled emotion according to the *Cambridge Dictionary*[12] online (hereafter as the Dictionary), the translators using this collocate to recharacterize Mary could give their target readers a reading experience similar to that of the original. Finally, it is noteworthy that even a minimal quantitative deviation from the original text, as observed in Huang and Finkelstein's rendition in this example, can still result in a significant contextual shift on a qualitative level, subsequently generating a distinct effect on target readers.

(30) **[ST]** "要男人的時候, 找男人去好了, 咱們逃不出天然律的管轄!" 瑪力說得有點嘲弄的意思,心裡並不信這個。

[James] "When I want a man, it'll be time enough to go look for one. We can't escape the domination of natural law". Mary's words were *meant to be funny*; she certainly did not believe them.

[H & F] "At times when I need a man, I can always get one. We can't escape from the laws of nature, can we?" Mary taunted her mother with a little *sarcasm*, though she herself would never have done what she was suggesting.

[Jimmerson] "I could just seek male company when the fancy struck me, after all—we can't ignore the laws of human nature!" Mary didn't really believe this herself but was *being facetious*.

[Dolby] 'Or when a man's needed, I'll just go and find one. Can't escape the laws of nature, can we?' Mary spoke *sarcastically*.

Example (30) demonstrates a part of Jimmerson's linguistic idiosyncrasies (functional styles) and their potential interpretational effects on target readers. The original collocate "有點嘲弄" (underlined and italicized) in the ST line conveys Mary's "sarcastic/cynical" stance towards the male–female relationship. Jimmerson renders this collocate as "being facetious", a term that means "not serious about a serious subject" based on the Dictionary. This apparently undertones original "sarcastic/cynical" stance taken by Mary, which is tinted with a touch of "hurtful" humor. In contrast, both Huang & Finkelstein and Dolby render the same collocate as "sarcasm/sarcastically" and James "meant to be funny". The Dictionary suggests that "sarcasm/sarcastically" and "meant to be funny" share certain semantic similarity with a comparable focus on being "humorous". This means that these renditions align with

[12] https://dictionary.cambridge.org/dictionary/english/

each other and differ from Jimmerson's translation. For target readers, Jimmerson's use of "facetious" is likely to elicit a different perception of Mary compared to the translations by the other translators. In Jimmerson's translation, readers may interpret Mary as displaying a *nonchalant* attitude towards the male–female relationship due to her disbelief. On the other hand, in the original text and the translations by the other translators, readers may perceive Mary as humorously *disregarding* the relationship because of the same disbelief. Furthermore, this example partially explains the highest deviation score observed in Jimmerson's translation.

(31) **[ST]** 如今溫都姑娘的愛的理想和經驗，與這種小說式的一點也不同了……
[James] Miss Wendell's experiences and ideals *of love* were not the least little bit like those in fiction.
[H & F] But Miss Winter lived in contemporary times and her ideals and experiences *regarding love* were totally different from this stuff of novels.
[Jimmerson] But her daughter's *love* experiences and dreams were a far cry from this kind of gothic fiction
[Dolby] Miss Wedderburn's *romantic* ideals and experiences had nothing in common with such literary notions.

Example (31) illustrates Dolby's linguistic idiosyncrasies (functional styles) and their potential interpretational effects on target readers. The ST line discussed in this example involves a narrator's comment on Mary's ideals and experiences of romantic love, conveyed through the collocate "愛的" (underlined and italicized). While Dolby translates this collocate as "romantic", the other translators render it simply as "love". This indicates that all translators deviate from the original collocate in a pragmatic sense. According to the Dictionary, both "love" and "romantic" are broad concepts. The term "love" covers a range of relationships, including romantic love and fraternal love, while the term "romantic" can refer to loving relationships as well as the notion of impracticality. In this example, despite the translators' attempts to pragmatically reproduce the original collocate, Dolby's choice of "romantic" carries a broader implication compared to the other translators' use of "love". As explained, "romantic" may semantically suggest something outside "loving relationships", but "love" is less potent in this regard. Therefore, this diversity distinguishes Dolby from the other translators, because her rendition could potentially lead to a different perception of Mary among target readers. Under Dolby's translation, Mary's ideals and experiences may be seen as "impractical" in relation to romantic love. However, under the translations by the other translators, such an impression is less likely to be developed.

(32) **[ST]** 瑪力才接著說:"媽, 不用護著中國人, 他們要是不討人嫌為什麼電影上, 戲裡, 小說上的中國人老是些殺人放火搶女人的呢?" 瑪力姑娘的……
[James] Mary added, "Mother, there's no point protecting Chinamen. If they didn't arouse suspicion, would the Chinamen in films, plays, and stories always be the ones who murder, set fires, and *ravish women*?" Mary had picked up...
[H & F] "Ma, you don't have to be an apologist for the Chinese. If they didn't deserve the contempt they get, they wouldn't be characterized as they always

are, in plays and movies and novels, murdering, pillaging, and *kidnapping women*". Her understanding of ...
[Jimmerson] ...she continues: "Mum, you shouldn't stick up for Chinese so—if they really weren't so awful then why would the novels and movies always have them murdering, setting fire to things, or *abducting women*?" Young Mary's ideas on...
[Dolby] ... she continued. 'It's no good you sticking up for the Chinese, Mum. If they weren't so horrible, why would all the Chinese in films and plays and books be murderers or arsonists or *rapists*?' Miss Mary's ...

Example (32) highlights a part of James' linguistic idiosyncrasies (functional styles) and their potential effects on the target readership through her translation of the original collocate "搶女人" (underlined and italicized). The ST line portrays Mary's stereotyping of the Chinese as criminals, with the collocate "搶女人" serving as a Chinese euphemism alluding to sexual assault on women. In James' translation, this collocate is rendered as "ravish women", which, according to the Dictionary, carries an old/literary euphemistic usage suggesting "forcing a woman to have sex against her will". On the other hand, Jimmerson and Huang & Finkelstein translate the collocate literally as either "abducting women" or "kidnapping women", thereby losing the original sexual implication. Dolby's translation, however, presents the collocate simply as "rapists"—a straightforward rendition that lacks the original euphemistic tone. As a result, James' translation sets her apart from the other translators, as it pragmatically and rhetorically aligns closely with the original. Consequently, the interpretational effects of these translations on the target readership may vary. James and Dolby have successfully conveyed the original connotation of sexual assault on women to their target readers through translation, whereas such connotation is toned down in the translations by Jimmerson and Huang & Finkelstein.

9.2.6 Reconstructions of the Original Discourse Presentation

According to Leech and Short (2007: 2), different types of discourse presentation, such as speech, thought, and writing presentation, encompass a "handful of interesting features" capable of encapsulating a writer's style. In translation, a translator's style is similarly represented by similar features in target text (TT) discourse presentation. Translating Chinese narrative fiction like *Er Ma* into English can be challenging due to an apparent mismatch of tense and person markers between the two languages (Huang, 2015: 64). Moreover, the inherent ambiguity of discourse presentation in Chinese (Shen, 1991: 76–77) further complicates the translation of Chinese fiction into English. Consequently, it is the translator's responsibility to select the appropriate tense and person when translating a Chinese novel into English. This decision-making process reveals the translator's linguistic idiosyncrasies and, therefore, functional styles.

Based on the analytic framework (Fig. 9.1) presented and the reasons explained in Sect. 9.3, the study explores these linguistic idiosyncrasies through the ways these translators recreate the original ambiguous discourse presentation. The following section will first present the choices made by different translators and then focus on some bilingual examples for further explanations. The analysis will primarily concentrate on the discourse presentation of the British story figures. This is because the findings indicate that there are more British figures involved in the story conversation compared to the Chinese figures. Therefore, focusing on the British figures enables a more effective examination of the translators' linguistic idiosyncrasies and functional styles as they recharacterize story figures in translation.

To gain an overall picture of these translators' choices of person and tense, the first step is to locate the ambiguous discourse presentation in the source text (ST). This is operationalized by searching for colons throughout the ST—a method that has been successfully applied in Huang (2014) and Huang (2015). Once the instances of discourse presentation related to the British story figures are identified, the study will categorize them according to the presentation types outlined in Huang (2015), Leech and Short (2007), and Semino and Short (2004), recording the numbers of instances of each type. As for the TTs, the study will locate the English translations of those ambiguous discourses, with extra attention paid to the translators' choices of persons and tenses. The results are reported in Tables 9.15 and 9.16.

Table 9.15 and 9.16 show that writing presentation/thought presentation (WP/TP) and speech presentation/thought presentation (SP/TP) are the two major types of ambiguous discourse presentation used in *Er Ma*, with a total of 173 instances. Specifically, WP/TP accounts for 89 instances, with 53 linked to the Chinese figures and 36 to the British figures. Conversely, SP/TP comprises 84 instances, with 71 related to the Chinese figures and 13 to the British figures. Regarding the use of person in the target texts (TTs), the total instances of the first person (I) employed to render the ST discourse presentation in the four TTs are 56, 72, 76, and 50, respectively. The frequencies of the second person (II) used are 14, 8, 6, and 21,

Table 9.15 Use of person by the translators of *Er Ma*

Discourse type	Number of instances												
	ST	James			H & F			Jimmerson			Dolby		
		I	II	III	I	II	III	I	II	III	I	II	III
WP/TP (Chinese)	53	5	1	48	6	1	46	4	0	53	1	6	46
WP/TP (Britons)	36	5	1	34	2	1	34	7	1	33	3	1	34
SP/TP (Chinese)	71	39	9	18	52	5	9	54	4	14	40	11	27
SP/TP (Britons)	13	7	3	4	12	1	1	11	1	3	6	3	5
Total	173	56	14	104	72	8	90	76	6	103	50	21	112

Table 9.16 Use of tense by the translators of *Er Ma*

discourse type	Number of instances								
	ST	James		H & F		Jimmerson		Dolby	
		Present	Past	Present	Past	Present	Past	Present	Past
WP/TP (Chinese)	53	16	38	13	40	11	46	12	42
WP/TP (Britons)	36	14	26	6	31	14	27	6	32
SP/TP (Chinese)	71	57	10	57	9	60	12	54	25
SP/TP (Britons)	13	12	2	12	2	13	2	10	4
Total	173	99	76	88	82	98	87	82	103

respectively, while the third person (III) occurs 104, 90, 103, and 112 times in the respective translations. In terms of tense, the present tense is utilized 99, 89, 98, and 82 times in the four TTs, while the past tense occurs 76, 81, 87, and 103 times, respectively.

Regarding the use of person, these translators' linguistic idiosyncrasies vary. The first person is mostly frequently employed in Jimmerson's version, whereas it is the least preferred in Dolby's version. In contrast, the third person is the most widely used in Dolby's version, but the least favored in Huang and Finkelstein's version. The second person is employed less frequently by these translators, with Dolby using it more often than the others. These variations in person choice can lead to diverse interpretational effects on target readers: Jimmerson tends to immerse her readers directly into the minds of the story figures, whereas Dolby creates more distance between the readers and the story figures. Regarding the use of tense, James and Dolby exhibit contrasting preferences. James predominantly opts for the present tense when translating the original ambiguous discourse presentation, whereas Dolby consistently employs the past tense.

Moreover, the translators' choices to render the original ambiguous discourse presentation into WP, SP, or TP have introduced various discourse forms, such as free indirect thought (FIT), direct thought (DT), free indirect speech (FIS), and direct speech (DS), in their TTs. This discovery aligns with previous research on Lao She's narrative fiction (e.g., Huang, 2014, 2015) and suggests that these diverse choices may lead to distinct interpretational impacts on target readers, thereby resulting in varied narrative effects. The results of these translator choices are presented in Tables 9.17 and 9.18.

When translating the WP/TP into WP, the translators predominantly use the narrator's writing (NW), displaying a clear preference for the past tense over the present tense. This preference is notably consistent across these translators, with both the frequencies of the present tense (ranging from 8 to 14) and past tense (ranging from 42 to 53) demonstrating this pattern. Nevertheless, Jimmerson's version stands

Table 9.17 Translators' choices of discourse types in the translation of WP/TP

Discourse type	Translators	WP: Narrator's writing		TP: Thought presentation			
WP/TP		Present	Past	IT	FIT	DT	FDT
	James	14	51	0	19	0	10
	H & F	11	53	1	16	4	5
	Jimmerson	13	42	5	29	5	4
	Dolby	8	52	6	15	0	9

Table 9.18 Translators' choices of discourse types in the translation of SP/TP

Discourse type	Translators	SP: Speech presentation				TP: Thought presentation			
SP/TP		IS	FIS	DS	FDS	IT	FIT	DT	FDT
	James	3	2	2	34	4	11	3	20
	H & F	1	1	25	9	2	5	28	7
	Jimmerson	1	1	17	17	0	12	32	7
	Dolby	6	1	7	33	8	15	0	21

out with just 8 instances of the present tense and 42 instances of the past tense. In translating the same WP/TP into TP, there is a shared preference for FIT over other thought forms among these translators. FIT is employed consistently, with frequencies consistently above 10, while other thought forms are used either infrequently or not at all. This aligns with previous research by Semino and Short (2004) and Huang (2015), which identified FIT as the most frequently used thought form in the translation of narrative fiction. In *Er Ma*, these translators' preferences for the past tense and FIT when rendering the original WP/TP have a distancing effect on target readers' interpretation of the story figures. This is because FIT often lacks an apparent reporting structure, and it is predominantly associated with the third person in *Er Ma*.

In translating SP/TP into SP, the translators exhibit a preference for direct speech (DS) and free direct speech (FDS) over indirect speech (IS) and free indirect speech (FIS). Huang & Finkelstein, in particular, employs DS extensively with 25 instances, but uses FDS less frequently with only 9 instances. In contrast, James predominantly uses FDS with 34 instances, but includes only 2 instances of DS. This choice has implications for the proximity of the story figures to the target readers, with Huang & Finkelstein's choice of DS creating a closer addresser-addressee pattern compared to James' use of FDS. When translating SP/TP into WP, both Huang & Finkelstein and Jimmerson prefer direct thought (DT), with 28 and 32 instances, respectively. Conversely, James and Dolby favor free indirect thought (FDT), with 20 and 21 instances, respectively. This variation in narrative approach results in varying degrees of psychological distance between the target readers and the story figures. The use of DT by Huang & Finkelstein and Jimmerson tends to immerse the readers inside the characters' minds, while James and Dolby's preference for FDT presents these characters' thoughts more directly to the readers. There are fewer differences in these translators' translation of indirect thought (IT) and free indirect thought (FIT), although Jimmerson's complete absence of IT instances is noticeable. In the following, we will provide some bilingual examples related to the discourse presentation of British figures to illustrate how the translators render the original WP/TP and SP/TP.

(33) **[ST]** 一邊看一邊想: 等著, 慢慢的長薪水, 買那包紅盒子的皮糖, 買那件綠綢子繡邊兒的大衫。越看越愛看,越愛看越不愛走, 把回家那回事簡直的忘死了。***[SP/TP (Briton)]***

[James] Wait—by and by I'll get a raise and buy that box of candy and that embroidered green silk dress. The more she looked the more she enjoyed looking. The more she enjoyed looking the less she liked leaving. The little matter of going home was simply forgotten. ***[I][present][SP (Briton)][FDS]***

[H & F] "I'll wait", she thought as she browsed. "Eventually I'll get a raise and then I'll buy that red box of sweets and that green silk dress with the embroidered fringe". The more she saw, the more she wanted to see and the more she wanted to see, the less she wanted to leave; and she simply forgot entirely about going home. ***[I][present][TP (Briton)][DT]***

[Jimmerson] As she poured over the window displays, she would think to herself, "Just be patient and wait awhile, my salary will go up soon ... so that I can buy that red box of liquorice candies, and that green silk wrap". The longer she dallied, the more difficult it was to tear herself away, and in a matter of minutes it would completely slip her mind that she was supposed to return home. ***[I][present][TP (Briton)][DT]***

[Dolby] Just wait! she'd tell herself as she looked. Someday I'll get a pay rise, and then I'll buy that box of crystallised fruit, and that green satin gown with the embroidered hem. The more she looked, the more she enjoyed looking and felt disinclined to move on, and she would completely forget about getting home. ***[I][present][SP (Briton)][FDS]***

(34) **[ST]**問完了, 心裡又後悔了: 這麼問, 豈不是明明的表示已經有意把房租給他們嗎?***[WP/TP (Briton)]***

[James] When she'd asked all her questions, she felt some regret. Weren't all these questions a clear indication that she had already decided to rent the rooms to them? ***[III][past][WP (Briton)][NW]***

[H & F] but no sooner had she asked than she regretted having done so. For in raising these issues wasn't she indicating clearly that she intended to rent the rooms? ***[III][past][WP (Briton)][NW]***

[Jimmerson] After all her questions were answered she felt a tinge of regret: what with so many questions, wasn't she giving the impression of already being inclined to rent to them? ***[III][past][TP (Briton)][FIT]***

[Dolby] But when she'd exhausted all her questions, she suddenly regretted ever having asked them. Didn't her questions show quite clearly that she already intended letting the rooms to them? ***[III][past][WP (Briton)][NW]***

(35) **[ST]**溫都姑娘看著他, 笑了, 好像是說: "中國人, 挨打的貨!就不會生氣!" ***[SP/TP (Briton)]***

[James] Miss Wendell looked at him, smiled as if to say, "These Chinamen, these doormats! Of course, they never get angry!" ***[III][present][SP (Briton)][DS]***

[H & F] Eyeing him, Miss Winter smirked, as if to say: "Chinaman, scum of the earth born for beating, and he doesn't even know enough to be angry". ***[III][preset][SP (Briton)][DS]***

[Jimmerson] Miss Wendell looked at him and smiled as if to say, "Chinese can be toyed with and not get angry". ***[III][preset][SP (Briton)][DS]***

[Dolby] Miss Wedderburn looked at him with a smile, as if to say, Cringing cowards, the Chinese. They can't even get properly angry. ***[III][preset][SP (Briton)][IS]***

In Example (33), the presence of the think-type verb "想" and the subsequent colon in the ST indicates that it is an instance of SP/TP, which could be interpreted as either the character's actual expression of her dreams or her internal monologue. In the four translations, both James and Dolby render the original line as speech presentation in the form of FDS with first person and present tense. In contrast, Huang & Finkelstein and Jimmerson render the same line as thought presentation in the form of DT, albeit with the same choice of person and tense. This may give their target readers the impression that this British figure is talking to herself. The finding in Example (33) corroborates the results regarding the translators' preferences for DT or FDT, as shown in Table 9.18.

With the indicator "心裡", Example (34) could be deemed as thought presentation. However, this example can also be interpreted as writing presentation, as the entire line may suggest a narrator's report of the character's thoughts. In the translations, all the translators except Jimmerson remove the original semi-reporting clause formed by the colon and render it as NW. In Jimmerson's translation, however, the colon is retained. This makes Jimmerson's translation a FIT, with "regret" followed by the colon serving as an indicator of the character's thought activity. Compared with the other translators, Jimmerson's use of FIT could bring target readers closer to the story figure.

Example (35) features an ambiguous discourse presentation that can be regarded as either speech or thought presentation. The apparent reporting structure initiated by the tell-type verb "說" and the colon plus quotation marks indicates a speech feature. Yet, the word "好像" suggests that it is not an actual speech, but an internal monologue of the story figure. In the translations, all translators, except for Dolby, maintain the structure of the original line as DS by retaining the tell-type verb "say", along with the colon and quotation marks. This choice creates the impression that the story figure is talking to herself. In Dolby's translation, although the tell-type verb "say" is retained, the colon and quotation marks are omitted, resulting in an IS form. This would weaken the self-talking effect in the translation.

9.3 Conclusion

The present chapter discussed and compared the translators' functional styles in the translations of *Er Ma* through the linguistic idiosyncrasies they have shown in the recharacterization of story figures. These idiosyncrasies are explored through the translators' renditions of figure labels, reconstructions of the original semantic fields, and recreation of discourse presentation.

Concerning figure labels, all the translators have employed a wider range of English words to render the Chinese figure labels, in contrast to a more limited range used for the British figures. Regarding semantic fields, differences exist in the translators' efforts to shift the proportions of semantic components when recharacterizing the British and Chinese figures. Jimmerson puts forth the most effort in altering proportions for the British figures, while James and Huang & Finkelstein make the least effort. However, when recharacterizing the Chinese figures, Jimmerson makes the least effort in modifying proportions, whereas Huang & Finkelstein and James make the greatest efforts. In terms of discourse presentation, the discourse forms of free indirect thought (FIT), direct speech (DS), and free direct speech (FDS) are clearly preferred by all these translators, with Huang and Finkelstein showing a particular inclination for the use of DS and James favoring FDS. Such diversities are likely to introduce varied narrative effects into their translations, imposing diverse interpretational impacts on target readers.

Before concluding this chapter, it is important to note that some underlying factors that contribute to the similarities and differences in the translators' linguistic idiosyncrasies and functional styles have not been explored. However, in Chapter 11, we will address this gap by engaging in a more comprehensive discussion of these factors. But before that, in the upcoming Chapter 10, we will conduct a quantitative-focused analysis to investigate these translators' functional styles when creating the textual function of textual panoramas building in target texts.

References

Dolby, W. (2013). *Mr. Ma and son.* Penguin Books.

Huang, L. (2015). *Style in translation: A corpus-based perspective.* Springer.

Huang, K., & Finkelstein, D. (1984). *The two Mas.* Hong Kong Joint Publishing.

Ji, M. (2009). Corpus stylistics in translation studies: Two modern Chinese translations of Don Quijote. *Language and Literature, 18*(1), 61–73.

Kong, Q. D. (2005). Lao She and national spirit. *Journal of Peking University (Philosophy and Social Sciences Edition), 42*(5), 62–70.

She, L. (1998). *Er Ma.* People's Literature Publishing House.

Leech, G. N., & Short, M. (2007). *Style in fiction: A linguistic introduction to English fictional prose* (No. 13). Pearson Education.

Louie, K. (2000). Constructing Chinese masculinity for the modern world: With particular reference to Lao She's the Two Mas. *The China Quarterly, 164*, 1062–1078.

Ma, X. D. (2004). Between self and other: The image of the British in Lao She's works. *Journal of Wenzhou University (Philosophy and Social Sciences Edition), 25*(1), 54–59.

Qian, Z. G. (1999). Comparison and exploration in diversity: On Lao She's cultural reflections in the novel *Er Ma*. *Journal of Literature, History and Philosophy, 5*, 113–117.
Semino, E., & Short, M. (2004). *Corpus stylistics: Speech, writing and thought presentation in a corpus of English writing*. Routledge.
Shen, D. (1991). On the idiosyncrasies of modes of speech presentation in Chinese narrative fiction. *Journal of Peking University (Philosophy and Social Science Edition), 4*, 76–82.
Shen, Q. L. (1999). A spotlight on Chinese and Western cultures: On Lao She's *Er Ma*. *Modern Chinese Literature Studies, 1*, 112–125.
Wen, R. M. (2000). The novel *Er Ma* from a cultural criticism perspective (Speech delivered at the International Comparative Literature Conference in the Netherlands, June 1997). *Modern Chinese Literature Studies, 4*, 123–128.
Wang, W. D. (1999). Exploring the path to rebuilding national ethical culture through comparison of Chinese and British national character: On the cultural connotations of Lao She's diaspora novel *Er Ma*. *Journal of Beijing Union University, 1*, 23–37.
Xiao, F. (2010). *On the British image in Lao She's writings*. Hunan Normal University.
Zhu, C. K. (2007). Postcolonial Lao She: Insight or prejudice? Centered on *Er Ma* and Xiao Po's Birthday. *Journal of Sun Yat-Sen University (Social Science Edition), 47*(2), 14–18.

Chapter 10
Functional Style as Textual Panorama Building

10.1 Introduction

The preceding chapters (Chapters 8 and 9) have examined the translators' functional styles through literary function. However, the insights derived from these two chapters offer only a partial glimpse of the stylistic landscape in the four English translations of *Er Ma*. To provide anther view of this stylistic landscape, this chapter investigates the translators' functional styles through textual function, using principal component analysis (PCA) and the multidimensional analysis (MDA).

Section 10.2 retrieves the parallel lists of words and word sequences in the four English translations, using Intelligent Archive 3.0. These lists will be to identify the most frequent words (MFW) and the most frequent word sequences (MFWS) in these translations. In Sects. 10.3, the functional styles of the translators are compared based on the textual panoramas represented by the MFW and MFWS through PCA. In Sect. 10.4, the functional styles are compared with respect to the discourse dimension of translated texts through MDA, following Biber's (1988) framework. Section 10.5 reflects on the findings, while Sect. 10.6 concludes the chapter.

10.2 MFW and MFWS in the English Translations of *Er Ma*

Stylometric attribution has a well-established tradition of employing MFW as an effective classifier to differentiate the stylistic features of one author from another (Burrows, 2002). Concurrently, word sequences or *n*-grams, which represent contiguous sequences of *n* items of words within a given text or speech, have found wide application in computational linguistics for predictive or attributive purposes (Broder et al., 1997: 1157). In empirical translation research, both MFW and MFWS have been successfully used either separately or in tandem to distinguish stylistic

K. Wu and D. Li, *Researching Translator's Functional Style*, New Frontiers in Translation Studies, https://doi.org/10.1007/978-981-95-1221-8_10

features across various translations of the same source text (e.g., Burrow, 2002; Rybicki, 2012; Mastropierro, 2018).

The present research uses both MFW and MFWS as the classifiers in analyzing the overall degree of differences and similarities of the translators' functional styles in the four English translations of *Er Ma*. In the analysis, frequency data of the two classifiers, which serve as the variables input in PCA, will be presented in parallel lists of words and word sequences generated by Intelligent Archive 3.0 (see Chap. 6). A parallel list for words or word sequences is a table that contains words or words sequences sorted in ascending or descending orders based on their raw frequencies within a given corpus (Hoover, 2015). In the four English translations of *Er Ma*, the parallel lists will consist of words, 2-grams, and 3-grams. The choice of including 2-grams and 3-grams word sequences is based on their representation of the most common word sequences in a text or speech (Barlow, 2013; Mastropierro, 2018; Rybicki, 2012). These n-grams are considered effective in capturing the overall textual characteristics from a quantitative perspective. Word sequences longer than 3-grams, such as 4-grams, 5-grams, or 6-grams, although potentially relevant for comparing translators' styles, are less efficient in distinguishing such styles due to their lower frequency in a text or speech. This rationale is supported by previous stylometric studies. For example, Hoover (2002) utilized 2-grams, while Barlow (2013) and Mastropierro (2018) employed both 2-grams and 3-grams. These studies concur that longer word sequences (beyond three) are not sufficiently frequent to be considered worthy of investigation.

Details regarding these lists are respectively presented in Tables 10.1, 10.2, and 10.3, though due to limited space, they only include partial results.[1]

In the parallel lists, the first row includes information about the MFW or MFWS and the names of the translators. The subsequent rows contain words or word sequences and their proportions in the four translations. Given the varying total sizes of the four English translations, proportional data (as opposed to raw frequencies) automatically generated by the software are employed for comparability.

Before data analysis, it's important to highlight a specific decision regarding the treatment of contractions in the four English translations. In contrast to prior studies (e.g., Laviosa, 2002; Mastropierro, 2018; Tognini-Bonelli, 2001), where contractions were treated as separate words due to morphological or phonetic reasons, this study adopts a different approach. The present research considers contractions such as "I've", "he'll", and "you'd" as single words. This decision is based on the premise that the varying usage of contractions in the four translations can reveal unique aspects of the translators' functional styles. For instance, Huang and Finkelstein (1984) employed the "'ll" form more frequently in their translation compared to the other translators, while Jimmerson (1991) featured the "'t" form more prominently in her rendition. Treating these contractions as separate words would overlook the potential linguistic idiosyncrasies in how the translators handle these forms, and

[1] The full lists, directly exported from Intelligent Archive 3.0, are in Figshare (10.6084/m9.figshare.29572907).

Table 10.1 Samples of TTs parallel wordlist with proportion

Word	James	Huang and Finkelstein	Jimmerson	Dolby
the	4.364996	4.5594735	4.37959	4.666213
and	2.74449	2.6037138	2.7251642	3.22718
to	2.830386	2.8627124	2.89138	2.60464
a	2.302439	2.4572835	2.5115964	2.641538
of	1.621554	1.93288	1.8100116	2.114555
he	1.781824	1.9868761	1.6515268	1.399296
his	1.317774	1.5237904	1.4128335	1.387943
in	1.385863	1.4341018	1.3384229	1.401188
ma	1.454999	1.3453285	1.4186317	1.316985
was	1.312537	1.1815095	1.2514496	1.069104
you	1.237116	0.8712603	1.0919985	1.092757
her	0.989902	1.0314184	0.9770004	1.033152
it	1.062181	0.95362735	0.96443754	0.900696
with	0.611749	0.95545775	0.89002705	0.897858
that	0.556231	0.9307476	0.88036335	0.757834
on	0.672505	0.8209249	0.8175493	0.806085
i	0.965809	0.73764265	0.7499034	0.581857
she	0.784589	0.8438046	0.6919211	0.614025
for	0.728023	0.7193389	0.71511406	0.74648
but	0.515378	0.70561105	0.7759954	0.619702
wei	0.669362	0.6397174	0.65519905	0.644301
at	0.711263	0.6214136	0.5363355	0.649031
as	0.372915	0.67449456	0.68805563	0.667953
had	0.622224	0.73947304	0.5334364	0.444672
mr	0.671457	0.55735034	0.5121763	0.593211
out	0.469287	0.43471497	0.6281407	0.394528
him	0.488142	0.45301875	0.45999226	0.521306
all	0.685075	0.25625303	0.47642055	0.519414
be	0.427386	0.4502732	0.45419404	0.422911
they	0.521663	0.4319694	0.4454967	0.354791
…	…	…	…	…

thus would significantly affect the analysis results. Hence, this research opts for an alternative approach and treats these contractions as single words.

Table 10.2 Samples of TTs parallel 2-grams list with proportion

2-grams	James	Huang and Finkelstein	Jimmerson	Dolby
ma.wei	0.667267	0.63239586	0.6513336	0.613079
mr.ma	0.598131	0.48962632	0.44742945	0.509953
in.the	0.378153	0.37431246	0.36045614	0.354791
of.the	0.269211	0.31482515	0.2638191	0.372767
on.the	0.254546	0.29560617	0.23772709	0.237474
to.the	0.294352	0.24801633	0.23289524	0.231797
at.the	0.166555	0.16290371	0.14592192	0.185437
he.was	0.153985	0.17846194	0.14882103	0.147593
it.was	0.137225	0.154667	0.20390414	0.124886
and.the	0.102657	0.14826068	0.117897175	0.159893
mrs.wendell	0.269211	0	0.2705837	0
with.a	0.081706	0.14185436	0.12562814	0.150431
in.a	0.124654	0.11897462	0.113065325	0.133401
a.few	0.084849	0.11073792	0.15172014	0.118264
for.a	0.077516	0.12263538	0.114998065	0.121102
was.a	0.125702	0.08877337	0.12852725	0.086096
to.be	0.102657	0.11897462	0.10243525	0.099342
a.little	0.183315	0.0951797	0.07924236	0.06812
he.had	0.131987	0.1647341	0.07924236	0.029329
with.the	0.058661	0.10524678	0.113065325	0.109749
the.chinese	0.123607	0.072299965	0.06957866	0.11921
for.the	0.093229	0.0951797	0.09567066	0.08988
in.his	0.098466	0.09243413	0.09083881	0.092719
his.head	0.082754	0.10433159	0.09180518	0.092719
of.his	0.076469	0.11348349	0.07537688	0.104072
the.shop	0.082754	0.0860278	0.09856977	0.095557
there.was	0.103704	0.0777911	0.0976034	0.080419
from.the	0.067041	0.097010076	0.09567066	0.087988
to.go	0.106847	0.07138477	0.07634325	0.066228
all.the	0.072279	0.04575947	0.08890607	0.10218
...	...	...	...	...

Table 10.3 Samples of TTs parallel 3-grams list with proportion

3-grams	James	Huang and Finkelstein	Jimmerson	Dolby
mr.ma.senior	0	0.27089605	0	0
in.front.of	0.039806	0.04575947	0.055083107	0.027437
the.reverend.ely	0	0	0	0.126779
ma.wei.was	0.028283	0.021049356	0.03962118	0.03406
the.elder.ma	0	0	0.082141474	0.035006
a.couple.of	0.003143	0.039353143	0.03768844	0.03406
mr.ma.was	0.039806	0.010982273	0.03672207	0.030276
to.the.shop	0.037711	0.021049356	0.026091998	0.023653
there.was.a	0.02514	0.010982273	0.03382296	0.032168
to.ma.wei	0.026188	0.027455682	0.026091998	0.020814
out.of.the	0.015713	0.028370872	0.025125628	0.029329
there.was.no	0.028283	0.028370872	0.023192888	0.012299
the.two.of	0.021998	0.02928606	0.017394666	0.021761
two.of.them	0.021998	0.027455682	0.015461925	0.021761
ma.wei.had	0.014665	0.024710113	0.025125628	0.019868
said.ma.wei	0.010475	0.020134166	0.003865481	0.049198
mr.ma.had	0.027235	0.009151894	0.017394666	0.029329
what.do.you	0.024093	0.01464303	0.029957479	0.011353
be.able.to	0.00838	0.023794925	0.020293776	0.024599
it.was.a	0.017808	0.013727841	0.03189022	0.015138
ma.wei.and	0.018855	0.019218978	0.021260146	0.018922
at.ma.wei	0.023045	0.018303787	0.018361036	0.017976
ma.wei.said	0.026188	0.021964546	0.020293776	0.009461
it.would.be	0.019903	0.023794925	0.026091998	0.006623
shook.his.head	0.023045	0.013727841	0.022226518	0.017976
to.have.a	0.01257	0.018303787	0.018361036	0.025545
go.to.the	0.035616	0.009151894	0.014495554	0.016084
mr.ma.and	0.013618	0.007321515	0.028991109	0.021761
asked.ma.wei	0.01257	0.011897462	0.006764592	0.03879
his.head.and	0.010475	0.018303787	0.020293776	0.020814
…	…	…	…	…

10.3 Functional Styles as Textual Panorama Building: Insights from PCA

This section examines the translators' functional styles by assessing how they build textual panoramas in their translated texts. The investigation hinges on the findings from the principal component analysis (PCA) based on the most frequent words (MFW) and most frequent word sequences (MFWS) in the four translations. The results centered on MFW will be discussed in Sect. 10.3.1, while the findings associated with MFWS will be explored in Sect. 10.3.2.

10.3.1 Principal Component Analysis of the MFW

The following part explores the translators' functional styles as they build textual panoramas in their translations through the MFW. Section 10.3.1.1 will present the results obtained through the PCA, and Sect. 10.3.1.2 will offer a concise interpretation of these results in terms of their potential impact on readers' comprehension of the story.

10.3.1.1 Results

The utilization of MFW in stylometric attribution for distinguishing authorial styles is well-established (Burrows, 2002; Rybicki, 2012; Segarra et al., 2016). This section employs the same technique for stylistic analysis, but with a focus on translator style. However, before conducting the analysis, it is crucial to establish a threshold for identifying the MFW contributing to the formation of a textual panorama. In other words, it's necessary to determine the number of MFW required to create a meaningful textual panorama. Nevertheless, this is not a straightforward matter and requires careful consideration.

Past studies lack consensus on the precise number of MFW needed to create a textual panorama. For example, Burrows (2002) experimented with different numbers, such as 60, 80, 100, and 150, to triangulate the most stable results. Similarly, Grabowski (2012, 2013) explored thresholds of 2000 and 1000, respectively. Rybicki (2012) considered a range from 100 to 5000 with increments of 100 for acceptable results. Rybicki et al. (2014) used 1000 as the threshold. Mastropierro (2018) employed 350. However, it's crucial to emphasize that these decisions regarding the number of MFW aren't arbitrary. They are guided by a fundamental principle: the stability of analysis results improves as the number of MFW increases, reaching a point of relative stability where the formation of a textual panorama is achieved. However, this point is not fixed and can vary across texts in different languages and genres. Therefore, conducting repeated pilot studies is necessary to determine this threshold and identify the optimal number of MFW for the analysis.

In the present analysis, attempts are made with the number of MFW ranging from 100 to 1000 with an increment of 50 to identify the threshold for achieving stable results that form a textual panorama. The threshold turns out to be the top 500 MFW. With numbers smaller than 500, the results are notably affected, while numbers larger than 500 remain largely stable. This finding aligns with previous research by Rybicki et al. (2014), Hoover (2015), and Mastropierro (2018), which suggests that multivariate analysis results based on relatively small numbers of MFW lack the consistency of those obtained from larger numbers of MFW. Hence, PCA is conducted using the top 500 MFW to find out the differences of these translators' functional styles in the four English translations of *Er Ma*. PCA is often employed to measure the metric distance and investigate the relatedness between populations (Abdi & Williams, 2010: 433). In this study, PCA is chosen for its effectiveness in capturing the overall similarities and diversities among texts with shared features. This decision is supported by previous studies (e.g., Mastropierro, 2018) with similar research objectives. The PCA results are presented in Fig. 10.1.

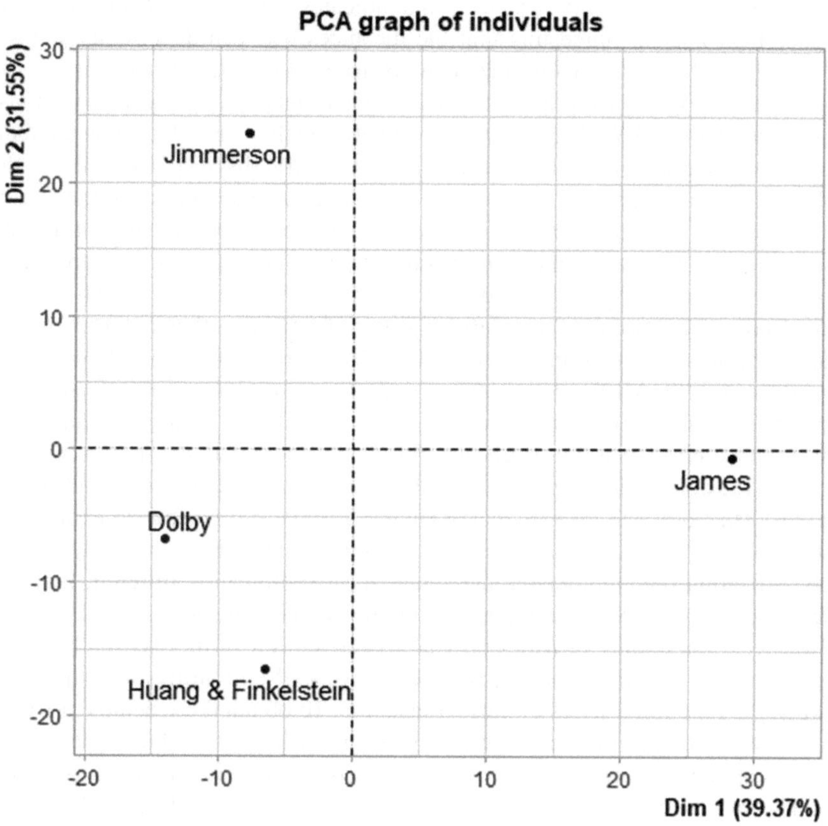

Fig. 10.1 PCA graph of individuals (Top 500 MFW)

Figure 10.1 provides an overview of the extent to which these translators' functional styles in the four translations differ based on the textual panoramas formed by the top 500 MFW. Since PCA is a multivariate statistical analysis that operates according to dimensionality reduction (Manly, 2016: 102–103), multiple dimensions in the analysis will be compressed into two dimensions—a more manageable scale for the present work. Specifically, the horizontal and vertical axes in Fig. 10.1 are the two principal components (dimensions) that are automatically generated during the PCA through dimensionality reduction. Additionally, PCA is an unsupervised machine learning technique, with datasets typically being unlabeled, unclassified, or uncategorized (Saslow, 2018). Hence, the two principal components that represent the majority of data variance in the parallel wordlist are likewise unlabeled. This is unlikely to impact the research results since the objective of this chapter is to ascertain the overall stylistic similarities and differences between the translators. Moreover, the two percentiles in the brackets along the axes signify the level of variance carried by the two components (dimensions): the first component (Dim 1) represents 39.37% of the variance across the data, while the second component (Dim 2) represents 31.55% of this variance. This indicates that Dim 1 captures more data variance than Dim 2, suggesting that the distances between data points along the horizontal axis bear greater variance than distances along the vertical axis.

The dots in Fig. 10.1 represent the textual panoramas of the translators' translations based on the MFW. The diversity level between them is reflected by the metric distance on the graph. Essentially, the longer the metric distance between two dots, the higher the diversity level between the textual panoramas of the two translations. It's evident that the dots representing the textual panoramas of James' translation (referred to as dot_Ja) and Jimmerson's translation (referred to as dot_Ji) are the only ones dispersed towards the right side of the horizontal axis or downwards along the vertical axis. These two dots are relatively distant from each other and from the other dots, indicating that James and Jimmerson exhibit distinct functional styles, particularly concerning the MFW, in comparison to the other translators. In contrast, the dots representing Dolby's translation (referred to as dot_D) and Huang & Finkelstein's translation (referred to as dot_H&F) are closely clustered with the shortest distances among all the dots. This suggests that Dolby's functional style in the English translation of *Er Ma* closely aligns with that of Huang & Finkelstein in the same translation. Lastly, both dot_Ji and dot_Ja are considerably distant from both dot_D and dot_H&F, indicating that Jimmerson and James have significantly different functional styles in terms of the MFW compared to Dolby and Huang and Finkelstein.

However, this finding provides only a broad overview of the stylistic landscape, lacking specific details regarding the exact levels of similarities and differences between the functional styles of these translators. To obtain these details, it's necessary to calculate the metric distances between each pair of dots. These metric distances are derived from the dot coordinates obtained during the PCA graph plotting. The results of these metric distances are presented in Tables 10.4 and 10.5, offering precise measurements corresponding to the metric information depicted in Fig. 10.1. According to Table 10.5, the average distance between the textual panorama of James' translated text (dot_Ja) and the rest of the translators' translated texts is the

Table 10.4 Coordinates of the PCA individuals (Top 500 MFW)

	Dim1	Dim2
Dolby	−14.02	−6.70
H&F	−6.51	−16.51
James	28.33	−0.57
Jimmerson	−7.80	23.78

Table 10.5 The metric distances between the PCA individuals (Top 500 MFW)

	Dolby	H&F	James	Jimmerson
Dolby	n/a	12.35	42.79	31.11
H&F	12.35	n/a	38.32	40.31
James	42.79	38.32	n/a	43.57
Jimmerson	31.11	40.31	43.57	n/a
AVG	28.75	30.32	41.56	38.33

longest, with a value of 41.56. In contrast, the average distance between the textual panorama of Dolby's translated text (dot_D) and the rest of the translators' texts is the shortest, with a value of 28.75. This indicates that, concerning the top 500 MFW, James' style displays the greatest divergence from the styles of the other translators, while Dolby's style demonstrates the smallest deviation. Regarding the textual panoramas of Jimmerson's translated text (dot_Ji) and Huang & Finkelstein's translated text (dot_H&F), their average distances from the rest of the translators' texts are 38.33 and 30.32, respectively. This suggests that Jimmerson's style displays a moderate difference compared to the other translators, while Huang and Finkelstein's style shows a mild difference.

10.3.1.2 Making Sense of the Results

To interpret the findings from the previous section, another R-plot is employed. This graph, shown in Fig. 10.2,[2] is generated during the PCA analysis based on the parallel wordlists. However, it differs from Fig. 10.1 as it elucidates the overall variance of the textual panoramas of the translations by showing the contributions of each MFW in the parallel wordlists, rather than their combined effects. Each MFW in Fig. 10.2 serves as a vector extending from the origin, with the angle formed between each vector and the axes representing the correlation between the vector (word) and the principal component (i.e., Dim 1 and Dim 2) carried by the axis. In simpler terms, the larger the angle, the weaker the connection between a vector and the corresponding principal component, or vice versa.

[2] A high-resolution version is attached in Figshare (10.6084/m9.figshare.29572907).

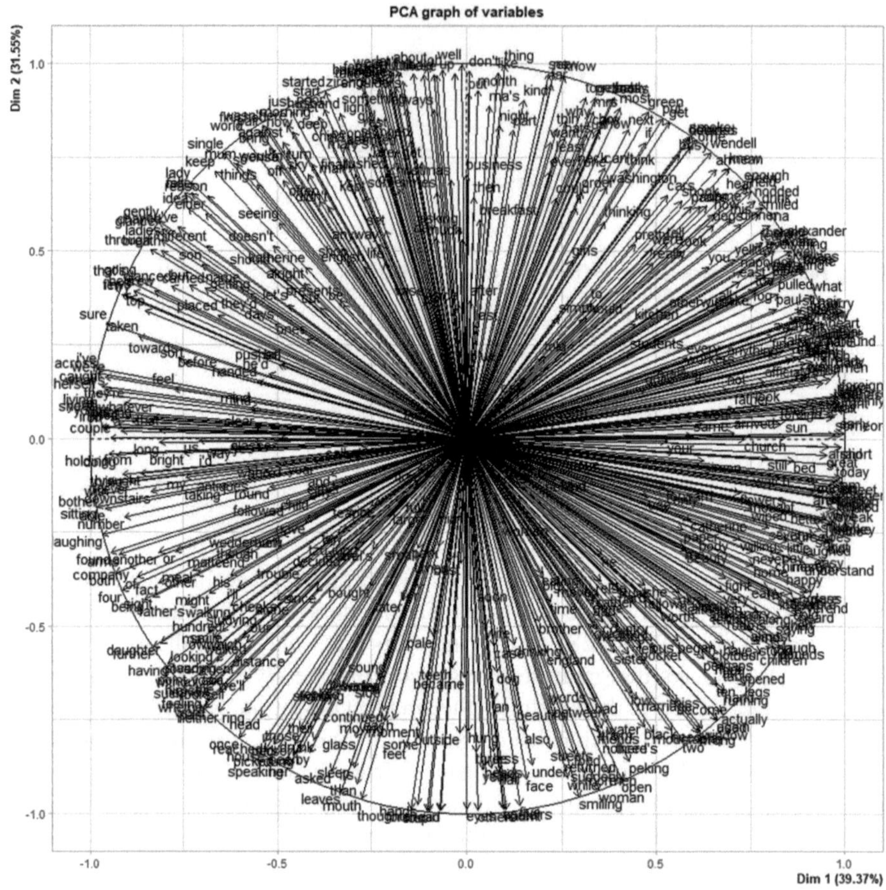

Fig. 10.2 PCA graph of variables that show individual words (Top 500 MFW)

From Fig. 10.2, it becomes apparent that one possible reason for the observed differences in the functional styles of these translators, as demonstrated in Fig. 10.1, is their varied translations of the story figure labels. For example, the label "子榮", referring to Mr. Ma's shop assistant, has three English versions: "zirong" by Jimmerson, "dze-rung" by Huang & Finkelstein, and "tzu-rung" by both James and Dolby. These variations in translation are immediately reflected in the graph. The vector "zirong" points towards dot_Ji, "dze-rung" points to dot_H&F, and "tzu-rung" falls between dot_Ja and dot_D. Notably, "tzu-rung" is closer to dot_D, indicating that Dolby (0.2384) uses this name more frequently compared to James (0.0523). It's worth noting that, except for Jimmerson's version, which is published in Mainland China, the copyright information of the four translations reveals that they are published in the US, UK, or Hong Kong. This explains why Jimmerson employs Mandarin Pinyin in her translation, while the other translators do not (for further details, see Chap. 11). Likewise, the label "伊牧師" is differently translated by these translators. Dolby and Huang & Finkelstein translate it as "Ely" and "Eden" respectively, while both James and Jimmerson translate it as "Evans". These discrepancies are clearly depicted in Fig. 10.2, with the vectors indicating the corresponding textual panoramas of each translation.

The translation of figure labels can offer target readers insights into different methods in the romanization of labels in Chinese. For instance, rendering "子榮" as "Zirong" immediately connects the reader to labeling conventions in mainland China (since 1949). Conversely, translating it as "Dze-rung" or "Tzu-rung" reflects labeling practices in pre-1949 or non-mainland Chinese regions, where the Wade-Giles system (e.g., "Tzu-rung") or Yale system (e.g., "Dze-rung") might also be employed alongside the Pinyin phonetic system.

Another possible reason for these stylistic diversities is the different use of auxiliary and modal verbs. For example, James uses notably more "will" than the other translators: the proportions of "will" in the four translations are James (0.1634), Huang & Finkelstein (0.0777), Jimmerson (0.0608), and Dolby (0.0690). Similarly, James has a special preference for "must" in her translation (0.1696), while Huang and Finkelstein (0.0567), Jimmerson (0.0318), and Dolby (0.0586) do not display a similar inclination in their respective translations. Furthermore, James (0.0408) uses "does" more frequently than Huang & Finkelstein (0.0228), Jimmerson (0.0183), and Dolby (0.0236) in their translations. This preference for auxiliary and modal verbs is evident in Fig. 10.2, where a cluster of such verbs can be observed in Quadrant I, aligning with the position of dot_Ja, as indicated in Fig. 10.1.

Concerning target readers, those who are attentive to the nuances of auxiliary and modal verbs may perceive differences in the translated texts produced by these translators. For instance, James's extensive use of "will" may evoke a sense of uncertainty among readers, as grammatically, it signifies the future. Additionally, James's higher frequency of "must" and "does" could imbue target readers with a heightened sense of emphasis or strong conviction, as these words are occasionally associated with emphatic expressions.

A third possible reason for these stylistic variations is the different use of body language words. According to Korte's framework (1997:15), body language in literary works can be classified into "modal" and "functional" classes. The former pertains to the kinetic presentation of body language, while the latter focuses on its impact in a narrative text (Mahlberg, 2013: 101). The study identifies a notable pattern in the translations of Dolby and Huang & Finkelstein, where they demonstrate a strong inclination to employ body language words such as "laughing," "arms," "sitting," "four," and "feeling." In contrast, this tendency is less prominent in the translations of Jimmerson and James. Figure 10.2 visually represents this, showing that many vectors representing body language words are directed towards the vicinity of dot_D and dot_H&F. Additional information obtained from the footnotes and prefaces of these two translations indicates that Dolby and Huang and Finkelstein aimed to faithfully capture Lao She's characterization techniques (Dolby, 2013: ii; Huang & Finkelstein, 1984: i-ii). Consequently, they made efforts to retain most of the original body language expressions used by Lao She in their translated texts.

As a result, when encountering Dolby's and Huang and Finkelstein's translations, target readers are more likely to develop a vivid impression of the story's characters, as the preserved descriptions of body language contribute to a sense of liveliness and perceptible human motion. In comparison, James' and Jimmerson's translations may not evoke the same level of vividness in readers' perception of the characters, as they may have omitted or altered some of the original body language descriptions, creating a greater psychological distance between the readers and the recharacterized story figures.

10.3.2 Principal Component Analysis of the MFWS

Similar to the MFW-based analysis, analyzing these translators' functional styles using the MFWS also necessitates determining the appropriate number of MFWS to include. After conducting repeated PCA experiments in RStudio, it has been determined that a minimum of 550 stable results are needed to form a cohesive textual panorama based on 2-grams. For 3-grams, the number required is 700. To ensure consistency and comparability, this study will employ 700 MFWS for both 2-grams and 3-grams. The PCA results for the 2-grams will be presented in Sect. 10.3.2.1, while the results for the 3-grams will be discussed in Sect. 10.3.2.2. Additionally, the R-plots for individual 2-grams and 3-grams will be provided in Sect. 10.3.2.3.

10.3.2.1 Results Based on 2-grams

In this analysis, the 2-grams extracted from the four English translations of *Er Ma* will serve as the variables for the PCA. The analysis techniques applied here are consistent with those used for the MFW analysis in Sect. 10.3. The results of this PCA are presented in Fig. 10.3.

The first principal component (Dim1) on the horizontal axis represents 38.88% of the variance across the data, while the second principal component (Dim2) accounts for 32.99% of data variance. This pattern is similar to the PCA results based on the MFW. Dots in this graph represent the textual panoramas of these translators' translations, and their tendencies to diverge or converge remain largely consistent with those based on the MFW. The findings from Fig. 10.3 suggest a potential similarity in stylistic patterns between Dolby and Huang & Finkelstein, while James and Jimmerson exhibit substantial differences from each other and from Dolby and Huang & Finkelstein. This observation is supported by the clustering of dot_D and dot_H&F in Quadrant III with a close metric distance, while dot_Ja is positioned in Quadrant IV with the greatest metric distance from dot_D. Similarly, dot_Ji is located in Quadrant II with a significant metric distance from all the other dots.

The precise levels of similarities and differences between the functional styles of these translators are obtained using the same methodologies as described in Sect. 10.3.1.1 and are presented in Tables 10.6 and 10.7. The findings in these tables

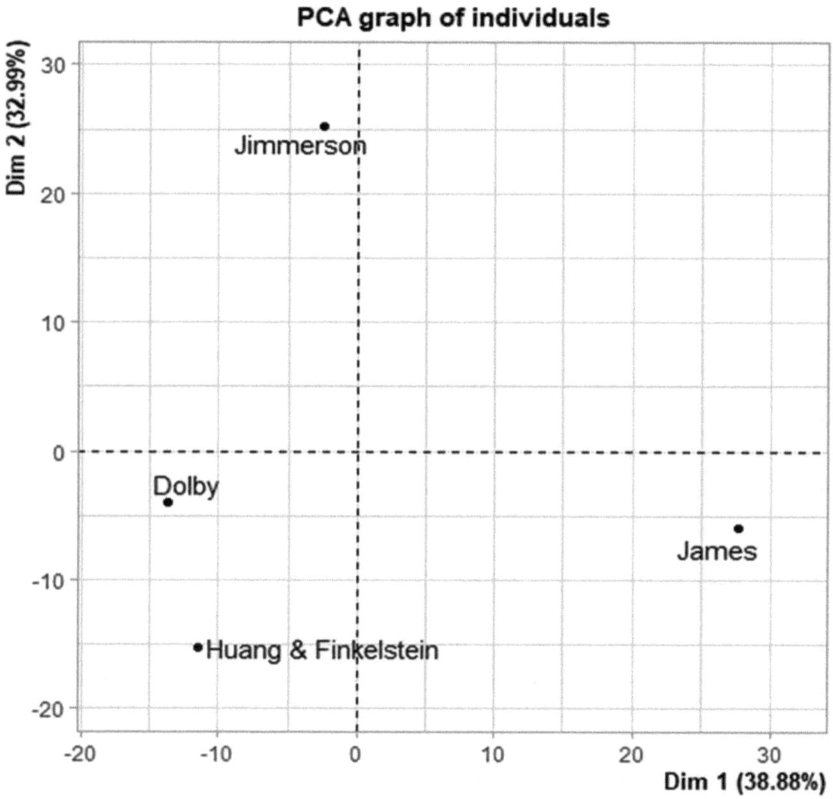

Fig. 10.3 PCA graph of individuals (Top 700 2-grams)

align with those in Tables 10.4 and 10.5. Specifically, the average distances of the textual panoramas reveal that James' translation (dot_Ja) has the longest average distance of 41.66 from the rest of the translators' translations, while Dolby's translation (dot_D) exhibits the shortest average distance of 28.07. This suggests that James' functional style differs the most from the other translators, whereas Dolby's functional style shows the least deviation from the rest, particularly concerning the 2-grams. Similarly, Jimmerson's translation (dot_Ji) and Huang & Finkelstein's translation (dot_H&F) have average distances of 38.75 and 31.09, respectively, indicating moderate and mild differences in their functional styles compared to the rest of the translators.

Table 10.6 Coordinates of the PCA individuals (Top 700 2-grams)

	Dim1	Dim2
Dolby	−13.68	−3.96
H&F	−11.45	−15.30
James	27.64	−6.00
Jimmerson	−2.51	25.26

Table 10.7 The metric distances between the PCA individuals (Top 700 2-grams)

	Dolby	H&F	James	Jimmerson
Dolby	n/a	11.56	41.38	31.28
H&F	11.56	n/a	40.18	41.53
James	41.38	40.18	n/a	43.43
Jimmerson	31.28	41.53	43.43	n/a
AVG	28.07	31.09	41.66	38.75

10.3.2.2 Results Based on 3-grams

Following the same procedures as the 2-grams analysis, this section conducts a similar analysis using the 3-grams. The purpose is to explore the variations in the translators' styles when translating *Er Ma* into English. The result of this analysis is illustrated in Fig. 10.4.

In this 3-gram-based PCA analysis, the first component (Dim 1) represents 37.06% of the data variance, which is slightly lower (less than 5%) compared to the PCA results based on the MFW (39.37%) and 2-grams (38.88%). Similarly, the second component (Dim 2) represents 32.93% of the data variance, which remains largely consistent with the analyses based on the MFW (31.55%) and 2-grams (32.99%). This similarity in data variance between the MFW and the MFWS (2-grams and 3-grams) ensures the comparability of our analysis results.

When it comes to the dots that represent the textual panoramas of the TTs, a highly similar pattern is detected between this 3-grams-based analysis and the 2-grams-based analysis. Again, dot_D and dot_H&F are situated in close proximity within Quadrant III, while being notably distant from dot_Ja and dot_Ji, which positioned in Quadrant I and Quadrant II, respectively, and far away from each other. Furthermore, the results from both the 2-grams and 3-grams based analyses indicate a certain similarity: dot_Ji and dot_Ja exhibit considerable metric distances from each other and from dot_D and dot_H&F, which are more closely clustered. This finding once again suggests that the functional styles of Jimmerson and James differ significantly from each other and from those of Dolby and Huang & Finkelstein. At the same time, the functional styles of Dolby and Huang & Finkelstein demonstrate greater similarities.

The data that provide precise measurements of the similarities and differences in functional styles among these translators are generated using the same methodologies

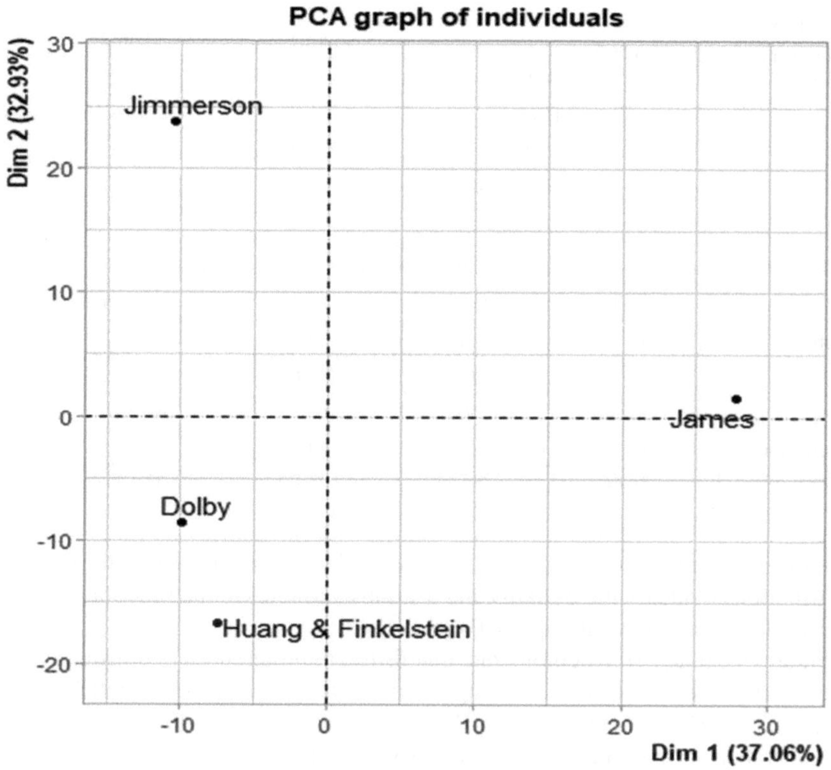

Fig. 10.4 PCA graph of individuals (Top 700 3-grams)

employed in Sects. 10.3.1.1 and 10.3.2.1. The results obtained from analyzing the 3-grams align with those derived from the MFW and 2-grams analyses. Specifically, as shown in Tables 10.8 and 10.9, the average distances of the textual panoramas indicate notable distinctions between James' translation (dot_Ja) and those of the rest translators, with the longest average distance of 41.02. Meanwhile, Dolby's translation (dot_D) exhibits the shortest average distance of 26.66, indicating a higher degree of similarity to the other translators' translations. Moreover, the average distances for Jimmerson's translation (dot_Ji, 39.12) and Huang and Finkelstein's translation (dot_H&F, 29.65) fall within the medium range, suggesting moderate variations in their functional styles compared to the other translators.

10.3.2.3 Making Sense of the Results

Similar to the maps in the MFW-based analysis, the variable factor maps for 2-grams (Fig. 10.5) and 3-grams (Fig. 10.6) are generated simultaneously with the

Table 10.8 Coordinates of the PCA individuals (Top 700 3-grams)

	Dim1	Dim2
Dolby	−9.94	−8.51
H&F	−7.43	−16.75
James	27.83	1.45
Jimmerson	−10.46	23.81

Table 10.9 The metric distances between the PCA individuals (Top 700 3-grams)

	Dolby	H&F	James	Jimmerson
Dolby	n/a	8.61	39.06	32.33
H&F	8.61	n/a	39.67	40.67
James	39.06	39.67	n/a	44.35
Jimmerson	32.33	40.67	44.35	n/a
AVG	26.66	29.65	41.02	39.12

individual factor maps during the PCA process.[3] These maps represent the individual contributions made by the 2-grams and 3-grams variables to the functional styles of the translators, as shown in Figs. 10.3 and 10.4.

Figures 10.5 and 10.6 demonstrate that different preferences in translating figure labels serve as the first differentiating factor in these translators' functional styles. For example, when translating "老馬" into English, Huang & Finkelstein (0.0210) demonstrate a stronger inclination towards rendering it as "Old Mr. Ma", compared to Dolby (0.0019) and James (0.0010). Additionally, Huang & Finkelstein stand out as the only translators who translate "老馬" as "Mr. Ma Senior" (0.2708). In contrast, Jimmerson (0.0821/0.0009) and Dolby (0.0350/0.0170) show an interest in translating it as either "Elder Mr. Ma" or "the Elder Ma". These diverse preferences are clearly illustrated in Fig. 10.6, where the vectors representing "Old Mr. Ma" and "Mr. Ma Senior" cluster in Quadrant III, pointing towards the vicinity of dot_H&F. Meanwhile, the vectors representing "Elder Mr. Ma" and "the Elder Ma" are located in Quadrant III, near the space between dot_D and dot_Ji. Additionally, James (0.5981) exhibits a particular inclination towards translating "老馬" as "Mr. Ma", compared to the other translators. This preference is evident in Fig. 10.5, where the vector representing "Mr. Ma" is located in Quadrant IV, close to dot_Ja on the border between Quadrant I and IV.

These diverse renditions of the same figure label are expected to provide target readers with different insights into the source and target cultures. For instance, when Huang and Finkelstein render "老馬" as "Mr. Ma Senior", target readers are exposed to the American way of labeling "the older of two people with the same name in the same family", according to the Macmillan Dictionary (https://www.macmillandictionary.com/dictionary/british/senior_1, last accessed on 16/09/2023). Similarly, Dolby's and Jimmerson's preferences for "Elder Mr. Ma" and "the Elder Ma"

[3] High-resolution versions of Figs. 10.5 and 10.6 can be found in Figshare (10.6084/m9.figshare.29572907).

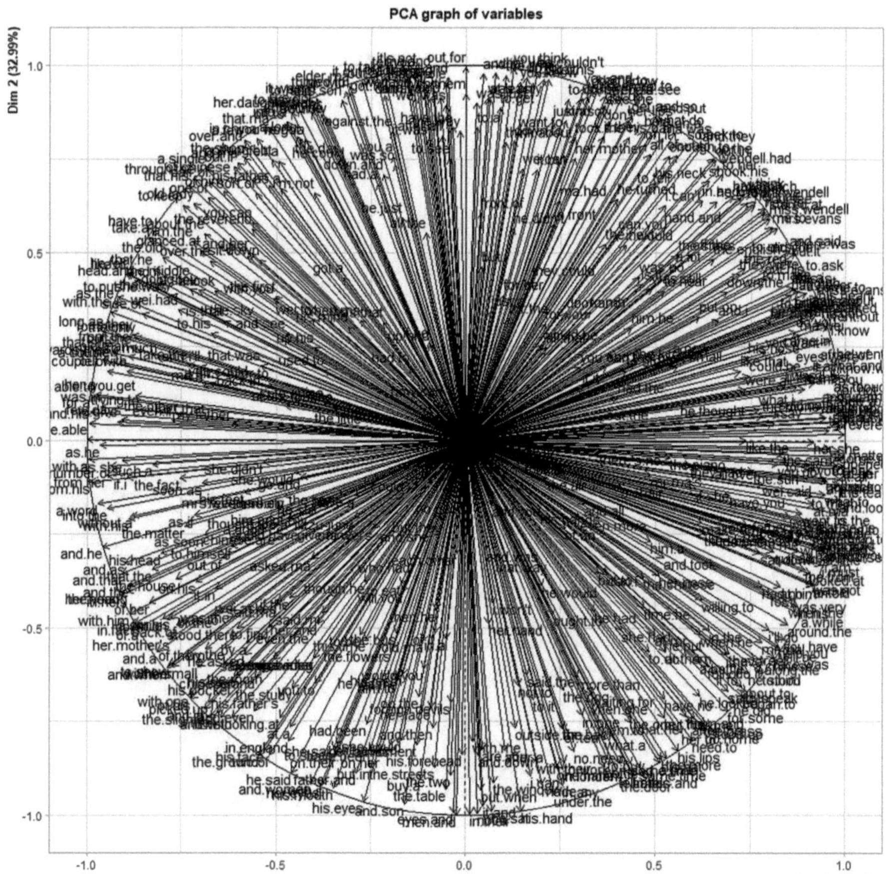

Fig. 10.5 PCA graph of variables that show individual words (Top 700 2-grams)

would present their target readers with a more old-fashioned British way of labeling "the aged" (https://forum.wordreference.com/threads/the-elder-mr-xy-mr-xy-senior.2565312/, last accessed on 16/09/2023).

The second differentiating factor in the functional styles of these translators pertains to their varied preferences regarding the use of contractions and the possessive case of nouns in translation. Parallel lists of 2-grams and 3-grams reveal that Jimmerson is especially devoted to using contractions compared to the other translators. In terms of percentiles, Jimmerson (0.0802) uses almost twice as many "I don't" as the other translators (James: 0.0555, Huang & Finkelstein: 0.0420, Dolby: 0.0321) do in the translation. Similarly, Jimmerson (0.0232) also uses significantly more "I've got to" than the other translators (James: 0.0000, Huang & Finkelstein: 0.0009, Dolby: 0.009) do in their translations. These trends are clearly reflected in Figs. 10.5 and 10.6, as most vectors of contractions gather within Quadrants I & II, pointing to the space near dot_Ji.

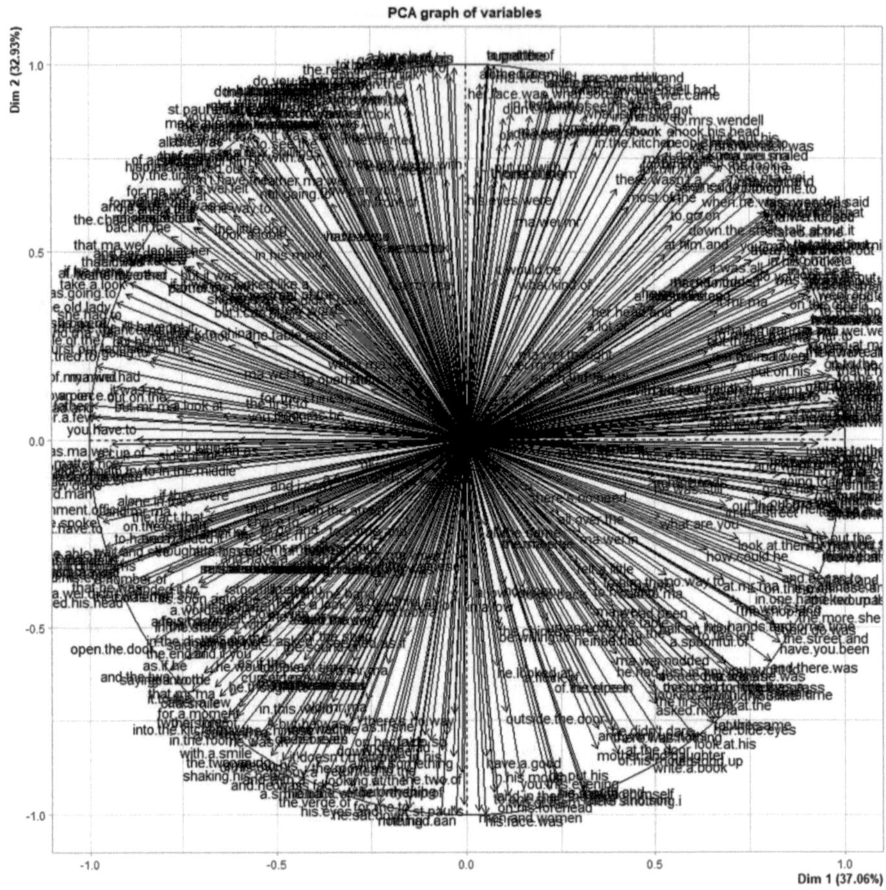

Fig. 10.6 PCA graph of variables that show individual words (Top 700 3-grams)

However, when it comes to the possessive case of nouns, the pattern is somewhat unexpected. The parallel lists reveal that there are only four "'s" possessive cases (i.e., "Ma Wei's," "Mr. Ma's," "his father's," and "her mother's") in the top 700 2-grams list, but James' translation, along with Dolby's translation, has three of them. Similarly, of the exclusive five "'s" possessive cases (i.e., "Ma Wei's face," "the Reverend Ely's," "of St. Paul's," "of Ma Wei's," and "St. Paul's Cathedral") in the top 700 3-grams list, James' TT and Dolby's TT have four of them. These tendencies are also clearly shown in Figs. 10.5 and 10.6, as these "'s" contractions are scattered either in Quadrant III near dot_D or Quadrant IV near dot_Ja.

We argue that such differences in the use of contractions in the translations may stem from the varied narrative strategies adopted by these translators when rendering the ST speech. This connection between a translator's narrative strategy and contraction use was also explored by Olohan (2003: 82), where she investigated Peter Bush's and Dorothy S. Blair's uses of contractions in their English translations. She found that the translators' different strategies in literary genres and narrative structures were the chief reasons for differences in contraction use. Nevertheless, when it comes to the effect of contraction use on target readers, it is less explored in Olohan's (2003) work. The present research holds that different uses of contractions would affect target readers' mental construction of a story figure. For instance, in comparison to phrases like "I have to" or "I do not", the use of expressions like "I've got to" or "I don't" in a character's speech may convey the impression of relatively informal language use or indicate a close relationship with the interlocutor.

The third differentiating factor in the functional styles of these translators pertains to their preferences in the use of "as if" 2-grams in translation. In this study, parallel lists of 2-grams (top 700) reveal that Huang & Finkelstein (0.1061) exhibit a stronger preference for the use of "as if" in their translation compared to James (0.0335), Jimmerson (0.0686), and Dolby (0.0567). This pattern is also depicted in Fig. 10.5, where the "as if" vector falls within Quadrant III, pointing to the space near dot_H&F. Further insights emerge from the parallel list of 3-grams (top 700), which includes six "as if" 3-grams (e.g., "as if he," "as if it," "as if the," "as if they," "as if she," and "seemed as if"), with the majority found in the translation by Huang & Finkelstein.[4] This trend is also evident in Fig. 10.6, where the vectors of these six 3-grams consistently fall within Quadrant III, pointing to the vicinity of dot_H&F.

According to Wikberg (1999), "as if" is a stylistic marker that occurs more frequently in texts of the prose genre than in informative texts. Mahlberg (2013: 131) argues that "as if" is especially common in fiction and serves the general function of introducing the narrator comments. In this study, we argue that Huang and Finkelstein's higher frequency in the use of "as if" compared to the other translators reflects their greater subjectivity in the English translation of *Er Ma*. Huang and Finkelstein tend to assume the role of the narrator more often when rendering source text details that they believe require clarification. In contrast, James and Dolby's relatively lower frequency in the use of "as if" indicates their lesser intervention as narrators when reconstructing the same details.

Concerning target readers, we posit that their reading experiences of a translation will vary based on the frequencies with which a translator employs "as if" 2-grams. Since "as if" introduces a narrator comments, its frequent appearance in a translation may suggest frequent interventions by the translator in the story's details. In such cases, target readers are likely to interpret the story's details differently, considering the translator (narrator) comments. For example, in the opening chapter of the novel, Lao She described the scene of the "Salvation Army" on a London street, writing, "有時候聖靈充滿，他們唱得驚天動地…" (She, 1998: 1). Huang & Finkelstein rendered this part as "Filled with the Holy Spirit, they sang at times as if to shake heaven and earth…." (Huang & Finkelstein, 1984: 1). In contrast, James, Dolby, and Jimmerson translated the same part as "Sometimes, filled with holy spirit, their singing startles heaven and shakes the earth…" (James, 1980: 1), "Sometimes, however, when they're filled with the Holy Spirit, they shudder all heaven

[4] Due to limited space, the specific proportions of these six 3-grams in the four translations are provided in the attached 3-grams list in Figshare (10.6084/m9.figshare.29572907).

and earth…" (Dolby, 2013: 1), and "There were moments when the soldiers were fired so with the holy ghost, that their singing would jar the earth…" (Jimmerson, 1991: 1), respectively. It is evident that while all the translators include "heaven and earth" in their translations, Huang and Finkelstein are the only ones who use "as if" to function as a narrator comments. Consequently, when encountering the phrase "as if" in Huang & Finkelstein's translation, target readers are more likely to perceive the subsequent content ("to shake heaven and earth") as a personal interpretation added by the translators or narrators. In contrast, in the translations by the other translators, similar content is more likely to be seen as the original description by the source text author, rather than the interpretation of the translators or narrators.

10.4 Functional Style as Textual Panorama Building: Insights from MDA

Biber's (1988) multidimensional analysis (MDA) is an exploratory study originally designed to uncover genre variations and text types in English texts. Founded on six dimensions[5] of variation, it has been influential in corpus linguistics, leading to numerous follow-up and replicative studies characterizing new registers (Gries, 2015: 68). In this work, each of the six dimensions is considered a set of linguistic features that tend to co-occur in a text. Together, these dimensions form a textual panorama capable of distinguishing one text from another. Despite the assumption of similar text types/genre variations in the four translations of *Er Ma*, MDA assists in observing their textual panoramas based on these dimensions, thereby revealing the translators' functional styles in the English translations of *Er Ma*.

To explore each of the six dimensions in the four translations, we utilize the Multidimensional Analysis Tagger (MAT) (2015), a freeware based on the Stanford Tagger (2013) designed for text-type or genre analysis. MAT automatically detects and tags a group of preset linguistic variables[6] (features) in a text and generates dimension scores through factor analysis. MAT also provides quantitative information, such as the (per 100) frequencies of each linguistic variable and their z-scores. However, this investigation will only consider the dimension scores for two reasons. First, the objective is to differentiate the functional styles of translators based on the textual panoramas of their translated texts, and the dimension scores would suffice for this purpose. Second, due to the extensive data available, including all the quantitative information on linguistic variables in this investigation is impractical. The results

[5] According to Biber (1988), the six dimensions are "D1: involved vs. informational production", "D2: narrative vs. non-narrative discourse", "D3: situation-dependent vs. elaborated reference", "D4: overt expression of argumentation" "D5: abstract vs. non-abstract style" and "D6: online information elaboration".

[6] The version of MAT used in the present work is v1.3.3, which contains numerous linguistic variables, ranging from "AMP", "TTR" to "WH-clauses". Details are available in https://sites.google.com/site/multidimensionaltagger/

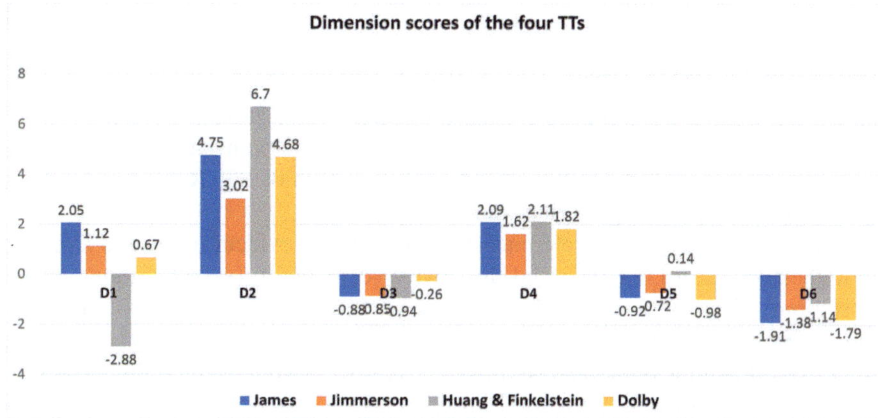

Fig. 10.7 Dimension scores of the four TTs

of the textual panoramas of the four translations based on the dimension scores are reported in Fig. 10.7.

Figure 10.7 reveals notable dimension scores of D2 above zero in all four translations, indicating that these translations fall under the text-type of imaginative narrative. This suggests that the translators of *Er Ma* have predominantly preserved the original text-type as narrative fiction, which aligns with our initial expectations.

However, upon closer examination, some nuances in genre preferences/inclinations can be observed in the dimension scores among the four translations. For instance, in Huang & Finkelstein's translation, genre preferences/inclinations are particularly evident across all six dimensions. The highest scores in D2 (6.7), D4 (2.11), D5 (0.14), and D6 (-1.14) suggest that their translation may contain more past tenses, third-person pronouns, modal verbs, passive clauses, and conjunctions, as described in the MAT manual (Nini, 2015: 7–8). Additionally, based on the manual, the lowest scores in D1 (−2.88) and D3 (−0.94) suggest that Huang & Finkelstein's translation also includes a higher proportion of nouns, long words, adjectives, and adverbs. These findings imply that, compared to the other translations, Huang and Finkelstein's translation may require more interpretational efforts from target readers. This conclusion is further supported by the highest values of standardized type-token ratio (STTR) (44.67) found in Huang and Finkelstein's translation.

By contrast, the aforementioned genre preferences/inclinations are less pronounced in the other three translations. Taking Jimmerson's translation as an example, genre preferences/inclinations are only evident in two dimensions, namely D2 (3.02) and D4 (1.62), with the lowest scores among all the translations. According to the manual, this suggests that Jimmerson utilizes fewer modal verbs, past tenses, and third-person pronouns. As a result, the narrative features in her translation might be less prominent compared to the other translations, but her target readers would experience a closer connection to the story figures with fewer narrative interventions and third-person pronouns.

In Dolby's translation, genre preferences/inclinations are only noticeable in D3 and D5, with the highest score in D3 (−0.26) and the lowest score in D5 (−0.98) among all the translations. This may indicate a relatively higher occurrence of nominalizations in her translation, implying a higher level of difficulty for readers and requiring greater interpretive efforts compared to the other translations. This conclusion is further supported by the second-highest values of STTR (43.81) found in Dolby's translation among all four translations.

As for James, the genre preferences/inclinations are evident in D1 and D6, with the highest score in D1 (2.05) and the lowest score in D6 (−1.91) among all the translations. This suggests that James' translation contains more verbs and fewer noun phrases according to the manual. Consequently, her translation may be relatively easier to read, with less demand for interpretive efforts from the target readers. This claim is supported by the lowest STTR value (41.77) found in James' translation among all four translations.

10.5 Reflection on the Findings

The results from the PCA and MDA present a relatively complete textual panorama of each translation from the perspectives of word, word sequences (n-grams), and the discourse dimensions. Together, these results reveal two patterns regarding these translators' functional styles in the English translations of *Er Ma*.

The first pattern is about the overall stylistic similarities and differences among the translators. The PCA, conducted based on the MFW and MFWS, highlights a remarkable similarity between Dolby's functional style and that of Huang & Finkelstein, despite a nearly three-decade temporal gap between their translations. In contrast, there is a noticeable contrast between James' style and Huang & Finkelstein's style, even though the temporal gap between their translations is relatively small (both in the 80 s, with a four-year gap). Examining specific details, it becomes evident that James' functional style exhibits the most significant deviation from the styles of the other translators. The average distance of the textual panoramas, based on the MFW and MFWS, between James' translation and the other translation is 39.03. Conversely, Dolby's functional style exhibits the least deviation from the functional styles of the other translators, with an average distance of 29.61. The MDA further corroborates this pattern, as Huang & Finkelstein's functional style stands out prominently, showing substantial deviations in five out of the six dimensions examined, in contrast to the remaining translators whose functional styles exhibit fewer deviations in only two of the six dimensions.

The second pattern concerns the potential relationships between the translators' interventions and the resulting interpretational effects on the target readers. This study posits that the translators' diverse usage of "as if" n-grams, body language words, figure labels, contractions, and "'s" possessive cases primarily constitute their interventionist manipulations. These manipulations have the potential to influence the mental construction of the original story details and/or figures (Cf. 10.3.1.2 and

10.2.2.3) and shape the exposure of target readers to the source/target cultures (Cf. 10.2.2.3). Moreover, these manipulations reflect the translators' subjectivities and may be linked to their different ethnic and cultural backgrounds, as well as personal preferences. For instance, translators from various regions might employ diverse English terms to translate the same body language expressions found in *Er Ma* (Cf. 10.3.1.2). This divergence highlights their idiosyncrasies and, consequently, the varying degrees of faithfulness to the source text. Similarly, the translators' varying frequencies of inserting "as if" as narrator comments may suggest their differing levels of narrative intervention in the target texts (Cf. 10.2.2.3). This observation partly reveals their subjectivities and, by extension, their visibility as translators.

10.6 Conclusion

This chapter conducts a comparative analysis of the translators' functional styles in the English translations of *Er Ma* by examining how the textual panoramas are built in the target texts. The analyses reveal significant variations in functional styles among the translators, with Jimmerson/James and Huang & Finkelstein demonstrating particularly noteworthy differences in the PCA and MDA, respectively. These stylistic distinctions can be attributed to various factors, including the translators' preferences in rendering figure labels, preferences for auxiliary/modal verbs and contractions, as well as their motivated use of body language words and "as if" n-grams. Furthermore, these stylistic differences have the potential to impact target readers' interpretations in diverse ways, influencing their mental constructions of story details and figures, as well as their exposure to the source/target cultures.

In this chapter, the research methodology follows the implementation of the "stylometric attribution" part of the framework (see Chap. 4), specifically developed for this study. In contrast, the analyses conducted in Chapters 8 and 9 focus on the "Corpus Stylistic Circle" part of the framework, which explores the translators' functional styles through their recreation of the two literary functions: thematic reconstruction and recharacterization. Conversely, the "stylometric attribution" part in this chapter examines the translators' functional styles by analyzing the ways in which they create the textual function of textual panorama building in target texts. While potential interpretational effects of these functional styles on target readers are discussed, some factors contributing to the diversities in these functional styles are not extensively examined. However, this gap will be addressed as comprehensively as possible in the subsequent chapter, Chapter 11.

References

Abdi. H., & Williams, L. J. (2010). Principal component analysis. *Wiley Interdisciplinary Reviews: Computational Statistics*. *2*(4), 433–459.

Barlow, M. (2013). Individual differences and usage-based grammar. *International Journal of Corpus Linguistics, 18*(4), 443–478.

Biber, D. (1988). *Variation across speech and writing*. Cambridge University Press.

Broder, A. Z., Glassman, S. C., Manasse, M. S., & Zweig, G. (1997). Syntactic clustering of the web. *Computer Networks & ISDN Systems, 29*(8–13), 1157–1166.

Burrows, J. (2002). 'Delta': A measure of stylistic difference and a guide to likely authorship. *Literary and Linguistic Computing, 17*(3), 267–287.

Dolby, W. (2013). *Mr. Ma and son*. Penguin Books.

Grabowski, Ł. (2012). Between stability and variability. A corpus-driven study of translation universals: The case of Polish translations of Lolita. In E. PiechurskaKuciel & L. Piasecka (Eds.), *Variability and stability in foreign and second language learning contexts* (pp. 2–24). Cambridge Scholars.

Grabowski, Ł. (2013). Interfacing corpus linguistics and computational stylistics: Translation universals in translational literary Polish. *International Journal of Corpus Linguistics, 18*(2), 254–280.

Gries, S. T. (2015). Quantitative designs and statistical techniques. In D. Biber & R. Reppen (Eds.), *The Cambridge handbook of English corpus linguistics* (pp. 50–71). Cambridge University Press.

Hoover, D. L. (2002). Frequent word sequences and statistical stylistics. *Literary and Linguistic Computing, 17*(2), 157–180.

Hoover, D. L. (2015). *Cluster analysis, principal component analysis (PCA), and T-testing in Minitab*. Retrieved from https://fles.nyu.edu/dh3/public/Te%20Excel%20TextAnalysis%20Pages.html (Last accessed 22/02/2025).

Huang, K., & Finkelstein, D. (1984). *The two Mas*. Hong Kong Joint Publishing.

Jimmerson, J. (1991). *Mr. Ma & son: A sojourn in London*. Foreign Languages Press.

Korte, B. (1997). *Body language in literature*. University of Toronto Press.

Laviosa, S. (2002). *Corpus-based translation studies*. Rodopi.

Mahlberg, M. (2013). *Corpus stylistics and Dickens's fiction*. Routledge.

Manly, B. F. J. (2016). *Multivariate statistical methods: A primer* (4th ed.). Chapman and Hall.

Mastropierro, L. (2018). *Corpus stylistics in Heart of Darkness and its Italian translations*. Bloomsbury Publishing.

Nini, A. (2015). *Multidimensional analysis tagger* (Version 1.3). Retrieved from http://sites.google.com/site/multidimensionaltagger.

Olohan, M. (2003). How frequent are the contractions? A study of contracted forms in the translational English corpus. *Target, 15*(1), 59–89.

Rybicki, J. (2012). The great mystery of the (almost) invisible translator: Stylometry in translation. In M. Ji & M. P. Oakes (Eds.), *Quantitative methods in corpus-based translation studies: A practical guide to descriptive translation research* (pp. 231–248). John Benjamins Publishing Company.

Rybicki, J., Hoover, D., & Kestemont, M. (2014). Collaborative authorship: Conrad, Ford and Rolling Delta. *Literary and Linguistic Computing*, *29*(3), 422–431.

Segarra, S., Eisen, M., Egan, G., & Ribeiro, A. (2016). Attributing the authorship of the Henry VI plays by word adjacency. *Shakespeare Quarterly*, *67*(2), 232–256.

Saslow. E. (2018). *Unsupervised machine learning*. Retrieved from https://towardsdatascience.com/unsupervised-machine-learning-9329c97d6d9f (Last accessed 13/05/2025).

She, L. (1998). *Er Ma*. People's Literature Publishing House.

Tognini-Bonelli, E. (2001). *Corpus linguistics at work*. John Benjamins.

Wikberg, K. (1999). The style marker as if (though): A corpus study. *Language and Computers, 26*, 93–106.

Chapter 11
Functional Styles and Beyond

11.1 Introduction

The previous three chapters (Chapters 8, 9, 10) have investigated the translators' functional styles in the four English translations of *Er Ma* using corpus stylistic methods. These chapters have demonstrated how the translators recreate the two literary functions, namely "thematic reconstruction" and "recharacterization", as well as how they create the textual function of "textual panorama building" in translation. However, these chapters provide limited exploration of important factors that contribute to these functional styles. These factors are crucial for corpus-assisted translator style research, as discussed in Chapter 2. Therefore, the present chapter specifically focuses on the discussion of these factors. Section 9.2 summarizes the previous findings regarding the functional styles of the translators in the English translation of *Er Ma.* Section 9.3 discusses the potential factors that contribute to their stylistic similarities and differences. Section 9.4 presents concluding remarks.

11.2 Functional Styles in the English Translations of *Er Ma*

The results of the translators' functional styles obtained from the previous three chapters (Chapters 8, 9, 10) are based on six types of analyses: keyword rendition analysis (KRA), semantic field analysis (SFA), lexical chain analysis (LCA), discourse presentations analysis (DPA), principal component analysis (PCA), and multidimensional analysis (MDA). These analyses can be categorized into two groups based on the types of comparisons they make.

The first category involves an "ST-TT comparison", where a translator's functional style is assessed by examining the deviation of their target text (TT) from the source text (ST). In this research, this deviation is represented by the linguistic idiosyncrasies shown by the translator in target texts, and it is measured based on the

K. Wu and D. Li, *Researching Translator's Functional Style*, New Frontiers in Translation Studies, https://doi.org/10.1007/978-981-95-1221-8_11

Table 11.1 Summary of the analyses based on ST-TT comparisons

	James		Jimmerson		Dolby		Huang and Finkelstein	
	CHN	*BRN*	*CHN*	*BRN*	*CHN*	*BRN*	*CHN*	*BRN*
SFA	3	2	1	4	2	3	4	1
LCA	4	2	2	1	2	2	1	4
KRA	Wade-Giles	n/a	Pinyin	n/a	Wade-Giles	n/a	Yale	n/a

following principle: the greater the deviation from the original, the more pronounced the linguistic idiosyncrasy. The KRA, SFA, and LCA fall into this category. Based on the results presented in the three chapters, the translators' linguistic idiosyncrasies are summarized in Table 11.1, with a deviation mark[1] assigned to each case in these analyses. A higher deviation mark indicates a relatively strong linguistic idiosyncrasy, while a lower mark suggests a weaker idiosyncrasy.

According to Table 11.1, in the reconstruction of theme "Diasporic Chinese" and the recharacterization of the Chinese figures ("CHN" in the table), James exhibits the most robust linguistic idiosyncrasies in the SFA and LCA, with deviation marks of 3 and 4, respectively. By contrast, Jimmerson demonstrates the weakest idiosyncrasies in the same analyses, with marks of 1 and 2, respectively. This suggests that James' intervention in reconstructing the theme and recharacterizing the figures is the most prominent, while Jimmerson's intervention in the same regards is the least noticeable. In the case of Dolby and Huang & Finkelstein, their respective interventions fall into the medium range, with deviation marks positioned between the extremes.

In the reconstruction the theme of "Local Britons" and the recharacterization of the British story figures ("BRN" in the table), the deviation marks reveal notable linguistic idiosyncrasies observed in the SFA and LCA for Jimmerson and Huang & Finkelstein. Jimmerson displays the most robust idiosyncrasies in the SFA (a deviation mark of 4) but the weakest in the LCA (a mark of 1), while Huang & Finkelstein show the exact opposite pattern (a deviation mark of 1 in the SFA and 4 in the LCA). This suggests that Jimmerson tends to be more interventionist in reconstructing the original semantic fields associated with the "British Keywords", while remaining relatively faithful when reestablishing the original lexical chain formed by these keywords. Conversely, Huang and Finkelstein make contrasting choices when they reconstruct these semantic fields and reestablish the lexical chain. Regarding Dolby and James, the SFA results indicate that Dolby is more interventionist (a deviation mark of 3) compared to James (a deviation mark of 2). Meanwhile, the LCA demonstrates that both translators exhibit similar levels of intervention in maintaining or breaking the original lexical chains related to the theme of "Local Britons".

[1] The deviation marks, ranging from 1 to 4, indicate the strength of linguistic idiosyncrasies, with a positive correlation (i.e., a "4" represents the most robust idiosyncrasy, while a "1" represents the weakest). In the case of SFA, the marks are assigned based on the overall proportional deviation scores presented in Chaps. 8 and 9. For LCA, the marks correspond to the percentages of disrupted lexical chains out of the total in the same chapters.

Before delving into the second category, it is important to highlight that while the KRA results distinguish the linguistic idiosyncrasies between the translators, they are less quantifiable. For instance, the use of different Chinese romanization systems by the translators to render Chinese figures' labels could partly illustrate their linguistic idiosyncrasies. However, it is challenging, if not impossible, to assign precise deviation marks to these variations. Similarly, the translators' utilization of different names in rendering the labels of British figures, although idiosyncratic, is difficult to quantify in terms of their deviations from the original.

The second category involves a "TT-TT comparison", which assesses a translator's functional style by examining its similarity or difference compared to that of other translators. This evaluation principle is based on analyzing the extent to which a translator's target text (TT) deviates from the TTs of other translators within the same comparison group in each analysis. In the present research, the DPA, PCA, and MDA analyses fall into this category. Based on the results obtained in Chapters 8, 9, and 10, we present a summary of the translators' functional styles using the "TT-TT comparison" in Table 9.2. The data in the "DPA" column describe the translators' preferences regarding "person", "tense", and "discourse form" in their rendition of the original ambiguous discourse presentation. The data in the "PCA" column represent the average metric distance between the textual panorama of a translator's TT and the TTs of the other translators. The data presented in the "MDA" column provide information about the readability levels of each TT based on the dimension scores.

Table 11.2 illustrates the patterns of similarities and differences in the translators' functional styles as analyzed through the DPA, PCA, and MDA. Regarding the DPA, all translators show a preference for the first (I) and third (III) persons and past tense. However, their divergence lies in their varied choices of discourse forms in their target texts. James and Dolby share similarities as they prefer free direct thought (FDT) and free direct speech (FDS), while Jimmerson and Huang & Finkelstein are similar in their preference for direct thought (DT) and direct speech (DS). This suggests that Jimmerson and Huang & Finkelstein tend to immerse their target readers within the minds of story figures, whereas James and Dolby present these figures directly to their target readers.

In terms of the PCA, the average metric distances in the table reveal a noticeable pattern of divergence and convergence. James and Jimmerson form a group with a similar distance range around 40, while Dolby and Huang & Finkelstein form

Table 11.2 Summary of the analyses based on TT-TT comparisons

	James	Jimmerson	Dolby	Huang and Finkelstein
DPA	I, III, past, FDT, FDS	I, III, past, DT, DS	I, III, past, FDT, FDS	I, III, past, DT, DS
PCA	41.42	38.73	27.83	30.36
MDA	High	High	Low	Low

another group with a range around 30. As discussed in Chapter 10, this pattern may indicate that James and Jimmerson show strong linguistic idiosyncrasies that differentiate their target texts from each other and from those of the other translators. In contrast, Dolby and Huang & Finkelstein possess weaker idiosyncrasies that are less effective in distinguishing their target texts from each other. In other words, the textual panoramas of Dolby's and Huang & Finkelstein's target texts are similar, while those of James and Jimmerson are not.

In terms of MDA, the dimension scores provided insights into genre preferences and readability levels of the four translations. Huang & Finkelstein's translation has high scores in D2, D4, D5, and D6, while scoring low in D1 and D3. Dolby's translation has a high score in D3, but a low score in D5. This suggests that Huang and Finkelstein's and Dolby's translations are relatively challenging to read, requiring greater interpretational effort from readers. In contrast, Jimmerson's translation scores low in D2 and D4, while James' translation has a high score in D1 but a low score in D6. This indicates that Jimmerson's and James' translations have relatively higher readability, requiring less interpretive effort compared to other translations.

The above summaries of the translators' functional styles based on the findings in Chapters 8, 9, and 10 reveal an important trend: the patterns of similarities and differences in their stylistic features can vary depending on the chosen analytical perspectives. This observation aligns with our expectations, as translation is a complex endeavor that encompasses various factors and considerations. The diverse patterns that have emerged from our analyses can be seen as partial reflections of these factors and considerations. In the following section, we will delve into some of these factors and considerations to gain further insights.

11.3 Factors Underlying the Functional Styles

In order to address the gaps left in the previous chapters (Chapters 8, 9, and 10) and gain deeper insights into the translators' functional styles in the English translations of *Er Ma*, this section explores underlying factors that contribute to their stylistic similarities and differences. Following the framework outlined in Sect. 2.4.3 of Chapter 2, this study classifies these factors as "translatorial" and "extra-translatorial" to examine how various elements surrounding the translators influence their stylistic decision-making. The purpose of this categorization here is to offer a better understanding of how various factors around the translators affect their stylistic decision-making. In this book, the "translatorial factors" refer to those factors primarily associated with a translator's personal ideologies and/or this translator's background, whereas the "extra-translatorial factors" are factors without such apparent associations. The following two subsections will discuss some of these "translatorial" and "extra-translatorial" factors.

11.3.1 Translatorial Factors

Firstly, a translator's background, including their nationality and mother tongue, could significantly influences their styles in translation. This influence is particularly noticeable in the translation by Huang & Finkelstein. As shown in Table 6.1 of Chapter 6, Huang, an overseas Chinese residing in the US, is the only native Chinese speaker among all the translators. According to Li (2016: 124), faithfulness to the source text has traditionally been the predominant criterion for evaluating translation quality among practitioners in China, although its importance may vary in overseas contexts. Therefore, it can be inferred that Huang's English translation is more likely to prioritize literal translation for a greater level of faithfulness. This could partially explain why the collaborative translation by Huang and Finkelstein closely adheres to the original construction of the theme "Diaspora Chinese", as illustrated in SFA. Moreover, this emphasis on faithfulness may also explain why the two translators consistently employ the term "Chinese" to translate "中國人" in the source text, as demonstrated in the LCA analysis. By contrast, the other three translators are either British or American, with English as their mother tongue. As a result, faithfulness to the original text and maintaining a style similar to the original may not be the primary considerations driving their translation strategies.

Secondly, a translator's personal stance, recognized as the critical point in translation decision-making (Munday, 2012), serves as another significant "translatorial" factor that could influence the translator's functional style. Translation, as a sociocultural practice, plays a role in negotiating and adopting a specific stance towards the values it conveys (Hermans, 2014: 293). This stance and value system of the translators are evident in the findings of the SFA and LCA, where significant translatorial interventions by James and Jimmerson are observed in their thematic reconstruction and recharacterization. For James, her linguistic idiosyncrasies (interventions) shown in the SFA/LCA reflect her stance on the fictional portrayal of the Chinese story figures. In the preface to her translation, she describes the novel as a Chinese perspective on the English view of the Chinese people (James, 1980: i). This suggests that James may perceive the English stereotypes in the story as one-sided representations perceived by the Chinese, which aligns with Lao She's technique of negative characterization. Therefore, it is plausible that James deliberately amplifies this negative effect by increasing the proportion of some semantic components within the semantic field of *General Negativity* (Cf. 8.3.2.2) and disrupts the original lexical chain established by "中國人" by extensively replacing "Chinese" with "Chinamen" (Cf. 8.3.3). Likewise, Jimmerson's prominent linguistic idiosyncrasies (interventions) reveal her personal stance towards the British characters in the story: Britons in the eyes of the Chinese (Witchard, 2009: 152). This is evident as Jimmerson reduces the proportional rates of several negative semantic fields (e.g., *Hypocrisy and Pretension*, *Colonialism and Conservatism*), while increasing those of positive semantic fields (e.g., *Rule and Law*, *Pride and Prejudice*), as discussed in Sect. 9.3.2.2.

Thirdly, the translators' personal preferences could also contribute to the similarities and differences observed in their functional styles. This is clearly shown in the PCA, where the similarities between Dolby and Huang & Finkelstein reflected in their MFW/MFWS-based textual panoramas owing a lot to their shared preference in the use of contractions. Since this shared preference lacks apparent "extra-translatorial" connections and likely originates from the translators' narrative strategies (Cf. 10.3.2.3), it can be attributed to their personal preferences, which are expected to remain consistent across different translations.

11.3.2 Extra-Translatorial Factors

Firstly, the sociocultural context in which the translation takes place is a key factor that shapes the translators' functional styles. Results from the DPA indicate that Jimmerson and Huang & Finkelstein exhibit stylistic similarity due to their shared preference for DS and DT in their renditions of the original WP/TP and SP/TP. We argue that this preference could be "inextricably bound up with the sociocultural context in which the act of translating takes place" (Hatim & Mason, 2014: 12).

The period from 1978 onwards marked the opening of mainland China to the global community both economically and culturally (Huan, 1986). Within this sociocultural context, it is reasonable to assume that some translators of Chinese fiction would likewise follow this "opening-up" process in translation. In Huang and Finkelstein's 1984 version, they explicitly state in the preface that their translation is to "improve the mutual understanding between China and the rest of the world" (Huang & Finkelstein, 1984: ii). In Jimmerson's 1991 version, although not explicitly stated, the objectives of the publisher, Foreign Languages Press of China (FLP), can provide a rationale for a similar motivation. The primary publishing goal of FLP in the early 1990s was to vigorously and decisively promote Chinese literature overseas (refer to http://flp.com.cn/about/history/). Therefore, we believe that the translators are more inclined to employ discourse forms that establish a closer connection between target readers and the story figures in terms of their speech and thoughts as originally presented. This approach aims to foster a stronger bond between target readers and the Chinese culture and way of life, thereby achieving the desired effect of "opening-up" to the rest of the world. This is evident in the MDA results, which indicate that both Jimmerson's and James' translations show a high level of readability.

Furthermore, the influence of sociocultural context on translation is also clearly reflected in the SFA and LCA results. This is particularly noticeable in the cases of Jimmerson and Huang & Finkelstein as they reconstruct the "Diasporic Chinese" theme. Jimmerson's translation shows low levels of linguistic idiosyncrasies (interventions) in the SFA/LCA, while Huang & Finkelstein's translation exhibits a low level in the LCA, but a high level in the SFA. We contend that Jimmerson's weak idiosyncrasies (interventions) might indicate her reluctance to alter the original construction of the theme "Diasporic Chinese" in the story. This reflects a faithful translation strategy that aligns with the sociocultural context of that time. Likewise, Huang and Finkelstein's weak idiosyncrasies (interventions) in the LCA may suggest a similar translation strategy, while their robust idiosyncrasies (interventions) in the SFA reflect this strategy from a different perspective.

Secondly, patronaging intervention is another important "extra-translatorial" factor that contributes to the differences in translators' functional styles. This is evident in the KRA, where the translators adopt different Chinese romanization systems (Table 10.1) in their renditions of the Chinese figure labels. We argue that this stylistic diversity is partly related to patronaging intervention, which is "one determinant of translation practice" (Tymoczko, 1999: 30) and could influence a translator's choices.

Copyright information reveals that Jimmerson's version, published by FLP in mainland China, aligns with the region where the promotion of Mandarin Pinyin has been an official language policy since the 1950s (Benjamin, 1997). Consequently, it is plausible to assume that Jimmerson may have been required to use Pinyin to pass patronaging censorship and secure publication. In contrast, the copyright details indicate that James' version was published by the Chinese Material Center, Inc. in the US in 1980, Huang and Finkelstein's version by Joint Publishing Co. in Hong Kong in 1984, and Dolby's version by Penguin Book in the UK in 2013. This suggests that, compared to Jimmerson's version, the influence of patronaging intervention on the choice of Chinese romanization systems may be less pronounced for these translators, as there are fewer official policies for Pinyin use outside mainland China. In such cases, publishers may opt to preserve the translators' original usage of romanization, as explicitly stated in the preface of Dolby's version (Dolby, 2013: iii) and potentially applicable to James' and Huang & Finkelstein's versions, although not explicitly mentioned.

Thirdly, the presence of post-translational influence, whereby an earlier translation affects the subsequent translator's work, is also a potential "extra-translatorial" factor contributing to the observed stylistic similarities between the translators. Although not extensively examined in the previous chapters, the diverse renditions of British figure labels by these translators draw attention to the potential impact of post-translational influence. As the labels for the British figures were originally devised by Lao She in Chinese, there are no established rules for their translation into English. In other words, it is up to the translator to decide how to render these labels in *Er Ma*, and the likelihood of two translators selecting the same translation is relatively low, given the absence of officially fixed translations for these labels.

However, both James and Jimmerson translate the original British labels "温都" as "Wendell" and "伊" as "Evans" in their respective versions. In contrast, the translators of the other two versions render the same labels as "Wedderburn/Winter" and "Ely/Eden", respectively. Considering that James' 1980 version is the first published English translation of *Er Ma*, the potential influence it carries in terms of post-translational impact cannot be overlooked. This conclusion is supported by the research conducted by Ji (2009), which explored and confirmed similar influences between different Chinese translations of *Don Quixote*. Regarding Jimmerson's 1991 version of *Er Ma*, given the shared renditions of certain British figures labels and the 11-year gap between the two versions, it is reasonable to believe that James' version exerted a certain influence on Jimmerson's translation, at least in terms of the renditions of these British figure labels.

11.4 Conclusion

This chapter has examined the potential factors contributing to the observed stylistic similarities and differences in the four English translations of *Er Ma*, based on a summary of the findings from Chapters 8, 9, and 10. These factors are broadly classified as "translatorial" and "extra-translatorial". Translatorial factors, including a translator's backgrounds, stances, and preferences, are considered to shape the translators' functional styles through their personal attributes, such as experiences and ideologies. On the other hand, extra-translatorial factors, such as sociocultural contexts, patronizing intervention, and post-translational influences, could impact these functional styles of translators through external influences, particularly of a social, cultural, and linguistic nature.

References

Dolby, W. (2013). *Mr. Ma and son*. Penguin Books.

Hatim, B., & Mason, I. (2014). *Discourse and the translator*. Routledge.

Hermans, T. (2014). Positioning translators: Voices, views and values in translation. *Language and Literature, 23*(3), 285–301.

Huan, G. (1986). China's open-door policy, 1978–1984. *Journal of International Affairs*, 1–18.

James, J. M. (1980). *Ma and son: A novel by Lao She*. Chinese Materials Center Inc.

Ji, M. (2009). Corpus stylistics in translation studies: Two modern Chinese translations of Don Quijote. *Language and Literature, 18*(1), 61–73.

Li, D. (2016). *Corpus-assisted translator style research: A corpus linguistic approach to literary translation*. Shanghai Foreign Language Education Press.

Munday, J. (2012). *Evaluation in translation: Critical points of translator decision-making*. Routledge.

Tymoczko, M. (1999). Post-colonial writing and literary translation. In *Post-colonial translation: Theory and practice* (pp. 19–40).

Witchard, A. (2009). Bloomsbury, Limehouse and Piccadilly: A Chinese sojourn in London. In P. Rastogi & J. F. Stitt (Eds.), *Before Windrush: Recovering an Asian and black literary heritage within Britain*. Cambridge Scholars Publishing.

Chapter 12
Conclusion

12.1 Introduction

The present research employs the corpus stylistic approach to investigate the functional styles of translators in the English translations of *Er Ma*, addressing the five research questions outlined in Chapter 6. This concluding chapter briefly summarizes the major findings of the study and outline possible directions in future research.

12.2 Major Findings

Using the corpus stylistic approach, the study examines and compares the translators' functional styles in the four English translations of *Er Ma* by analyzing their recreation of literary functions and the creation of textual function in target texts. Specifically, the study explores how translators reconstruct the literary themes of "Diasporic Chinese" and "Local Britons" and how they recharacterize Chinese and British story figures in target texts. The study also assesses the degree of similarity and difference in the textual panoramas built in these target texts, using principal component analysis and multidimensional analysis.

The overall results (Cf. 11.2) have demonstrated that the translators' functional styles in the four English translations exhibit both similarities and differences when we analyze them from the perspectives of literary and textual functions. These various analytical viewpoints lead to distinct interpretational effects, which subsequently may influence how target readers perceive and comprehend the original story figures. Moreover, the potential factors contributing to these functional styles are diverse, incorporating both "translatorial" factors like backgrounds, stances, and preferences, as well as "extra-translatorial" factors such as sociocultural contexts, patronage intervention, and post-translational influences.

K. Wu and D. Li, *Researching Translator's Functional Style*, New Frontiers in Translation Studies, https://doi.org/10.1007/978-981-95-1221-8_12

These findings, together with the corpus stylistic methodologies used in the study, have offered some reflections for corpus-assisted translator style research:

1. By adopting the corpus stylistic approach, we can explore both the formal and functional aspects of translator style. This allows us to triangulate translator style by analyzing the same corpora form different methodological perspectives, yielding a relatively comprehensive profile of the translator style being examined.
2. By viewing translator styles as the recreation of functions, we can capture and compare these translators' stylistic profiles based on their diverse methods of reenacting the original literary functions (e.g., thematic reconstruction, recharacterization) from source texts into target texts, and how they perform textual functions (e.g., textual panorama building) in their target texts.
3. The potential factors that influence the stylistic similarities and differences in translators' functional styles are numerous and complex. It may be challenging, if not impossible, to trace all of these factors within a single study. Therefore, the focus of a single study should be directed towards those "translatorial" and "extra-translatorial" factors that can effectively explain these stylistic similarities and differences.

12.3 Further Research

As emphasized by De Sutter and Lefer (2020:6), existing corpus-assisted translation studies, including research on translator style, have encountered limitations such as limited research designs, methodological narrowness, and isolation from other disciplines. To address these limitations, De Sutter & Lefer (ibid.) have put forth a new research agenda that underscores methodological pluralism, interdisciplinarity, and multifactorial research designs.

Hence, future research on functional style could develop a comprehensive and systematic analytical framework that encompasses a broader range of literary and textual functions, while incorporating a diverse set of stylistic indices capable of effectively capturing the translator's stylistic profiles. This approach promotes methodological pluralism.

Furthermore, researchers might consider employing analytical tools from related disciplines, such as digital humanities and computer science, in addition to existing tools from translation studies and corpus linguistics. This broader toolkit might enhance both the depth and breadth of investigations into translators' functional styles, contributing to interdisciplinarity.

Finally, future research could explore the evolution of a single translator's functional styles across multiple works, over different time periods, and possibly involving various translation directions (e.g., English to Chinese and Chinese to English). This approach facilitates a multifactorial research design.

Reference

De Sutter, G., & Lefer, M. A. (2020). On the need for a new research agenda for corpus-based translation studies: A multi-methodological, multifactorial and interdisciplinary approach. *Perspectives, 28*(1), 1–23.

MIX
Papier aus verantwortungsvollen Quellen
Paper from responsible sources
FSC® C105338

If you have any concerns about our products,
you can contact us on
ProductSafety@springernature.com

In case Publisher is established outside the EU,
the EU authorized representative is:
Springer Nature Customer Service Center GmbH
Europaplatz 3, 69115 Heidelberg, Germany

Printed by Libri Plureos GmbH
in Hamburg, Germany